To Complete the Jigsaw

British Military Intelligence in the First World War

NICHOLAS VAN DER BIJL

Foreword by Major-General
Julian Thompson

The
History
Press

This book is dedicated to the Intelligence Corps and members of the armed forces who have been involved in military intelligence and security.

First published 2015

The History Press
The Mill, Brimscombe Port
Stroud, Gloucestershire, GL5 2QG
www.thehistorypress.co.uk

British Library Cataloguing in Publication Data.
A catalogue record for this book is available from the British Library.

ISBN 978 0 7509 5613 0

Typesetting and origination by The History Press
Printed in Great Britain

Contents

Foreword

Nick van der Bijl's meticulously researched book provides a much-needed corrective to the popular view of the First World War. This too often consists of a potpourri of ideas characterised by expressions such as, 'lions led by donkeys', and 'futility', based on watching *Oh! What a Lovely War*, and reading some fiction of questionable accuracy. Even serious and balanced historical works on the war make scant reference to the role of intelligence. The author has a wealth of experience in intelligence and security in both conventional war and counter-insurgency; and brings his expertise to an in-depth analysis of the part played by intelligence between 1914 and 1918.

That the First World War was a 'first' in the introduction of tanks, aircraft, and chemical weapons is widely acknowledged by military historians. Less well known are intelligence techniques such as air photography and wireless (radio) intercept, which remain with us in vastly more advanced forms. In giving us fascinating insights into the developing intelligence techniques, the author unearths many intriguing nuggets of information. For example, in the early days on the Western Front, the Germans were reluctant to comprehend that wireless traffic could be monitored, and therefore they did not bother to encode their messages, thereby revealing their plans to the listening French and British. The Germans made the same mistake during the Second World War when they assumed the Allies would be unable to decipher traffic encoded on their Enigma machines.

As the author points out, information must be collated and disseminated as graded intelligence to those who need it. Failure to disseminate intelligence is an intelligence sin. General Hamilton, who commanded ground operations in Gallipoli, later claimed that, 'The Dardanelles and the Bosphorus might be in the moon for all the military information I have got to go upon'. He had not been given access to a wealth of regularly updated information going back to 1807 held in War Office and Admiralty. Also not told was the First Lord of the Admiralty, Winston Churchill, the moving spirit behind the Dardanelles campaign. Telling commanders what they want to hear is another intelligence sin. Haig's Chief of Intelligence, Brigadier-General Charteris, was guilty of just that. Nevertheless, as the author tells us, the much-maligned Charteris was responsible for converting the 'BEF intelligence infrastructure from the muddled organisation of August 1914 to a function that exploited intelligence and security resources and enabled the dissemination of daily intelligence summaries from every division, corps and army'. The 'flip side' is the commander or political leader rejecting intelligence that does not fit with his preconceived notions. In the opening months of 1918, Lloyd George refused to reinforce Haig despite intelligence, mainly from agents, accurately indicating a massive German offensive because he believed Haig to be an alarmist and intent on enlarging the BEF.

In most works on the First World War, intelligence gathering by agents behind enemy lines is covered sparsely, if at all. It gets due attention in van der Bijl's book. One factor was getting the information out to their handlers. Since portable radios first made an appearance during the Second World War, one method was to use homing pigeon. These could be back in the GHQ loft in France within eleven hours of being released in occupied Belgium or north-eastern France. The author tells us how carrier pigeons were delivered to agents in baskets, sometimes parachuted from Royal Flying Corps aircraft. Some of the adventures of those delivering the pigeon baskets read like a James Bond novel. Especially interesting are intelligence operations in the campaigns against the Turks in Mesopotamia, Arabia, the Sinai, Palestine and Syria and against the Germans in East Africa. These, in contrast to the Western Front, were mostly wars of manoeuvre and frequently involved deception operations and the landing of agents from the sea, in methods that foreshadowed Second World War clandestine operations.

One character always associated with the Middle East intelligence operations is T.E. Lawrence. An opinionated meddler and not wholly highly regarded, he was a relentless self-publicist. One of his critics remarked, 'he backed into the limelight'. As the author suggests, there were others deeply involved in intelligence gathering, such as Lieutenant-Colonel Leachman in Mesopotamia, Captain Weldon who spent the war landing on Asia Minor beaches to collect information and the NILI group of young Jews in Palestine. Their activities are barely known. Perhaps the most famous deception in the Middle East was the 'haversack ruse', in which a haversack containing false information was deliberately abandoned by a British officer for the Turks to collect. For years, Colonel Meinertzhagen, an intelligence officer on General Allenby's staff, professed that he had conceived the operation. Years later, it emerged that another officer had conceived the plot. That said, as the author points out, the ruse was the forerunner to two famous Second World War deceptions – MINCEMEAT (the Man Who Never Was) preceding the invasion of Sicily; and FORTITUDE before the invasion of Normandy.

This book is a tour de force, and a splendid piece of work. By covering all the major campaigns in the First World War, we get a far more comprehensive view of intelligence in that war than we would have done had the author followed the stereotype and written only about trench warfare on the Western Front.

MAJOR-GENERAL JULIAN THOMPSON

Acknowledgements

In August 1914, Great Britain and France went to war in Europe with Germany, a country that had embraced military technology and had a General Staff that had conducted a thorough intelligence assessment of the politics, likely opposition and the ground. In contrast, Great Britain was about to fight a major war in Europe for the first time since the end of the Napoleonic wars in 1815. Most of its wars fought since that time had been to expand and defend the Empire from weakly armed opponents. While modern technology was investigated by some dynamic officers, strategic management tended to rely on the whims of individual commanders, as opposed to a General Staff. The country learnt the sharp lesson in Crimea, Afghanistan and South Africa that intelligence was crucial. Matters improved during the post-Victorian era with the development of intelligence and security, for instance the use of aircraft by the army and the first stirrings of signals intelligence by the Royal Navy. This book is not an academic study but a glimpse into how unconventional officers and men laid the foundations for defeating Germany and Turkey and their allies.

Thanking those who contributed to such projects as this is always a pleasure. To Marion Freudenthal, of the Beit Aaronsohn Museum Nili, for supplying information and photographs relating to Jewish espionage in Palestine. To Harry Fecitt for his knowledge of the campaign in East Africa. To Mike Mockford and Peter Jefferies of the Medmenham Museum for information on the early days of air photo reconnaissance. To Joyce Hutton, Sally-Anne Reed and Fred Judge of the Military Intelligence Museum for giving me access to Intelligence Corps archives. To Peter Woods, of GWR, for the maps. To Kate Baker and Andrew Latimer and their teams at the History Press for their expertise and guidance. I am indebted to Major-General Julian Thompson, a colleague at HQ 3rd Commando Brigade during the Falklands War, for finding the time in his busy schedule to write the 'Foreword'. To those who provided photographs. While every effort has been made to trace ownership of all photographs and information, this has not always been possible, nevertheless, I am content to make amends, if appropriate, including acknowledgement in future editions.

Finally, but not least, I must thank my wife Penny, for her patience and support in this project.

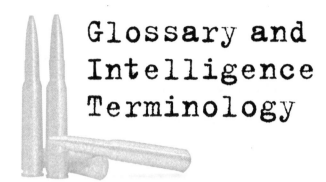

Glossary and Intelligence Terminology

ANZAC	Australian and New Zealand Army Corps
BCI	*Bureau Central Interallie* (Inter-Allied Central Bureau)
BE	Blériot Experimental – part of the designation of an aircraft
BEF	British Expeditionary Force
BGGS	Brigadier-General, General Staff
CIGS	Chief of the Imperial General Staff
CMG	Companion of Order of St Michael and St George
DH	De Havilland – manufacturer of aircraft
DMI	Director of Intelligence
EAEF	East African Expeditionary Force
EEF	Egyptian Expeditionary Force
EMSIB	Eastern Mediterranean Special Intelligence Branch
GHQ	General Headquarters
GOC	General Officer Commanding
GS	General Service
GSO	General Staff Officer. Three grades of GSO1 (usually a lieutenant-colonel); GSO2 (major) and GSO3 (captain)
HQ	Headquarters
I	Intelligence
I(a)	Operational Intelligence
I(b)	The Secret Service and Counter-Intelligence
I(c)	Topography and Mapping
I(d)	Control of Press
I(e)	Wireless and Control of Ciphers and Codes
I(f)	Control of Visitors
I(g)	War Trade – an offshoot of the War Trade Intelligence Department of the War Office (WTID)
I(h)	Postal and Telegraphic Censorship
I(x)	Administration of the Intelligence Corps
IC	Intelligence Corps
IEF	Indian Expeditionary Force

I-Toc	Telephone Interceptor – used to gather information from field telephones
MC	Military Cross
MEF	Mediterranean Expeditionary Force
MI	Military Intelligence
MM	Military Medal
MO	Military Operations
MP	Member of Parliament
NCO	Non-Commissioned Officers – in the British army, private equivalent to a colour sergeant
NILI	*Netzakh Yisrael Lo Yishaker.* A Jewish espionage network in Palestine.
No-man's-land	The ground between opposing trenches
O	Operations
PoW	Prisoner(s) of War
RAMC	Royal Army Medical Corps
RFA	Royal Field Artillery
RFC	Royal Flying Corps
RHA	Royal Horse Artillery
RNAS	Royal Naval Air Service
RNVR	Royal Navy Volunteer Service
SE	Santos Experimental – refers to a British aircraft
US	United States
VC	Victoria Cross
VIP	Very Important Person
YMCA	Young Men's Christian Association

MAP 1 - THE WESTERN FRONT

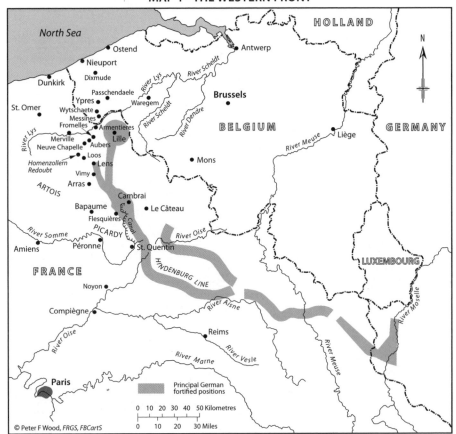

North Sea

Ostend
Nieuport
Dixmude
Dunkirk
St. Omer
Passchendaele
Ypres
Wytschaete
Messines
Fromelles
Merville
Neuve Chapelle
Aubers
Loos
Homenzollern Redoubt
Lens
Vimy
Arras
ARTOIS
Armentieres
Lille
Bapaume
Cambrai
Flesquières
Le Câteau
River Somme
PICARDY
Amiens
Péronne
St. Quentin
FRANCE
Noyon
Compiègne
River Oise
Reims
River Marne
River Vesle
Paris

HOLLAND
Antwerp
River Lys
River Scheldt
Waregem
Brussels
River Scheldt
River Dendre
BELGIUM
Mons
River Meuse
Liège
GERMANY
River Oise
HINDENBURG LINE
River Aisne
LUXEMBOURG
River Moselle
River Meuse

Principal German fortified positions

| 0 | 10 | 20 | 30 | 40 | 50 Kilometres |

| 0 | 10 | 20 | 30 Miles |

© Peter F Wood, FRGS, FBCartS

N

MAP 2 - THEATRE OF WAR: EAST AFRICA

Miles 0   100   200   300 Miles
Km 0   100   200   300   400   500 Km

N

BELGIAN CONGO

Lake Albert

U G A N D A

K E N Y A

Lake Edward

Kisumu

Victoria Nyanza

Nairobi

Lake Kivu

RUANDA

URUNDI

Mt Kilimanjaro

Moshi

Tsavo

Taveta

Kigoma

G E R M A N

Tabora

Usambara Railway

Mombasa

Tanga

Pemba Island

5°

Lake Tanganyika

E A S T   A F R I C A

Central Railway

Zanzibar

Da es Salaam

Kilossa

Lake Rukwa

Ruaha R.

Rufiji R.

Mafia Island

Lake Mweru

Abercorn

Indian

Liwale

Lindi

10°

N O R T H E R N

Masasi

Newala

Ocean

R H O D E S I A

N Y A S A L A N D

Lake Nyasa

R. Rovuma

P O R T U G U E S E

E A S T   A F R I C A

R. Lurio

15°

30°   R. Zambezi   35°   40°

© Peter F Wood, FRGS, FBCartS

MAP 3 - GALLIPOLI

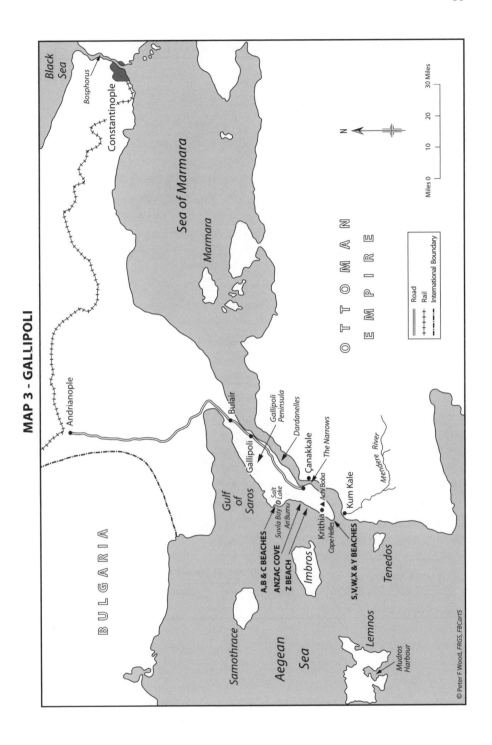

© Peter F.Wood, FRGS, FBCartS

MAP 4 - THE NEAR AND MIDDLE EAST

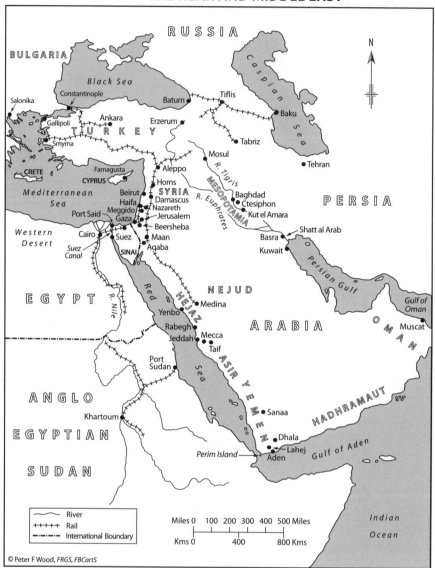

© Peter F Wood, *FRGS, FBCartS*

MAP 5 - THE FIRST BATTLE OF YPRES

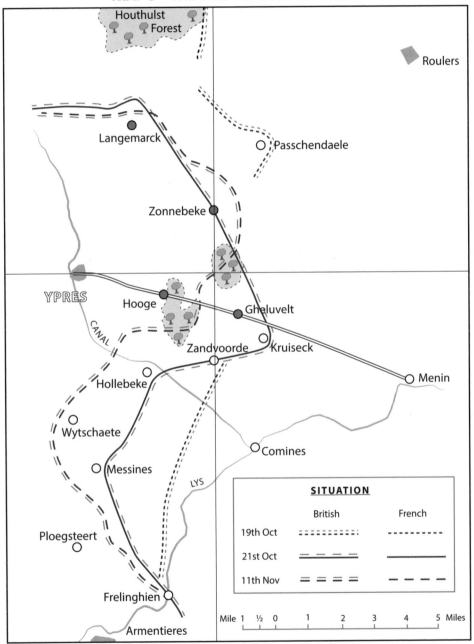

Houthulst Forest

Roulers

Langemarck

Passchendaele

Zonnebeke

YPRES

Hooge

Gheluvelt

CANAL

Zandvoorde

Kruiseck

Hollebeke

Menin

Wytschaete

Comines

Messines

LYS

Ploegsteert

Frelinghien

Armentieres

SITUATION		
	British	French
19th Oct	··············	------------
21st Oct	—————	—————
11th Nov	= = =	– – –

Mile 1 ½ 0   1   2   3   4   5 Miles

14

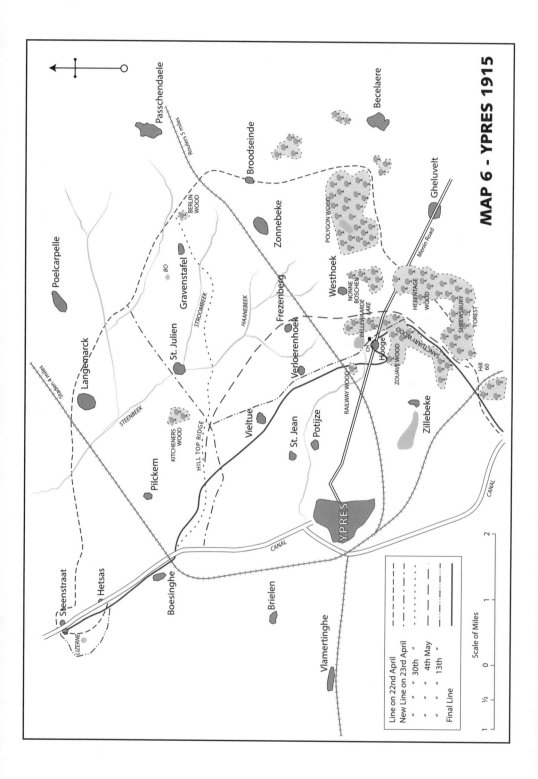

MAP 6 - YPRES 1915

Line on 22nd April
New Line on 23rd April
"   "   " 30th   "
"   "   " 4th May
"   "   " 13th   "
Final Line

Scale of Miles

1

Setting the Scene

On 10 October 1899, 21,000 Dutch South Africans, commonly known as Boers, crossed into Natal in four columns in pursuit of independence from Imperial Great Britain and trapped the British army in three towns and defeated it in several battles. Lieutenant-General Sir George White, commanding British forces in Natal, abandoned his logistics base at Dundee, leaving behind his map store and intelligence library. In 1901, the Boer President Kruger authorised the raising of *Theron's Verkenners Korps* (Theron's Intelligence Corps) to conduct intelligence operations behind British lines. This is thought to be the first use of the nomenclature. When Louis Botha, a senior Boer commando, met General Lord Herbert Kitchener, the commander-in-chief, at Middelburg to discuss peace talks on 28 February 1901, Botha sent a telegram to Kruger in Holland suggesting that their cause was hopeless. Botha was unaware that the telegram was routed through Aden Settlement where it was read by the British after its code had been broken. However, when Kruger replied that the war should continue as 'Europe felt the Boers were doing very well', particularly Germany, the intelligence was passed to Kitchener, who favoured terms. But the high commissioner in Cape Town, the expansionist imperialist Sir Alfred Milner, demanded defeat and for the next seventeen months, Kitchener used a well-organised intelligence function to conduct a systematic 'sweep-and-scour' strategy against the commandos. Although their families were confined to appallingly administered camps, the Boers were resilient; for example, Jan Smuts and his commando of 250 ragged horsemen embarrassed the British for three months in 1901 with a long raid into Cape Colony. A scapegoat for the early disasters was needed and one emerged before the war ended on 4 November 1901.

After an order in council had condemned the War Office Intelligence Division, the Earl of Hardwicke, Undersecretary of State for War, reviewed 'The Permanent Establishment of the Mobilisation and Intelligence Department' and recommended in 1903 that:

Intelligence should remain advisory.
Commanders, at all levels, are entitled to accept or reject intelligence.

Staff intelligence officers should receive specialist training.

Military attaches should be involved in intelligence collection.

Closer links between Military and Naval Intelligence should be established.

But, first – what is intelligence? As Speaker Robert Harley said in 1704, 'Information is the soul of business'.

Intelligence is widely used. Information on customer and client practices is called market research. Police and lawyers call it evidence. Doctors call it prognosis. Sports team managers scout for players and analyse opponents. Journalists scoop. Members use it to get the best deal. Some information is open to all while other information is discreet and protected from unauthorised access using classifications, such as top secret and confidential, permitting access to those who need to know and providing physical protective security measures. Carelessly handled information can be catastrophic and thus protection is rarely as expensive as insecurity in terms of loss of life, loss of position and loss of credibility. In military terms, intelligence sets out to collect information on armed forces and convert the product into assessments and predictions in time for it to be of use. There is substantial basic information available via the web, publications and displays and exhibitions. There is also selective information which nations wish to protect, such as plans and policies, equipment capabilities, operational orders of battle and personal information.

Intelligence organisations set out to breach enemy defences, in peace and war, so that they have up-to-date information and can gain strategic and operational advantage. Systems on the battlefield include 'document exploitation', collected prisoners and the dead, and intercept of mail. 'Human intelligence' includes the ancient but widely misunderstood art of interrogation of prisoners of war, refugees, spies and well-placed sources and informants. Gossip should not be discarded. 'Signals intelligence' refers to the intercept of communications, which has graduated over the centuries from interpreting messages passed by flags and semaphore lights to the intercept of radios and telephone and, in the modern context, social media, email and mobile telephones. 'Imagery intelligence' and 'topographic intelligence' of the ground can be very revealing, particularly when viewed from the air, and are a crucial in mapping.

Related to intelligence acquisition is the defence and protection of information using protective security and counter-intelligence to protect political, military, research and development and critical assets, such as key buildings and infrastructure from the effects of espionage, sabotage, subversion and terrorism. 'Protective security' sets out to build defensive cocoons of assets by organising a series of defensive barriers arranged in depth to detect, divert, deflect, deter actual and potential attack. 'Counter-intelligence' is the offensive mechanism used to discover and undermine attacks. Security is rarely as expensive as insecurity.

Countries employ cohorts of intelligence and security officers tasked to convert information into intelligence for immediate to long-term use. Key to their skill set is the application of the intelligence cycle, the continuous collection, evaluation, analysis, collation and timely dissemination of information, each item graded according to the reliability of sources and collateral to other information. It is vital that when intelligence is presented, it is done without bias and tailored to please the decision-maker, who should, in turn, consider the conclusions dispassionately. Unfortunately, some intelligence is ignored, not infrequently with disastrous political, military and commercial results.

Recommendations by the 1903 Elgin Committee led to the creation of the Committee of Imperial Defence as an advisory body to the prime minister. The 1904 War Office (Reconstitution) Committee, which is usually known as the Esher Committee, made major recommendations to reorganise the War Office, including:

The Secretary of State for War to have the same political power over the Army as the First Lord of the Admiralty had over the Royal Navy.

The War Office to use the Admiralty Board as a model to establish the Army Council as the principal military policy-making body of the Secretary of State for War.

The Commander-in-Chief to be replaced by the Chief of the Imperial General Staff (CIGS).

A General Staff to control Military Operations, Staff Duties and Military Training and prepare the Army for war.

The Adjutant-General be responsible for administration, recruiting, organisation, medical services and the Auxiliary Services.

The Quartermaster-General be responsible for logistic support to include transport, movements, barracks and quartering, supplies and clothing.

The Master-General of the Ordnance be the Director of Artillery and Director of Fortifications and Works.

Administrative Military Districts to be formed, thereby leaving Army commanders to train for war.

Military Operations (MO) at the War Office was reformed as follows:

MO1: Strategical Section
MO2: Foreign Intelligence
MO3: Administration and Special Duties
MO4: Topographical

Esher also recommended the selection of some General Staff as intelligence officers. The 1904 'Regulations for Intelligence Duties in the Field' stated:

> Whenever possible, the interpreters, permanent guides, scouts, and other employees of the Field Intelligence should be formed into a corps. In civilised warfare they should be temporarily commissioned or enlisted and should wear uniform.
>
> That a Regular officer stationed at headquarters should be detailed to perform the duties of Adjutant of the Intelligence Corps.

Skills of the proposed Intelligence Corps included languages.

Meanwhile Lieutenant-Colonel David Henderson, who had been one of four heads of intelligence during the Boer War, wrote in his 1904 *Field Intelligence Its Principles and Practice* that:

> The successful Intelligence officer must be cool, courageous, and adroit, patient and imperturbable, discreet and trustworthy. He must understand the handling of troops, and have a knowledge of the art of war. He must be able to win the confidence of his General, and to inspire confidence in his subordinates. He must have resolution to continue unceasingly his search for information, even in the most disheartening circumstances and after repeated failures. He must have endurance to submit silently to criticism, much of which may be based on ignorance or jealousy. And he must be able to deal with men, to approach his source of information with tact and skill, whether such source be a patriotic gentleman or an abandoned traitor.
>
> The spectacle of an Intelligence man entering camp in the early morning on a tired horse tends to raise the Intelligence Corps in the esteem of the Army, and there will always be occasions when the display of a little personal gallantry, or the cheerful endurance of exceptional fatigue or discomfort on the part of the Intelligence officers or men, will have a good effect in inspiring that confidence which is required.

In 1904, Lord Bruce, a former viceroy of India, chairing a commission investigating the conduct of the Boer War, concluded that the politics of avoiding discussion of hostilities had meant that intelligence assessments prepared by the Intelligence Division had not been passed to the Cabinet Office and that memoranda had been altered after dissemination. Lieutenant-General White admitted that he had not met with Major-General Sir John Ardagh, the director of military intelligence, before he sailed for South Africa. It then emerged that while the Boer Intelligence Service had spent £170,000 annually on clandestine intelligence operations since 1897, Ardagh had asked for £10,000 but was grudgingly given £100. In a period when press opinion was valued, the *Times* editor George Bell emphasised that while the German General Staff employed over 300 officers and spent £270,000 on intelligence, the War Office Mobilisation and Intelligence Division employed seventeen officers at a cost of £11,000:

> We did not spend nearly enough money, or send enough officers. The eight or ten who went out did very good work, but they were fewer than the men I employed myself as *Times* correspondents, and I should have been ashamed to have sent correspondents anywhere, or even a commercial traveller with the sums of money they were given. Far worse than the starved condition of the Intelligence Division was its lack of authority. It was a mere information bureau with absolutely no control over military policy. Its investigations were not directed with the sense of responsibility that belongs to those who inquire in order to act upon their own information, nor had it the power to insist upon the taking of those measures of the necessity of which its special knowledge convinced it.

The vitriolic attacks on Ardagh and his intelligence officers were quickly replaced by praising the 'quiet backroom boys who had worked so diligently and successfully to predict the outbreak of the war', a cause that has resonated since under several circumstances. When Prime Minister Arthur Balfour spoke in the House of Commons in 1905 of the 'profitless wrangle between the advocates of different schools' and said that the Royal Navy and the army should be available for the defence of the British Empire anywhere, he was referring to the patronising culture promoted by the former commander-in-chief, the late Duke of Cambridge, who advoated rivalry between those officers with substantial experience of campaigning in Africa, the 'Africans', and those who had served largely in India, the 'Indians'. The change in government in 1906 meant that many of Esher's recommendations were not implemented and it took the progressive Secretary of State for War Lord Richard Haldane to establish the British Expeditionary Force (BEF) of two regular corps and a cavalry division, a Territorial Force of fourteen reserve divisions and fourteen yeomanry brigades, the Imperial General Staff and the Advisory Committee for Aeronautics to investigate powered flight.

By 1907, the Directorate of Military Operations consisted of:

MO1:   Imperial Defence: Strategy and Operations
MO2:   Foreign Intelligence: Europe, Near East, USA, Mexico, Central and South America and parts of the Caribbean (North Africa added by 1914)
MO3:   Foreign Intelligence: Asia and the Americas
MO4:   Topography and the study of potential overseas theatres of operations
MO5:   Special Duties: covert intelligence gathering and counter-intelligence
MO6:   Medical Intelligence associated with overseas operations

During the year Major-General Henderson enhanced his reputation as a progressive proponent of tactical intelligence by writing the *Art of Reconnaissance* in which he promoted patrolling and long-range skirmishing. In a debate organised by the Aldershot Military Society, he reinforced his conviction for the need for an Intelligence Corps:

> All persons, except staff officers and secret service agents, permanently engaged on intelligence duties in a campaign should be formed into an Intelligence Corps. The advantage of such an organisation are many; subordinates are more directly under control and know to whom they are responsible; their accounts, and the care of their horses and equipment, can be more easily dealt with; and there is the probability of the growth of an *esprit de corps* which may be invaluable.

The War Office was slow to respond; nevertheless, when Henderson became Director of Training, he insisted that MO5 should, as part of the Army Mobilisation Plan, develop a register of men capable of intelligence duties. The problem was that the War Office believed that since there were no hostilities, then there was no need for intelligence, a culture that prevailed until 1948. Asking the rhetorical question 'what is the army for?' Haldane concluded that it was to match the military threat with sufficient numbers to undertake the task. The problem was it is not always possible to predict the threat.

By the nature of their appointments, military attachés must balance their diplomatic status against the military mission of collecting information. Spread across the globe before the First World War, they stayed in the same country for several years and learnt the culture and language, knew influential people socially and were able to attend military displays, exercises and exhibitions as invited guests. They were thus able to keep the War Office informed of the application of science and technology to the armed forces of the host nation. Officers filling consulates and vice-consulates also had an intelligence role. One intriguing source in Germany was the young daughter of Colonel Arthur Brookfield who chatted with people involved with building warships in Danzig and then shared the content of her conversations with her father. Brookfield, the consul in Danzig, presumably sent the information to the director of Military Intelligence. In any event, it does seem that the information led to the 1909 naval scare that Germany was winning the naval arms race, and to the British ordering eight Dreadnought battleships. Several attachés from Eastern Europe and the Middle East became intelligence officers during the war.

During the early twentieth century, Great Britain had two principal enemies: Germany and the Ottoman Empire. For the sake of simplicity, the latter will hereafter be referred to as Turkey.

The German Threat

When in 1902 William Robertson, once a private and now a lieutenant-colonel, returned to the Intelligence Division from South Africa as head of Foreign Intelligence, he believed that the German expansionist ambitions and belligerence towards Great Britain was caused by an inability to challenge the Royal Navy and 'instead of regarding Germany as a possibly ally, we should recognise her as our most persistent, deliberate and formidable rival'. He then asked the Foreign Office for an assessment of British obligations to Belgium should its neutrality be challenged either by France or Germany. Robertson's comments were noted in government circles and in April 1904 centuries of hostilities between Great Britain and France ended when both countries signed the Declaration Respecting Egypt and Morocco, otherwise known as the *Entente Cordiale*. As Britain drew up contingency planning for hostilities with Germany, Foreign Secretary Sir Edward Grey had several 'conversations' with the French to discuss strategic planning.

After the Prussian statesman Otto von Bismarck had persuaded most of the Teutonic states to merge into Germany under his chancellorship, he then altered the balance of power in Europe by defeating France in 1871. His two principal strategists, Helmuth Karl Bernhard, Graf von Moltke, who had developed the concept that 'no plan survives contact with the enemy' and 'strategy is a system of expedients', and Field-Marshal Albrecht, Graf von Schlieffen, the chief of the Imperial Staff, devised the Schlieffen Plan to defend Germany against a Franco-Russian attack.

Their strategy was to hold the Russians while the majority of the army would bypass the French fortified frontier, strike across the plains of Belgium and northern France, capture Paris and corner the remnants of the French against the Swiss border. While the French army was not as large as the German army, it was highly regarded. The Russian army was large but not well organised. To prevent the British uniting with the French, a corps would seize the Channel ports. The German army was a formidable fighting machine controlled by an efficient General Staff of professional officers focused on fighting in Europe. In comparison, the British had spent seventy years fighting colonial campaigns. By 1914, an efficient national service system had developed requiring all men between the ages of 17 and 44 years to serve two years in the standing army, seven years in the reserves, eleven years in the *Landwehr* (second-line reserve) and, finally, seven years in the *Landsturm* (home guard). The field and foot artillery were the elite. Infantry regiments were generally organised into three battalions, each of four companies of four platoons, the lowest tactical unit being a section of eight men commanded by a lance-corporal. Most regiments had a machine-gun company of six guns.

Invasion had been strong in the British psyche for centuries and when Erskine Childers wrote his novel *Riddle of the Sands* (1903) focusing on Germany sending an army in shallow-draught craft across the North Sea without warning – a bolt from the blue – 'spy fever' gripped the country. An Irish nationalist, Childers was the maritime secretary of the League of Frontiersmen, a 'civil, self-supporting, self-governing Field Intelligence Corps' of patriots and imperialists with frontier, military and naval experience. The populist author William Le Quez exploited the fear with several novels such as *The Invasion of 1910* (1906) and *Spies of the Kaiser* (1909). Inevitably, shallow-minded journalists stoked up fears, to the extent that almost every German in the country became suspect.

An investigation by the Committee of Imperial Defence found that national counter-intelligence was weak and that Special Branch concentrated on domestic threats, principally Irish Fenians. The committee also found that the credibility of the Admiralty and War Office was at risk when it received information gained through espionage, as opposed to through a deniable intermediary. William Melville, a County Kerry-born founder of Special Branch, advocated a counter-intelligence department akin to those formed by most European governments as an interface to protect the governance of departments. Melville had previously been recruited by the Intelligence Division to collect information on German military capabilities and had obtained mobilisation plans and had investigated German financial support to the Boers. In October 1909 a Committee of Imperial Defence subcommittee considered the nature and extent of foreign espionage in Great Britain and reported that since 1907, seventy cases of espionage had been detected with Germany considered to be the prime suspect in the majority of cases investigated. When it also concluded that the acquisition of information on foreign countries was weak, this resulted in the Secret Service Bureau being formed to serve as a cut out between the Admiralty, War Office and foreign spies who might have information for sale; to maintain links between the Home Office, police and agents sent to ascertain the scope of the foreign espionage; and to serve as an intermediary between the Admiralty and the War Office and friendly agents employed in foreign countries.

So secret were the findings that they were not printed nor distributed to the subcommittee, except for a single copy handed to the director of military operations. In 1911, the 1898 Official Secrets Act strengthened the protection of official information, places and activities. The bureau was soon broken into two departments: Home Intelligence and Foreign Intelligence. Home Intelligence was commanded by Captain Vernon Kell (South Staffords), a linguist in several languages who had served in the 1900 Boxer Rebellion in China before ill-health ended his active service in 1902. He had also served in the German Section, Intelligence Division. Foreign Intelligence was managed by Lieutenant-Commander Mansfield Cumming-Smith, who had been forced to retire from the Royal Navy with chronic seasickness.

While Kell inherited an efficient counter-intelligence structure in Great Britain, there was no formal espionage organisation. Most information came from military attachés and the observations of patriotic amateurs collecting information. One such amateur was Captain Bertrand Stewart, a wealthy solicitor educated at Eton and Oxford who had served as a trooper in the Imperial Yeomanry during the Boer War and was a reservist officer in the West Kent Yeomanry. Volunteering to discover German military and naval defences in 1911, he was arrested in a toilet in Bremen reading several documents passed to him. Although the British press claimed the evidence relied on the testimony of a penniless ex-criminal in the pay of the prosecution, Stewart was convicted in January 1912 and sentenced to three years and six months imprisonment. He and two other officers were released in May 1913 when King George V visited Berlin. In German South-West Africa, Captain Edmund Ironsides (Royal Field Artillery) served for two years in the German army collecting information on the German and Boer alliance. Between 1908 and 1911, Brigadier-General Sir Henry Wilson, while commanding the Staff College and as director of military operations, explored the possible axis for a German invasion of France and noted German railway construction close to the border.

When Germany dispatched a warship to the Moroccan port of Agadir in June 1911, ostensibly to protect German interests in a period of localised tension, France and Great Britain regarded this as provocation. In London, Prime Minister Asquith summoned the Committee of Imperial Defence on 23 August at which Brigadier-General Wilson presented a paper on the threat recommending that if Germany attack France through Belgium, the BEF should be sent to fight on the left flank of the French army under its command. By 1912, the General Staff issued the *Handbook of the German Army* describing its conditions of service, war and peace organisation, tactics and orders of battle of the infantry, cavalry, artillery, signals, supply and technical troops and medical services, and its colonial military organisation. Annexes included pay, military terminology, map reading symbols and abbreviations.

The Turkish Threat

The Ottoman Empire emerged from the dynasty founded by Othman I (1258–1326) in north-west Anatolia in modern Turkey. After the Ottomans captured Constantinople (now known as Istanbul) in 1453, their political, economic, maritime and military power empire that grew from the sixteenth to the nineteenth centuries covered the Middle East, south-east Europe, the Caucasus, north Africa and eastern Africa. The main threat to the British was the loss of control of Suez Canal and the potential transfer of lines of communication to India, south-east Asia and Australasia around the Cape of Good Hope. Turkey was regarded as a threat.

Three years after the British had defeated Egyptian nationalist threats in 1882, an Intelligence Branch was formed within the Egyptian army to take over regional intelligence from the War Office-controlled army of occupation, depriving it of an intelligence function. Major Reginald Wingate was appointed head of intelligence and held the post for ten years from 1887 during which he organised an efficient system embracing Sudan and the Suez Canal/Red Sea Egyptian border. But it lacked co-ordination with the Intelligence Division, largely because colonial armies were independent of the War Office. By the end of the wars against the Mahdi in 1898, the branch was reporting to two masters, the *Sirdar* (governor-general) of Sudan and the consul-general in Cairo. While the greater threat was assessed to be from Sudan and not the Turks in Palestine, the military attachés of the Levant Consular Service in Aleppo, Beirut, Damascus and Jerusalem provided sufficient intelligence for the first handbook on the Turkish army, published in 1877. The defence of Egypt relied on preventing the enemy from crossing the Suez Canal.

During the mid-1870s, the declaration by Turkey that part of southern Arabia was to be the province of Yemen induced several border clashes with the British settlement of Aden. Garrison life was grim with Anatolian folklore suggesting a soldier posted to Yemen was as good as dead. The British seizure of Aden in 1839 as the first colony in the reign of Queen Victoria was significant because its port was an important link in the maritime lines of communications to and from India. The settlement was governed from India. The British adopted a strategy of forward defence by agreeing alliances with several emirs and sultans to the north. Yemen had previously been dominated by the imam of the Shi'ite Zaidi tribes, in the northern mountains, who regarded the Sunni Turks to be invaders, and consequently insurrections were not uncommon, particularly after 1891 when the Hamid al-Din family gained the imamate and expanded its political influence into a near-feudal monarchy. By mid-1900, Aden was receiving reports that the Turks were encouraging incursions by Yemeni tribesmen, and tension increased when Turkish troops crossed the border on several occasions. This inevitably led to confrontations, even after Great Britain and Turkey formed a border commission. In February 1902 Turkish soldiers surrounded the British camp, harassed survey parties and strengthened their border garrisons. Aden garrison retaliated a year later by forming the Aden Movable Column, as a flying column, and India sent 2,200 British and Indian troops and artillery to the border with a further 1,400 men available in Aden. Meanwhile, the Turkish garrison of the 30,000-strong VII (Yemen) Corps had been tied down by another insurrection by the Zaidi, citing poor harvests, and two Royal Navy cruisers were sent to the region to dissuade both sides from crossing the border. Having experienced mass surrenders, attempted defections and 27,500 casualties, the Turks agreed to a one-year armistice and Ahmed Fezi Pasha, commander of IV Corps in Baghdad and with thirty years' experience of Yemen, was appointed to command VII (Yemen) Corps.

The rebellion gave the British valuable insight into the Turkish army, a key observer being Lieutenant-Colonel Francis Maunsell (Royal Artillery), the military attaché at the British Embassy in Constantinople. In anticipation of the political and military threat from Turkey, MO2 asked Maunsell to conduct an intelligence survey of Syria, with particular emphasis on Tripoli, Damascus, Deraa, Haifa and the Hejaz Railway, and to identify beaches suitable for amphibious operations. He seems to have shrouded any clandestine intelligence collection by camouflaging his travels as jolly japes; nevertheless he had watched the Turkish army struggle to solve shortages of troopships by sending reinforcements overland from Syria to Yemen and had noted that discontent, desertion, disease, heat and dispatch of East Europeans degraded morale. He noted that the Fifth Army was severely understrength from supplying reinforcements to operations in Macedonia and Yemen. He published his findings in *The Military Report on Syria* (1904), but when he sought financial reimbursement from the War Office on cash spent on *baksheesh* (bribery), the matter was referred to the Foreign Office because the War Office did not have a budget for such skulduggery.

Travellers, archaeologists and officers travelling overland to and from India also provided information. During the late nineteenth century Germany had developed closer links with Turkey by rearming its navy, reorganising the army and the most symbolic of all, financing the Berlin-to-Baghdad railway as a challenge to the Suez Canal. Great Britain had rejected the idea of investing in the project; however, it became the subject of political disagreement with Germany and of intelligence interest. In 1903, the War Office asked Captain Herbert Smyth, on leave from his regiment in India and planning to return overland, to conduct a survey of the railway. Warned that his report would be circulated to the Foreign Office and the government of India and advising him to be open about returning to his regiment, Smyth was given a list of intelligence requirements. During his journey, he noted that the Bedouin did not welcome the railway because it meant repression and confiscation of grazing grounds in favour of the development of fields. He also collected military information on the Sixth Army in Baghdad and bribed an official for troop deployments. Smyth's progressive reports provided accurate intelligence on the effect that the railway had on the indigenous economies and details of its infrastructure, such as bridges and provision of water, and were fully supported with photographs.

When Major Roger Owen was head of Egypt intelligence in 1906 he gave Wilfred Jennings-Bramly a detachment of camel-mounted police and asked him to establish a tripwire of agents centred around wells, Bedouin campsites and caravan routes from Aqaba north to Rafa, on the Mediterranean coast, to give warning of any Turkish incursion. Jennings-Bramly was a desert explorer who had surveyed northern Syria and the western Negev Desert between 1896 and 1901 for 'administrative purposes'. When Turkish troops occupied Taba, an Egyptian town in the Sinai Peninsula, the presence of British troops persuaded them to withdraw; nevertheless, the incident provoked a wave of nationalist unrest challenging Britain's right to negotiate Egyptian territory.

Meanwhile, Jennings-Bramly and Colonel Alfred Parker, the acting governor of Sinai, conducted an intelligence assessment of the desert in the event of a Turkish invasion. Six months later, Owen asked Parker to ensure that the camel police post at Al-Nakhl keep local Bedouin on side and tracks heading towards the Suez Canal be monitored. He ensured quick passage of information by establishing a network of heliographs. A year later, the Committee for Imperial Defence assessed that a Turkish invasion was unlikely because preparations would soon be evident; however, a raid on the Suez Canal was more probable. Internal unrest was considered likely because of instability and the possibility of German subversion and finance fermenting *jihad*. The committee criticised the lack of an intelligence section in the army of occupation and the failure of the Egyptian Intelligence Department to share intelligence.

In 1913, reasoning that it would be easier to obtain a clandestine threat assessment for the defence of the north-east frontier of Egypt, the Foreign Office agreed to a proposal by Major-General Sir Henry Wilson that the War Office finance a survey by the Palestine Exploration Fund of the Wilderness of Zin in southern Palestine. The fund was founded in 1865 specifically to study Palestine and was keen to extend its knowledge from archaeology, survey, photographing sites and inscriptions and mapping place names from the Dead Sea west to Beersheba and Gaza and from Rafa south to Aqaba. However, the fund was not infrequently used as a front for espionage and consequently the fact the proposed location had previously been surveyed was ignored. The Turks agreed to the proposal and Stewart Newcombe, an expert surveyor, was appointed project leader. His team included the archaeologist Leonard Woolley and the topographer Thomas Lawrence. The Royal Geographical Society also contributed to the fund. On completion of the survey in March 1914, Newcombe drafted an academic paper but when the Foreign Office and GHQ Egypt prevented him from publishing it, he solved the impasse by producing an open report entitled *The Wilderness of Zin* with the maps drawn by Lawrence.

The refusal of the Turkish army to quell rebellion in Salonika in 1908 led to the nationalist Committee of Union and Progress (CUP), commonly known as the Young Turks, sharing governance with the army. The Young Turks were determined to recover territory seized by Russia, but were hindered by a government with punishing debts to European banks. After Great Britain had rejected three approaches from the Young Turks in 1911 and during the disastrous 1912–13 Balkans War, during which the equivalent of the two armies of the four German-organised regular armies had been destroyed, the Young Turk leader and minister for war, Ismail Enver Pasha, approached the German ambassador in mid-July 1914. However, the ambassador rejected his suggestion on the grounds that an alliance would invite hostility from Russia, France and Great Britain. Kaiser Wilhelm disagreed and on 2 August both countries signed a secret treaty pertinent to war with Russia.

Lieutenant-Colonel Gerald Tyrell (Royal Artillery), assessing the catastrophic losses, believed that Germany would re-equip the Turkish army. He had served three years with the Macedonian Gendarmerie and four years as the military attaché in Constantinople and Athens. Although the reorganisation in 1913–14 was comprehensive, deficiencies in strategy, material and operational readiness led to Major-General Wilson judging that the Turkish army could no longer be regarded as a serious, modern army. Of concern was that a German military mission commanded by General Liman von Sanders had been seconded to the Turkish army and that German officers held senior appointments. For instance, the appointment of von Sanders to command the 1st Army Corps in December 1913 caused an outcry in Europe and Russia because it meant that a German would control the defence of the approaches to the Sea of Mamara through the Dardanelles.

The era was one of increasing technology and industrialisation, including the development of combustion engines, rifled barrels, steam, iron and barbed wire. It also saw the exploitation of air as the third flank. Balloons had been used during the American Civil War and by the Royal Engineers during the wars in Sudan and in South Africa as observation platforms. The Royal Engineers established the Balloon Section and Depot School at Farnborough in 1906 and experimented with airborne wireless, kites, gliders and dirigibles. A year later, Army Airship No.1 *Nulli Secondus* was launched, and a year later, Army Aeroplane No.1 was built. War Office budgetary constraints curtailed further experiments until Louis Blériot crossed the English Channel three months later. Among those inspired was Major-General David Henderson, who realised that air was a flank and its supremacy was reliant on height and distance. In 1911, aged 49, he became the country's oldest pilot. During the same year, the Royal Engineers formed the Air Battalion of the Headquarters and No.1 (Balloon) Company at Farnborough and No.2 (Aeroplane) Company at Larkhill equipped with a mixture of about twelve aircraft. The reconstruction of Blériot's crashed aircraft at Farnborough in 1911, under the pretext of repairing it, and its emergence as the Santos Experimental-1 (SE-1) reignited War Office interest in the air. Henderson then chaired a technical subcommittee reporting to the Committee of the Imperial Defence from which emerged the Royal Flying Corps (RFC) and its naval wing at Eastchurch on the Isle of Sheppey, the Central Flying School at Upavon and the Royal Aircraft Factory at Farnborough.

The principal role of the RFC of twelve balloons and thirty-six aeroplanes was artillery observation and serving as an intelligence platform. Henderson was appointed the first director of military aeronautics a year later and Lieutenant-Colonel Frederick Sykes the first commanding officer. A former trooper in the Imperial Yeomanry during the Boer War and briefly captured before being badly wounded during the advance to Pretoria, Sykes was commissioned into the 15th Hussars in 1901. His interest in aviation in 1904 saw him awarded his ballooning certificate while posted to the Balloon Section and then, in 1911, he was awarded his pilot's licence. Posted to the Directorate of Military Operations, he promoted the feasibility of aerial reconnaissance and sat on the Committee of Imperial Defence subcommittee. When the RFC sought a motto, Lieutenant J.S. Yule was one of two officers walking from the Farnborough officers' mess and suggested *per ardua ad astra* ('through adversity to the stars'); King George V gave his approval. The Air Battalion reformed first as No.1 Airship and Kite Squadron in May and took over balloon, airship and kite operations from No.1 Airship Company. A month later, the first three aeroplane squadrons were formed. Since the British aviation industry was in its infancy, the pilots flew a variety of aircraft, mostly foreign intermingled with British designs, particularly from de Havilland. The large propellers and wing struts of early aircraft prevented the mounting of a machine-gun and consequently armaments were confined to pistols and rifles.

In October 1912 the War Office published its *Duties of the General Staff in War*. The twenty-three pages of chapter three listed detailed aspects of military intelligence in the field. In essence, commanders-in-chief had overall responsibility for Intelligence and General Staff officers (GSO) would supply sufficient intelligence to enable their commander to fight his battle. In terms of passage of information, the War Office Intelligence Branch would keep the BEF head of intelligence regularly supplied with assessments of enemy intentions, tactics, orders of battle, topography, dispositions and morale – and vice versa. Although the circulation of BEF intelligence to commanders was generally the responsibility of their intelligence sections, the BGGS (I) had direct responsibility for their performance. The basic organisation was:

BEF GHQ	
I(a)	Information
I(b)	Secret Service
I(c)	Topography
I(d)	Censorship and Publicity
Corps HQ	GSO2 and a GSO3
Divisional HQ	GSO3
Brigade HQ	Brigade Major
Regiment/battalion	Intelligence officers

Addressing the threats from espionage, sabotage and subversion to the army in the field, the staff duties stated that: 'All persons (except secret service agents) permanently engaged in intelligence duties will be formed into a special Intelligence Corps for the time being, under the Brigadier-General in charge of the Intelligence Section at General Headquarters.'

The Corps was formed under the provisions in the Staff Manual 1912:

Paragraph 33: Control and Organisation of the Intelligence Service in War
Paragraph 42: Codes and Ciphers
Paragraph 44: Relationship between the Intelligence Section at GHQ and
Intelligence Sections in Subordinate Commands and Intelligence Police

While the Intelligence Corps would report to GHQI(b), intelligence sections in subordinate commands were expected to maintain close links to I(b) but were not to deploy secret agents unless specifically approved by GHQ. An Army Pay Department officer would help with pay and accounts. Civilians recruited into the corps could be granted honorary commissions, be issued with uniforms and be classed as agents. A year later, Lieutenant-Colonel George Macdonogh (Royal Engineers) was commanding MO5 (Secret Service). Commissioned in 1884, he had found Staff College so insufficiently strenuous that he studied law and was called to the Bar. Major Walter Kirke (Royal Artillery), his GSO3I(b) had developed clear instructions for the Intelligence Corps:

- Provide experienced officers with linguistic qualification mounted on horses or on motor cycles or in cars.
- Supplement Intelligence staffs of various headquarters which were obviously inadequate both in numbers and in two essential foreign languages, those of French and German.
- Provide officers for the anticipated expansion of the Secret Service.
- Provide the nucleus of a counter-espionage organisation for the BEF.

Since the Intelligence Corps were not expected to command, except in exceptional cases, Macdonogh created the post of commandant with responsibility for administration, training and discipline. The commandant was to keep in close touch with the requirements of the General Staff (Intelligence) and to provide suitable personnel at short notice for special duties.

HQ Royal Fusiliers at Hounslow Barracks was conveniently close to the War Office to be selected to administer the corps. When talent-spotting for potential Intelligence Corps from the army and civilians, Macdonogh and Kirke largely followed this principle in the 1922 *Manual of Military Intelligence in the Field*: 'The best sources of supply for the Intelligence Corps will be the professional and literary classes, also public schools, universities, banks and commercial houses with overseas branches or trade connections with foreign countries.'

Knowledge of French and German, at the very least, was considered vital. Among those talent-spotted was Albert Sang. Born in 1876 to Anglo-German parents and raised in Paris where his father was a landscape artist, he trained as an analytical chemist and metallurgical engineer and, while writing a book entitled *The Corrosion of Iron and Steel*, built a successful business with offices in London, Pittsburgh, Paris, Frankfurt and St Petersburg. He married the daughter of a Pittsburgh steel magnate and fathered two children. Pittsburgh had become a centre for the 'sherardising' (or dry galvanising) process in which articles heated in zinc dust were given a zinc–iron alloy that prevented rust. Sang returned to Paris where in 1909 with the 'sherardising' patents for France he planned to expand his business. However, in 1914, it seems his marriage was weakening.

Meanwhile, shifting balances of power and political tensions and challenges in Europe and Russia, in particular Russia and Serbia competing for influence, led to Archduke Franz Ferdinand of Austria being shot by a Serbian student. When Prime Minister Herbert Asquith warned a belligerent Germany to acknowledge Belgian neutrality by respecting the 1839 Treaty of London, the Kaiser dismissed it as 'a scrap of paper' and invaded on 3 August. At 11 p.m. on 4 August Great Britain declared war on Germany and orders were despatched to mobilise the BEF.

The defence of Great Britain was entrusted to Home Intelligence and the constabularies and on receiving a prearranged coded message and using information filed on the Special War Lists, Captain Kell and the Secret Service Bureau (Home) co-ordinated the arrest of the twenty-two German agents known to be operating in the UK and began active monitoring of about 200 suspects. Of the thirty-one agents tried between October 1914 and September 1917, twelve were executed; seven had their death sentences commuted to penal servitude, ten were imprisoned and two were discharged. 'Cover' occupations used included businessmen, journalists, employees, no occupation and travelling for 'health reasons'.

In a single blow Germany lost its information flow from Great Britain. Among those arrested was Gustav Stenhauer, the head of the German Intelligence Service in Great Britain and a former member of the US Pinkerton Detective Agency. Knowledge of his activities was deduced from intercepted letters.

The passing of the Defence of the Realm Act on 8 August gave the authorities unprecedented power to ensure public safety, suppress public criticism, requisition economic resources, impose censorship, imprison without trial and give the War Office and Admiralty powers to take over engineering works, introduce conscription and take measures to defend the realm. This last included restricted pub opening times, the introduction in 1916 of British Summer Time to save energy costs, and food rationing in January 1918 to prevent panic buying during shortages caused by the action of U-boats. Anyone of alien origin had to register, a total of about 66,000 people. Of these, 34,500 considered to be enemy nationals or related by blood or marriage were found during the war, which included serving personnel. On 8 September, Bow Street Magistrates sentenced Special Constable Max Curtis to six months' imprisonment for failing to register, even though he had lived in England for six months and had changed his name from Duntz because it sounded like 'dunce'. In mid-October, a wealthy recently married Austrian couple committed suicide rather than be separated by internment.

Major-General Sir Charles Callwell (late Royal Field Artillery), an experienced intelligence officer, who had written several intelligence-related books, replaced Wilson as director of military operations with responsibility for intelligence. Wilson was appointed the BEF chief of staff. Callwell would find that Lord Kitchener, the Secretary of State for War, a political post, frequently bypassed the General Staff and interfered with decisions of a military operational nature. On 15 August 1914, the Directorate of Military Intelligence consisted of:

MILITARY OPERATIONS (INTELLIGENCE)

MO1   **Strategical Intelligence**

MO2   **Collection of Intelligence**
MO2(a)   Italy, Portugal, Spain, Central America, USA, Libya
MO2(b)   Abyssinia, Austro-Hungarian Empire, Balkans, Ottoman Empire, Switzerland
MO2(c)   Germany, Holland, Luxembourg

MO3   **Collection of Intelligence**
MO3(a)   Belgium, France
MO3(b)   Russia, Scandinavia, Morocco
MO3(c)   China, Japan, Korea, Tibet

MO4   **Geographical and Library**

MO5   **Special Intelligence**
MO5(a)   Submarine cables, intercept, martial law
MO5(b)   Intelligence library
MO5(c)   Personnel
MO5(d)   Cable censorship
MO5(e)   Investigation of enemy cipher
MO5(f)   Translation
MO5(g)   Secret Service Bureau
MO5(h)   Postal censorship

MO6   **Special Intelligence**
MO6(a)   Collection of war intelligence
MO6(b)   Liaison with espionage sevices
MO6(c)   Medical disbanded

MO7   **Military Assistant Services**
MO7(a)   Control of Press Services
MO7(b)   Control of BEF Press
MO7(c)   Press cable censorship

MO8   **Cable censorship**

MO9   **Postal censorship**

In terms of home defence, the Ministry of Munitions Labour Intelligence Division was formed to protect munitions factories from espionage and sabotage. In order to shield its purpose, it was later renamed the 'Parliamentary Military Secretary Department No. 2' and absorbed into MI5. Indeed, nearly every ministry developed an intelligence department during the war, which proved cumbersome. Military Port Control was started during 1915, and later joined MI5, to monitor access to Great Britain via ports and harbours.

2
The Western Front, 1914

As Belgium stubbornly resisted the German invasion, on 5 August telegram boys delivered telegrams to eighty-one men talent-spotted to join a military force which existed in name only: the Intelligence Corps. And as the BEF mobilisation plan developed, Major Kirke later wrote:

> Immediately an ultimatum to Germany was decided upon, steps were taken to organise an Intelligence Corps in accordance with the provisions of the Staff Manual 1912, paras 33 and 44. Although the need for an Intelligence Corps was already accepted in the War Office, nothing of its kind had ever before existed in practice. When the word to mobilise came on 4th August, I was ordered to take charge of Secret Service arrangements for the Expeditionary Force and to organise an Intelligence Corps forthwith. The page here was completely blank, and the puzzle was how to fill it.

As the replies were returned, he constructed its order of battle thus:

Headquarters Wing of 20 all ranks
>   Commandant
>   Adjutant
>   Quartermaster
>   Section Commanders
>   Six drivers
>   Four cooks

Scout Wing of 25 officers
>   Dismounted Section
>   Mounted Section
>   Motor-Cycle Section. The motorcycles were a mix of Douglas, Premier, Rudge and Triumph machines.

Security Duties Section of 25

HQ Royal Fusiliers formed the 10th (Intelligence) Battalion at Hounslow Barracks to administer the new unit. The regiment formed forty-seven battalions including seven Labour, four Public Schools and two Sportsmen battalions.

Major Thomas Torrie (17th Light Cavalry) was the brigade major of the Lucknow Cavalry Brigade and, as was customary for officers on leave from the colonies, he reported to the War Office and was offered the post of commandant, Intelligence Corps and GSO2 by his cousin, Lieutenant-Colonel Macdonogh, even though he had no direct experience of intelligence. After leaving Macdonogh, Torrie met an acquaintance, Captain John Dunnington-Jefferson (Royal Fusiliers) in a corridor, also on leave from India, and was convinced by his uncertain linguistic skills in French and German to invite him to join the Intelligence Corps. Second-Lieutenant A.E. Richardson (Rifle Brigade), who had been very recently commissioned from the ranks, was appointed quartermaster. Torrie also visited the Metropolitan Police Special Branch and arranged for the Special Duties Section of sixteen sergeants and seven constables to be mobilised. Its role would be:

> To prevent the collection and transmission to the enemy of information bearing on military operations, the detection of enemy agents and the control of the movements of suspects and undesirables. They should not make enquiries respecting larcenies and cases of desertion and it is not part of their duties to detect the illicit sale of spirits to troops or drinking during prohibited hours or to interfere with the morality and discipline of the British Military.

Essentially, it was to protect the lines of communications, which can be defined as a route, either land, water or air, which connects an operating military force with a base of operations and along which supplies and military forces move. The policemen were commanded by Inspector Curry; he was assisted by WO2 Rendall and CQMS Byart. PC Percy Smith had written to Lord Kitchener offering his services and had been directed to 10th (Intelligence) Battalion.

Several serving officers attached to the Intelligence Corps wore their regimental uniform. As the preselected new officers arrived, they were given temporary commissions in the General Service Corps either for six months or the duration of hostilities and issued with 'other rank' uniforms, Royal Court of Arms insignia and a £50 uniform allowance, which most used to purchase a service dress uniform or the jacket, not infrequently second-hand. Twelve applicants subjected to a French examination failed. Those who passed were ranked as Staff Lieutenants 2nd Class (Interpreters) and given a .303 Lee Enfield rifle and 100 rounds. The General Service Corps was a holding unit for specialists, usually reservists, yet to be assigned to a regiment or a corps. Their ages ranged from 24 to 46 years; several had seen active service in South Africa and in the 1900 Boxer Rebellion and knowledge of German was common. Given the rank of staff sergeant, PC Smith was issued with a uniform, a Webley revolver and twenty-five rounds of ammunition, a large tin of bully (beef), about 5lb of cheese, some hard biscuits and a rail warrant to join the BEF at Le Havre.

By 9 August 1914, as the Germans were powering through Belgium against plucky resistance and as they subsequently entered France, the leading elements of the 120,000 Regulars of the BEF under the command of Field-Marshal Sir John French began crossing the English Channel protected by the Royal Navy in such secrecy that the German High Command doubted British commitment. Unpopular and with some doubting his ability to command the BEF, French had been Chief of the Imperial General Staff (CIGS) before handing the appointment to General Sir Charles Douglas. One problem faced by senior commanders was that Field-Marshal Lord Kitchener, who was the Secretary of State for War, disagreed with the concept of the General Staff and insisted on being involved in military strategy, as opposed to managing the politics. It was not unusual for him to attend meetings dressed his uniform. Military Operations was expanded to:

MO7   Collate information from all branches of the War Office and pass it to the Admiralty and the War Office Press Bureau
MO8   Cable censorship
MO9   Postal censorship

After transferring his appointment as director of military intelligence to Captain Archibald Wavell, a Russian Section desk officer and one of the few officers without a defined mobilisation role, Lieutenant-Colonel Macdonogh, now BEF colonel General Staff (Intelligence), and his staff took the train to Southampton on 11 August. With him was Captain Edgar Cox (Royal Engineers), who became responsible for tracking the German order of battle from interrogations, documents and information from the Secret Service Bureau. Their vacated desks were filled by retired officers, irreverently known as 'dug outs', and enthusiastic amateurs. Wavell used powers reserved for the Army Council to conduct investigations, in one instance for the loss of a cipher. A key expert was Major Basil Bowdler (Royal Engineers) who had been in the directorate since 1910 and had written the *Handbook of the German Army*, a reference book regularly updated and distributed and covering:

- Recruiting and recruit training
- Officers and non-commissioned officers
- Mobilisation and the expansion of the German army
- Command and staff
- Infantry
- Machine guns and automatic rifles
- Cavalry

- Artillery: field, foot, mountain, trench and ammunition supply
- Technical Troops: engineers, pioneers, signals, railway and motor transport, survey units
- Air services
- Administrative services: medical services and veterinary services
- *Landsturm* units: coastal defence, frontiers, fortresses, lines of communication guards, prisoner of war guards, occupied country garrisons, labour units and unarmed units
- Uniforms
- Appendices of new equipment
- Photographs

Conjunctivitis prevented Bowdler from active service; nevertheless, he was mentioned in dispatches five times between 1914 and 1919 and was awarded the DSO in January 1916 and CMG the following year for his work.

At Southampton, Torrie organised his Intelligence Corps by appointing Dunnington-Jefferson as corps adjutant and dividing his officers into one of the sections. Major John Lawrence Baird MP, aged 40, held a Territorial Force commission in the Scottish Horse and was a diplomat of some distinction. When he arrived in Southampton he found some Intelligence Corps personnel 'grousing because they thought they had joined as officers, but had been told to look after their own horses'. Baird records that the strength of the cohort that arrived in France was sixty officers, of whom thirteen were regular officers and forty-two were second-lieutenants. Collectively, they became known as the 'Original 55'. The Security Duties Section and a clerk and batmen are not included.

The Honourable Maurice Baring, a widely travelled noted dramatist, linguist and essayist, had seen his friend Major-General David Henderson, then commanding the RFC, and was commissioned into the Intelligence Corps as his intelligence officer. After spending the night on the Queen's Hotel billiard table in Farnborough, he took the train to Newhaven on 11 August, crossed the Channel in the passenge-cargo ship the *Canterbury*, and joined a train going to Amiens, where he essentially became a staff officer to Henderson. Captain Frederick Hunt had been commissioned into the Leicestershire Regiment before transferring, in 1909, to the 19th Bengal Lancers (Fane's Horse). On leave in England with three colleagues, he was directed by the War Office to the Intelligence Corps. His regiment later arrived in France in 1914 as part of the Indian Expeditionary Force A. In 1914, the Indian army was the largest regular army in the world with a total strength of 240,000 men and was the Imperial Strategic Reserve; at the outbreak of war it deployed eight Indian Expeditionary Forces (IEF), usually of at least two divisions, lettered A to G. In most cases, they were replaced in India by British Territorial Army battalions.

In the Scouts Section, Second-Lieutenant Rolleston West had just left Cambridge University with an engineering degree and was on a motorcycling holiday in Wales when war was declared. Rejected by a Birmingham unit seeking motorcyclists, he made his way to a unit in Battersea but was again rejected. Nothing ventured, nothing gained, he returned to Birmingham and still finding there were still no vacancies, he rode to Cambridge and joined a friend with the intention of enlisting in the Royal Engineers in Chatham. However, his gallant motorcycle broke down near Baldock; nevertheless, he reached Chatham only to be told that the Royal Engineers were up to establishment and was advised to go to the War Office, which was also seeking motorcyclists. Admitting that he could speak French and German and was an experienced motorcyclist, he was commissioned into the Intelligence Corps by Captain Cox on 10 August and assigned to the Motor-Cycle Section. Rolleston West purchased a second-hand uniform at Moss Bros in London, was given overnight leave and next day posed for a portrait photograph with his family, complete with his motorcycle goggles.

After a long day waiting to embark, at about 5 p.m., the majority of the Intelligence Corps embarked on the SS *Olympia* for the night crossing to Le Havre, along with a battalion from the Coldstream Guards and the Royal Sussex Regiment. Captain Baird gives a flavour of the crossing: 'Men in splendid spirits, cheering and singing "God save the King" and patriotic songs. The route across was patrolled by three warships, so disposed that if a ship gets through the line in the dark, she cannot reach the third before daybreak. The ships were ten miles apart.'

Early the next morning the ship hovered in the port waiting for an empty jetty to emerge from the marching infantry, horses and piles of stores. Difficulties were then experienced unloading a lorry and disembarkation began at 9 a.m. Leaving the Mounted Section to follow, Torrie instructed the Motor-Cycle Section to ride the 2 miles up a steep hill to a mobilisation camp overlooking Harfleur that later became known as No.7 Infantry Base Depot. But so rapid had been the deployment that while lines of ten-man bell tents had been erected, there was no cookhouse and a tap dripped a feeble flow. The following day it rained heavily and the camp became a sea of mud, a foretaste of conditions encountered over the next four years. Since he felt that the corps needed to be flexible, Torrie dispensed with most of the horses because they required water, food and rest and strengthened the Motor-Cycle Section with more machines and a staff car for him. On 15 August Macdonogh sent Baird to the Adjutant-General Department as its intelligence officer and then he and Major Kirke met Captain John Cuffe, the British liaison officer to HQ Second French Army. Cuffe and Baird then drove to Mons to set up an intelligence collection system among the local population. Meanwhile, the second-lieutenants were given rudimentary training in weapon handling, reconnaissance and demolition, in between sending French speakers to interpret with the local and port authorities.

No one really knew how to employ the Security Duties Section and so they reverted to investigating crime and established a good relationship with the local *Gendarmerie* in Le Havre. When an epidemic of horse-stealing broke out at the Remount Depot, the former police officers recognised several well-known 'lags' among the troops, and after establishing an observation post overlooking the horse lines they arrested a soldier acting suspiciously. His interview unearthed a racket in which a French farmer was buying British horses, which he then sold as meat to the French army. It then emerged that several of the 'lags' had given false names on enlistment and so they were escorted back to England to be discharged. Smith believed most would re-enlist under aliases.

Meanwhile, the BEF made its way by train and road to its concentration area on the left of the French Fifth Army among the coal mines, slagheaps, factories and shabby cottages south of Mons between Le Cateau and the fortress at Mauberge. The left flank was exposed by undefended ground stretching 50 miles to the Channel coast. On the left, II Corps took up defensive positions along the Mons-Condé canal in Belgium, while I Corps was positioned along the Mons-Beaumont road on the right. The dominant geographical feature was a loop in the canal. The Intelligence Corps left Le Havre on 19 August and arrived at Amiens two days later. The only accident was Second-Lieutenant C. Fairbairn managing to entangle his rifle into the spokes of his motorcycle front wheel. When Lieutenant-Colonel Macdonogh instructed Major Torrie to deploy the Scout Section to the divisions, Torrie dispersed them with the instruction 'Make yourselves useful'. Most of those with motorcycles became dispatch riders.

The newly commissioned officers of the Intelligence Corps, most older than the average second-lieutenant and some distinctive in their other rank uniforms, joined a tightly knit regular army in which culture, tradition and history was strong and Intelligence, as a military discipline, purely incidental. Since the philosophy of commanders on seeing the enemy tended to be to take some form of action, perhaps to charge, as opposed to considering enemy intentions, their credibility was somewhat undermined and they were regarded as a spare pair of hands. Lieutenant-General Sir Douglas Haig, commanding I Corps, saw no reason for the Intelligence Corps. On the other hand, when Second-Lieutenant William Gabain was sent to Major-General Edmund Allenby's Cavalry Division and Second-Lieutenant E.H. Barker to the 18th Hussars, both were instructed to follow the expected counter-attack and collect information.

The French dispensed with their defensive strategy of using their fortresses in favour of an offensive strategy to blunt the German advance, first in Lorraine and then in the Ardennes. But little was known about German dispositions and intentions and consequently caution overruled élan. Meanwhile, two German armies swept aside the Belgians and, advancing south, forced the French commander-in-chief, Marshal Joseph Joffre, to divert forces to protect Paris.

Brigadier-General Henderson had mobilised four of his seven RFC squadrons, No.1 Squadron re-equipping with aircraft and Nos 6 and 7 Squadrons still forming up. The Naval Wing had transferred to the Royal Navy as the Royal Naval Air Service (RNAS). Four Australians formed the embryonic Australian Flying Corps. In a deployment that tested aircraft, pilot navigation and the ground deployment, the corps concentrated first at Netheravon and then reassembled near in a field flat enough for fragile undercarriages on the outskirts of Mauberge, about 9 miles from the Belgian border, with reasonable access to a road. During the morning of 19 August Captain Philip Joubert de la Ferte (Royal Field Artillery) flying a Blériot of No.3 Squadron, and Lieutenant Gilbert Mapplebeck (King's Regiment) in a No.4 Squadron BE-2c took off to locate the enemy or the Belgian army; however, their navigation skills were weak and they got lost.

During the day, as German cavalry patrols threatened the lines of communications, 19th Infantry Brigade was formed as an independent brigade and was supported by an Intelligence Corps detachment that consisted of Second-Lieutenants Fletcher, Sang and Rolleston West from the Motor-Cycle Section, King from the Mounted Section and Sergeant Woodhall from the Special Duty Section. Second-Lieutenant Walter Fletcher was an Eton College King's Scholar, who had graduated from Oxford University in German and had taught at Schleswig Gymnasium, Shrewsbury School and Eton.

The BEF relied on the Royal Engineers Signal Section to provide divisional signal companies of a headquarters section and three cable platoons of twenty-six men equipped with a horse-drawn cable layer, field telephones and reserve semaphore. Wirelesses were found in senior HQs and in wireless troops of cavalry brigades using wagons. Before the war, the French had erected a network of wireless intercept stations along its eastern borders and were able to deduce German intentions by direction-finding and could identify units by call signs and whether they were cavalry or slower infantry. While the Royal Navy exploited wireless intercept, the British army had no such capability; nevertheless, the BEF director of signals instructed, in mid-August, that information intercepted from German wireless transmissions were to be forwarded to GHQ Intelligence. But the concept of interception was generally not understood and IV Corps compromised its advance to St Omer by asking in clear speech on a wireless for maps of the region. At the end of the month on the Eastern Front, the German intercept of a Russian wireless message detailing orders for planned attacks gave General Paul von Hindenburg and his deputy, General Erich Ludendorff, time to shift troops from East Prussia and thus to defeat the Russians at the Battle of Tannenberg. The French broke German codes a month later and by the First Battle of Ypres in October and November they were circulating wireless intercepts of German intentions.

By the third week of August 1914, the BEF were deployed along a 26-mile front with II Corps on the left and I Corps on the right alongside the French Fifth

Army. The Cavalry Division protected the left flank. Although the Mons–Conde canal was not a major obstacle and the ground on the north bank was strewn with woods and clusters of buildings, II Corps defended the several bridges, but most were half-heartedly prepared for demolition.

During the first clashes on 21 August, an unnamed Intelligence Corps officer collected information as the German 9th Cavalry Division clattered into Nivelle and then left by car. His exploits are recorded in *Military Operations, France and Belgium 1914* written by Brigadier-General James Edmonds, a Royal Engineer, who had served as an intelligence officer during the Second Boer War. After the first clash between British and German forces in the twentieth century between two troops of the 4th Royal Irish Dragoon Guards and a 2nd Kuirassiers patrol near Mons, the next day, during which five Germans were captured, the RFC launched several reconnaissance flights.

Pilot Lieutenant Vivian Wadham (Royal Hampshires) and observer Captain Lionel Charlton (Lancashire Fusiliers), from No.3 Squadron RFC, took off on a reconnaissance from Mauberge on a circular route towards Brussels and then Mons. Noting many fires in the countryside south of Brussels and seeing several Taube fighters, which they knew operated with German Uhlan cavalry, they landed in a meadow and learnt from villagers that German troops were everywhere; indeed, as they took off, they were shot at by resting soldiers. Climbing to 4,000ft to avoid more ground fire, they noted Germans were moving south-west toward the BEF left flank. Their report and others received at GHQ led Lieutenant-Colonel Macdonogh to assess that the BEF was faced by three German corps and that Mons was their objective; however, Field-Marshal French was not going to accept intelligence from a modern and untested technology that contradicted his belief that he was facing a division and proposed to advance to Soignies. He had interviewed Charlton, but was more interested in his aircraft. He had also rejected the cavalry screen reports of large German formations near Nivelle. The troops were the German First Army advancing south and laying waste everything in its path.

Sergeant-Major David Jillings, a No.2 Squadron observer, became the first British airman to be wounded when he was shot in the leg by ground fire. Lieutenant Vincent Waterfall (East Yorkshires) and his South African observer, Lieutenant Charles Bayly (Royal Engineers), from No.5 Squadron, were the first RFC to be killed in action when they left Mauberge in an Avro 504 on a reconnaissance over Mons and Soignes during the morning and were shot down near Enghien thirty minutes later by ground fire. Bayly's written notes of a cavalry column found by some Belgians eventually reached the War Office.

In bitter fighting, the French lost 27,000 men during the day and when the French Fifth Army asked the BEF to attack the German right, French refused to expose his left, nevertheless, he still did not appreciate the gravity of the situation, even after meeting his two corps commanders for an early morning briefing before he left to visit 19th Brigade.

At dawn the next day a 1st Middlesex private who had previously been a bugler at the British Embassy in Peking noticed that troops emerging from a wood on the northern bank of the canal near Oburg were wearing German uniforms. Artillery then shelled the loop in the canal; however, the parade ground advance towards several bridges was shattered by British infantry firing fifteen rounds per minute from their .303-in Short Magazine Lee Enfield rifles and ten-round magazine and from Vickers machine guns. With Mons under serious threat and the French Fifth Army set on withdrawing, French prepared to counter-attack and regain ground lost, but when air reconnaissance indicated that the Germans intended to surround the BEF, a view supported by Macdonogh and Captain Edward Spears. an intelligence officer attached to the French Secret Service, he had no alternative but to order a withdrawal. At Le Cateau near the French border, Lieutenant-General Sir Horace Smith-Dorrien, one of the very few survivors of the Battle of Isandlwana during the Zulu War, and commanding II Corps, said 'I'll fight it out.'

Since no enemy cavalry had been seen, the Cavalry Division was tasked to find II Corps, who had been busy protecting the BEF right flank. The 15th Brigade in 2nd Division was commanded by Brigadier-General Count Albert Gleichen (Grenadier Guards), a former intelligence officer. When 5th Division was hit hard by the German IV Corps on 24 August, a rearguard of two infantry battalions and 119th Battery RFA was formed to shore up the defence. Allenby responded to the request for help by sending 2nd Cavalry Brigade to take up positions around the village of Elouges and helped to protect L Battery RHA west of the village. Attached to the 9th Lancers was Second-Lieutenant Julian Smith (Intelligence Corps). When the 14th and 15th Cavalry Brigades came under intense German pressure and Gleichen sought help from the 2nd Cavalry Brigade, in a scene reminiscent of the Charge of the Light Brigade during the Crimean War, its three regiments wheeled and charged into a hail of shelling and machine gun and rifle fire but were then trapped by a wire fence. Having scattered the British cavalry screen, the Germans advanced under intense shelling, which prevented the 119th Battery horse teams linking up with their guns. Major Earnest Alexander, the battery commander, refused to abandon them and asked Captain Francis Grenfell, of the 9th Lancers, to recover them. Grenfell, who had been wounded in the charge and was rallying his squadron behind a railway embankment, agreed and Alexander, Grenfell and forty volunteers manhandled the guns to a place where they were attached to their limbers. Alexander and Grenfell were both awarded Victoria Crosses.

The arrival of twenty-seven reinforcements in the third week of August bought the strength of the Intelligence Corps to nearly 100. Among them was Bertram Stewart, now a Territorial Force captain in the West Kent Yeomanry. In 1913, he had written the *Active Service Pocket Book* and a well-regarded article in the June 1914 *National Review* entitled 'Germany and Ourselves'. He was sent to the 1st Cavalry Division. Lieutenant Alistair Smith-Cumming (Seaforth Highlanders) was the son of Lieutenant-Commander Smith-Cumming. The Irish aristocrat Lord Ian Basil Gawaine Temple Hamilton-Temple-Blackwood was the third son of the 1st Marquis of Dufferin, the noted prominent colonial administrator in Canada and India. At Oxford University, he had become involved in the Cecil Rhodes–Alfred Milner cartel promoting British global domination. Lieutenant James Marshall-Cornwall (Royal Field Artillery), an interpreter fluent in Dutch, French, German, Italian and Norwegian and an instructor in military topography at the Royal Military Academy, Woolwich, arrived at St Nazaire on a horse named Sunbeam, requisitioned from the Grafton Hunt. He had been touring the Peninsular War battlefields in Portugal and was dining with the British consul in Oporto when a telegram arrived announcing that Great Britain was at war with Germany. Returning to England and reporting to the War Office, he was instructed to join the Intelligence Corps, about which he knew nothing, and was assigned to the Mounted Section.

Delays were experienced in unloading the horses and when Lieutenant Cornwall claimed that he could ride a motorcycle, he persuaded Second-Lieutenant William Blennerhasset to allow him to be pillion. The son of an Irish earl and a German mother, Blennerhasset knew most of the Bavarian aristocracy, including Crown Prince Rupprecht of Bavaria, one of the German army commanders on the Western Front. After coaxing the engine into life, they wobbled along the road for about 50 yards until it became clear that Blennerhasset was equally unfamiliar with motorcycles and eventually lost control, unceremoniously dumping both officers into a French gutter. Leaving the motorcycle behind a hedge, they hitched a lift in a lorry to the camp. The ability to ride a motorcycle was a requirement for Intelligence Corps; indeed, by June 1916 its officers at army and corps level were issued with one. Inevitably there were accidents. In August 1916, Blennerhasset was judged to be so severely injured when he was run over by a tram after he skidded in front of it that his wife was summoned to his bedside; he recovered within a few days, much to the indignation of his wife who considered her journey to be pointless.

After several days helping the port movements staff, Cornwall was sent by lorry to GHQ at Le Cateau where he helped II Corps with prisoner interrogations until corps headquarters was ordered to retire to Compiègne and he guided some sixty-five horses along roads congested by retreating French troops and refugees, while their owners travelled by car. He then joined HQ 3rd Division as an intelligence officer until the Corps GSO1, Lieutenant-Colonel Maurice, asked him to command the Divisional Mounted Troop provided by A Squadron, 15th Hussars after it had lost its officers, except for an inexperienced second-lieutenant.

On 25 August, when three No.2 Squadron aircraft forced a German Taube aircraft to land, the crew of one British aircraft landed and chased the Germans into nearby woods and then set fire to the enemy aircraft. On 28 August Lieutenant L.A. Strange of No.5 Squadron dropped a home-made petrol bomb on a German truck near Mons, which then caught fire and ignited petrol that set other vehicles on fire.

The following afternoon Lieutenant-Colonel Macdonogh sent Second-Lieutenants Le Grand and A.D. Harvey to collect stragglers near Wassigny. The two officers persuaded several civilians owning bicycles to look for German patrols and direct stragglers to them. By the next morning they had gathered several soldiers. When a civilian reported a mounted Uhlan patrol leaving Le Cateau, Harvey sent six hussars to deal with them and then both officers set off for St Quentin. En route, they met a car containing several French officers heading toward Le Cateau and warned them of the enemy patrols. Le Grand and the French were captured soon afterwards. Harvey was instructed to link up with HQ 5th Cavalry Brigade and, after refuelling his machine at Vaucennes on 1 September, set off to rejoin Brigade HQ at Villers-Cotteret. Two miles short of the village, he saw German infantry and as he accelerated away from them and sped around a corner, an Uhlan galloping towards him lanced his wrist, causing him to crash and be captured. Second-Lieutenants Breen – usually a clerk at the High Sheriff's office in Dublin – and Bevan, an officer cadet at Sandhurst, were also captured by German cavalry, their motorcycles no match for the flexibility of horses.

The Intelligence Corps earned its first gallantry decoration on 30 August. Second-Lieutenant Roger Rolleston West had been instructed by Colonel Ward, the 19th Brigade commander, to take a message to 1st Middlesex, which was providing the rearguard in the village of Pontoise-le-Noyon. Shortly after leaving Battalion HQ, he realised that he had forgotten his maps and was crossing the suspension bridge over the River Oise to retrieve them when he noted that demolition charges had failed to detonate. His observation was crucial because the bridge was the last that needed destruction in order to prevent von Kluck's cavalry crossing the river. Ignoring orders from Ward to return to Brigade HQ, he reported the problem to 59th Field Company, where Major G. Walker instructed Lieutenant James Pennycuik RE to destroy the bridge by placing charges on its piers. When West offered to help, they loaded West's motorcycle with a box of fourteen gun-cotton slabs and set off, with Pennycuik, his pockets full of primers and detonators, sitting on the explosive. Forcing their way through retreating troops and refugees, they reached the bridge and prepared the bridge for demolition, but again the charges failed. Pennycuik replaced the detonators and watched as the explosion ripped the cable between the piers and collapsed the trackway into the river. Both men were awarded DSOs.

Having held off numerically superior forces during the retreat from Mons, on 31 August Field-Marshal French threatened to withdraw the BEF for rest and reorganisation behind the River Seine, until Lord Kitchener persuaded him not to do so, agreeing with the proviso that the French did not expose his flanks by withdrawing without warning. At the end of August, Brigadier-General Henderson was transferred to command the 1st Infantry Division, leaving Lieutenant-Colonel Sykes, his chief of staff, to command the RFC; however, Kitchener objected to the move and a month later he resumed command of the RFC.

After an exhausting 200-mile retreat during which the BEF had fought, marched and briefly slept on hot days and warm nights, it crossed the River Marne on 3 September, ready to defend Paris, and bloew up bridges behind it. Most officers had left England in the expectation of transport to carry tents, camp beds, tables and chairs and crockery, but were relegated to carrying only the equipment they needed. The *Times* dated 5 September described that at crossroads, bridges and high ground:

> The retreating British left a detachment lining both sides of the road. The Germans appeared and were allowed to come within a few hundred yards. Then, as if by magic, two British machine guns in command of a British officer with a dozen men swing into the road and the machine guns and rifles blaze at short range into the Germans. A few minutes later, the British are marching along the road, whistling to the next 'station' … Our men, though cheerful, are angry at the continuous retreat, the need of which they do not understand, and the unending numbers of Germans.

In a letter printed in the *Times* on 12 September, a 3rd Coldstream Guardsman described his experiences at Mons:

> One machine-gun was placed on each corner, and about 60 of us lay cross the street, and as they advanced, we poured fire into them. This commenced at 8 p.m. on Tuesday and we lay there until 4 a.m. on Wednesday. The Germans had one big gun about 600 yards down the road and when they fired this we could see the shell leave the gun and pass over our head … There was a barbed wire fence about 75 yards from where we were lying. When they advanced too near this, the captain said 'Fire!' and the boys didn't half let go.

The German First and Second Armies also needed to rest after a month advancing against determined opposition. Their logistic tails were beginning to creak as the road and rail lines of communication that were moving men, ammunition and supplies lengthened, in spite of 26,000 railway construction workers struggling to repair damaged railways. The pivotal railhead at Liège was also congested and road convoys were hampered by refugees. To some extent, the rapidity of the fighting can be attributed to the cavalry moving quickly, to motor vehicles on the battlefield and German armoured cars able to carry squads of about ten riflemen. Both sides complained that 'dum dum' bullets, which expand on impact, were causing serious wounds. The reality was that both sides were using sharp-pointed bullets.

As is so frequent during retreats, the collection of intelligence had been difficult; nevertheless, astute interpretation of fragmentary information from prisoner interrogations and of captured documents translated by the Intelligence Corps had helped. The rudimentary air photography achieved a significant coup when three fresh German corps on the right flank of the BEF were identified. Throughout the retreat, the Security Duties Section were at something of a loss. Unfamiliar with the army and its culture and with no counter-intelligence policies to follow, the manoeuvre warfare meant that counter-intelligence was a low priority, although in September a French farmer was unearthed telephoning the Germans with details of British troop movements, and so the section was largely relegated to escort VIP escorts and as couriers.

Shortly before midnight on 1–2 September, the French had gained a priceless intelligence scoop when a knapsack containing a map showing German intended lines of march and objectives south-east of Paris, thereby exposing their right flank to attack from Paris, were found in the car of a divisional staff officer killed in a French ambush. Next day, a No.3 Squadron reconnaissance aircraft piloted by Lieutenant George Pretyman discovered a 30-mile gap between the German armies and that the German First Army was advancing in south-easterly direction. Although staff procedures required him to plot his observations on a map and submit a written report, the five photos he took proved invaluable. Field-Marshal French passed the information to General Joffre who realised that the German right would be exposed to the French armies defending Paris.

At first light on 6 September the advance to the River Aisne began when the BEF and the French, strengthened by 10,000 reinforcements including a Tunisian division rushed from Paris in taxis, counter-attacked across the River Marne. Joffre later said that:

The British Flying Corps had played a prominent, in fact a vital part, in watching and following this all-important movement on which so much depended. Thanks to the aviators he had been kept accurately and constantly informed of Kluck's movements. To them he owed the certainty which had enabled him to make his plans in good time.

On the same day, the famous poster depicting Lord Kitchener demanding 'Your Country Needs You' was circulated. This resulted in a new army of volunteers being raised, including, in 1915, the 10th Service (Stockbrokers) Battalion, Royal Fusiliers. The Intelligence Battalion title was abbreviated to 10th (B) Royal Fusiliers, the letter 'B' indicating counter-intelligence. It was perhaps not surprising that it became known as the 'Hush Hush Brigade' and the 'Spy Battalion'.

Next day, Second-Lieutenant Julian Smith (Intelligence Corps) was severely wounded in the spine; he died two days later after an operation. He is commemorated in Canterbury Cathedral on a list of 9th Lancers officers who died in the Great War. On the same day, Lieutenant-Colonel Macdonogh, Major Kirke and Major Torrie were in their staff car when the driver failed to negotiate a right-hand bend, collided with a tree and ended up in a ditch. Macdonogh suffered a broken collarbone while Torrie, who had just engineered a transfer to the 9th Lancers within the fortnight, was knocked out. The driver had a hurt knee. Kirke borrowed a bicycle to seek help and later wrote to his wife that being under fire was far safer than being driven by an Intelligence Corps driver. Two days later Torrie departed to take command of 2nd Life Guards, leaving the corps without a commandant at a time when its young officers needed leadership. He was killed in action during the Battle of the Somme while commanding 7th East Lancashires. Second-Lieutenant Sang was mortally wounded in the head by a shell splinter on 8 September near Signey-Signet.

By 9 September the BEF was advancing towards the River Aisne. Lieutenant Marshall-Cornwall, still commanding the Divisional Mounted Troop with the advance guard, proved his worth as an intelligence officer by constructing the order of battle of General von der Marwitz's II Cavalry Corps from interrogations of exhausted prisoners captured in barns and ditches and from documentary intelligence of billets and requisition notes left with the village mayors. When a 15th Hussars captain arrived to take command of the troop, Marshall-Cornwall remained with it until the BEF reached the River Aisne. From this emerged a fundamental principle of intelligence assessment: that of calculating the state of the enemy's order of battle in terms of 'fresh', 'exhausted', 'front-line' and 'reserve' divisions.

After Second-Lieutenant J.T. Seabrook, who was attached to the 5th Cavalry Brigade Signal Troop as a motorcyclist dispatch rider was killed, Lieutenant John Ffrench Blake, who commanded the troop, wrote to his mother on 11 September that the previous day, the brigade had been in contact with the Germans since the early morning. He had instructed her son to take a dispatch to HQ Second Army and that he had been briefed by another motorcyclist on routes to avoid; however, it appeared that he took a wrong road and was shot. The news of his death was sent from the Intelligence Department, 5th Cavalry Brigade.

In his book *From Mons to Ypres with General French* (1917), Frederick Coleman notes that Captain Bertram Stewart was with the 1st Cavalry Brigade near Braisne on 16 September. As Coleman negotiated a slope during the crossing of the River Velde, he came across a wounded trooper propped against a milestone and nearby was the body of Captain Stewart. In a letter to Stewart's parents, Trooper Burbridge, who was one of two West Kent Yeomanry whom Stewart took with him to France, described that as Stewart arrived on the outskirts of the village in his car, he noticed the advance guard in some houses on the outskirts was under attack. Seizing his rifle, he ran to rally them but was shot in the chest and later buried in the village cemetery. Officers and men of his regiment later presented his widow with a commemorative bronze tablet and an annual prize for an essay awarded in his name. One winner was Enoch Powell, the future intelligence officer and MP.

Meanwhile Colonel Richard Hentsch, a senior intelligence officer, arrived at HQ German First Army from the GHQ with the following assessment:

The situation is not favourable. The Fifth Army is held up in front of Verdun and the Sixth and Seventh in front of Nancy-Epinal. The retreat of the Second Army behind the Marne is unalterable: its right wing, the VII Corps, is being forced back and not voluntarily retiring. In consequence of these facts, all the Armies are to be moved back: the Third Army to north-east of Chalons, and the Fourth and Fifth Army, in conjunction, through the neighbourhood of Clermont-en-Argonne towards Verdun. The First Army must therefore also retire in the direction Soissons-Fere-en-Tardenois, and in extreme circumstances perhaps farther, even to Laon-La Fere.

Using charcoal to draw on the operations map the position to be reached by First Army, he mentioned that a new army was being assembled near St Quentin. Major-General Herman von Kuhl, the chief of staff, remarked that a retreat would be very delicate, particularly as the army was exhausted and its units intermingled. Emphasising that he had overriding powers to order the withdrawal, Hentsch suggested the best option was to cross the River Aisne and anchor the left flank at Soissons. As the Germans then withdrew and attacks against their positions on high ground overlooking the river made only negligible progress, both sides dug in, initially in weapon pits. During the fighting, the RFC used air photography and wireless telegraphy for artillery observation for the first time. The British front line stretched from Flanders south to the French provinces of Artois and Picardy. In a written briefing to King George V, Field-Marshal French wrote that the spade would now be as necessary as a rifle. On 13 September, the German commander-in-chief, Colonel-General Moltke, told the Kaiser that Germany had lost the war.

The reinforcement of the BEF with regular and territorial force divisions and Indian Expeditionary Force A of a corps allowed Field-Marshal French to form the First Army under command of Lieutenant-General Haig and the Second Army led by Lieutenant-General Smith-Dorrien. The arrival of the reinforcements also saw an increase in the establishment of the Intelligence Corps to about 300 men. Haig took with him as his head of intelligence Lieutenant-Colonel John Charteris (Royal Engineers). Fluent in French and German, Charteris had served on the North-West Frontier, had been an outstanding graduate at the Staff College at Quetta and had held the unusual appointment of war correspondent with the Bulgarian army. When Haig was appointed to command I Corps in Aldershot in 1912, Captain Charteris was one of several trusted Indian army officers known as 'the Hindoo Invasion', but Charteris had no formal intelligence training. Whereas Haig was dour and inarticulate, he was loquacious, quick-witted and good company.

Meanwhile, Captain Wavell, at the War Office, calculated that if he joined the Intelligence Corps, he could legitimately be posted to France. He arrived at GHQ, then at Fère-en-Tardenois, on 20 September. Lieutenant-Colonel Macdonogh promoted him and confirmed him as commandant. He found a disparate crowd of about thirty-five officers with a smattering of languages, mostly hurriedly recruited and largely leaderless after the confusion of the retreat. Although his prejudice as a regular officer against amateur reservists was strong, he needed to bring stability to the corps: 'Once I had got a grip on the purpose of the Intelligence Corps, got it organised, cleared up one or two scandals and dismissed one or two totally unsuitable types, I found there was only one or two hours' work.'

On 1 October Lieutenant Smith-Cumming was driving his father, Mansfield Smith-Cumming, to Paris in a Rolls-Royce Silver Ghost for ten days' leave when, in the darkness, the car hit a farm cart and careered into a tree. Mansfield Smith-Cumming's leg was trapped. On seeing that his son was very seriously injured, however, he amputated his own leg using a penknife. His son's injuries were too severe and he eventually died. French surgeons later tried to save the leg of Mansfield Smith-Cumming, without success. He was fitted with a wooden one and used a child's scooter to propel himself along War Office corridors.

With their southern flanks secure, both sides transferred their focus of operations to the Channel coast. In the confused fighting that became known as the 'race to the sea' between September and November, the Germans largely held the initiative by forcing the Allies to fill breaches threatening the Channel ports and their vital communications with Great Britain. When the Belgian government asked for Allied assistance to help defend its temporary seat of government at Antwerp, reservist sailors assembled into 63rd Royal Navy Division landed at Dunkirk to bolster the defence of Antwerp. The Intelligence Corps provided Captain Sigismund Payne Best, who had landed in France on 23 August and had arrived at Le Cateau just as the retreat from Mons began. The son of an Anglo-Indian daughter of a Maharajah and a Cheltenham doctor, he had left Munich University in 1913 convinced that war was imminent and spent 4 August in the Café Royal in London. He tried to enlist the next day, citing fluency in French and German and a knowledge of Europe from travelling by motorcycle, but failed because he needed a monocle. About a fortnight later he was offered a commission in the Intelligence Corps, along with about twenty-five other applicants, which had been reduced to ten by the time he left to join the Motor-Cycle Section.

Although 7th Division landed at Zeebrugge and was taken by London buses to Antwerp, it arrived too late to prevent the capture of the port on 9 October. During a confused withdrawal in which some sailors were captured and others interned in Holland, Payne Best advised a Royal Marines Brigade against using a withdrawal route because of German troops. He escaped capture by a German cavalry patrol by using his fluency in German and reached Bruges where he used the Belfry to advise GHQ by public telephone of German encroachments into the city. Ostend fell on 15 October. Meanwhile a German strike at Calais and Boulogne had been held up after the British recaptured Ypres and then both sides dug in, in a sector that would see some of the harshest fighting of the war.

The uneasy relationship between commanders expecting the enemy to dance to their tunes and the intelligence picture was amply illustrated by an incident shortly before the First Battle of Ypres when the British defended the approaches to Calais and Boulogne in October and November. Captain Leopold Amery (Intelligence Corps) was interrogating prisoners when he noted that a French intelligence officer was concentrating on morale in Germany and the location of the Kaiser. Amery intervened and discovered from two 215th Infantry Regiment cyclists captured near Dikmuide on 24 October that the German army had been increased with reserve regiments numbered 201 to 270. When he discovered deployments within their 46th Reserve Division, GHQ regarded the intelligence as suspect, but when more prisoners from the same division were captured, and he received orders that they be interrogated in depth at GHQ, Amery asked if they would like to see the 700 captured so far. In fact, the Germans had formed XXII to XXVII Reserve Corps with the 43rd to 54th Reserve Divisions predominantly from wartime volunteers. When Lieutenant-Colonel Macdonogh briefed General French that three new German corps were advancing through Flanders towards the BEF, French shouted, 'How do you expect me to carry out my plan if you will bring up these bloody divisions!' The rejection of the intelligence led to Lieutenant-General Haig and his I Corps clashing with overwhelming German forces near Ypres. During heavy fighting that began on 19 October, the Germans attempted to outflank the Belgians and British in 'the race to the sea'.

As Major-General Sir Edward Spears (late Royal Dublin Fusiliers) later wrote in his book, *Liaison 1914*:

Operations said, 'What can be the use of intelligence knowing our plans? Their sole duty is to watch the enemy and report his movements and number.'

'That's all very well', Intelligence would argue, 'but we have to divine the enemy's intentions. These are based largely on what he can guess of ours.'

Kirke later wrote that Intelligence and Operations must work together and not as two staffs. The attitude was that Intelligence was manoeuvring the German army with the express intention of upsetting the general's plans. The problem was the British army was generally ambivalent to military intelligence, an antipathy that was neatly summarised by Major Brian Parritt, historian and director, Intelligence Corps in the 1980s, in his book *The Intelligencers*:

The British Army has never liked or wanted professional intelligence officers. It has continually been held that the best man to help a commander assess the capabilities of enemy infantry is an infantryman, the best man to judge the potential threat of cavalry, is a cavalryman. To have an officer devote his military career to Intelligence was, in most Generals' opinion, a short-sighted policy which would lead to the officer having a specialised and narrow outlook to problems which require a wide and practical background of military experience.

The risk of the Germans outflanking the Allies became so high that on 27 October the Belgians flooded the land along the 20-mile strip between Dikmuide and Nieuwport, creating a 2-mile-wide water barrier that forced Falkenhayn to change his strategy to attacking the city of Ypres on 31 October.

After a wireless intercept on 28 October from the German Fourth Army ordering XXVII Reserve Corps to attack at 5.30 a.m. next morning was then confirmed by air reconnaissance, bitter fighting developed at Gheluvelkt, during which Captain Frederic Hunt, Intelligence Corps attached to the 4th Hussars, was killed. Sergeant George Fairclough mentions Hunt in his diary:

19 October: went out with Captain Hunt and three men to burn two farms in front of the trenches. We were afraid of the enemy getting hold of them. It was distasteful work, everything looked so neat and comfortable – good furniture etc. I went upstairs while Captain Hunt and men kept watch. I poured a tin of kerosene over the floor and set it alight, the place was burning all night, and by morning nothing but ruins was left. There must have been five or six hundred pounds of stuff including barns hay etc.

30 October. We had a terrible time and had to retire to the second line of trenches behind the canal – the enemy brought up a dozen heavy guns and blew what was left of Hollebeke to an atom. The church was knocked to the ground and they then commenced to shell the trenches and we had to crawl away. One shell hit the machine gun trench killing Lieutenant North. Captain Hunt went in and brought him out, then went back in to fetch the gun, the enemy put five shells into the trench blowing both Captain Hunt and the gun to pieces. I had to go back afterwards and cover him up.

The unrelenting fighting petered out three weeks later when the Belgians anchored the Allied left flank a few miles from Nieuwport on the coast. The cost to the BEF since mid-August was high. Eighteen battalions of the eighty-four sent to France had less than 100 men and fifty-seven had between 300 and 100 all ranks.

Captain Julian Grenfell later wrote to the *Times* on 3 November that he had a half troop in his trench while the remainder of the squadron was spread about 100 yards each side of him. He had only taken his boots off once in the previous ten days and their horses remain saddled behind hedges to the rear. Rations were sent up after dark and although the diet of 4,193 calories daily for those in the front line was plain, it was better than many reservists had at home. Tea was a mainstay of morale. One drawback was that the food was brought from field kitchens through communication trenches to the front line. His men he described as 'splendid' although 'they use the most awful language'. He was thoroughly enjoying the war as a 'big picnic'. The residue of the manoeuvre warfare meant that reports of spies were prolific, indeed the *Times* dated 14 November said that an individual speaking perfect English and dressed in a Belgian uniform and claiming to be an interpreter had been caught in the British lines. As November turned to December a sharp winter spell brought considerable hardship. Some pilots and observers flying air reconnaissance missions were so cold they had to be lifted from their aircraft. On the other hand, enemy positions, gun positions and entrenchments were clear against the white snow and often bathed by bright sun.

A Cambridge University graduate, described as a motorcyclist dispatch rider, had a letter published in the *Times*, on 20 November 1914, describing his experiences after being wounded: he was first carried by stretcher bearers from his trench to a first aid post and was then taken in unsprung, slow, jolting horse-drawn ambulance wagons to a field ambulance station in large hall filled with wounded lying on mattresses. Here he was visited by a padre and then a lieutenant medical officer and an orderly who tended his wounds with iodine. It is conceivable that this soldier was a member of the Intelligence Corps.

Like Major Torrie, Wavell used the Intelligence Corps to reach France and within five weeks he claimed that intelligence was not a full-time job. On 16 November he was posted to be the brigade major of 9th Infantry Brigade at Ypres. He had been commandant for three weeks and three days. Wavell lost an eye in the Second Battle of Ypres. During the Second World War, he defeated the Italians in North Africa in 1940 but was defeated by Rommel in April 1941 and by the Japanese in Burma in 1942; nevertheless, he was promoted to field-marshal in 1943. His departure meant that in its critical early months when stability was essential, the Intelligence Corps had lost two commandants. On 8 December Dunnington-Jeffries, promoted to major, was appointed commandant by Lieutenant-Colonel Macdonogh. When other officers were invited to join regiments, he reminded them that transfer applications were to be authorised by him.

As the fighting raged in France, in the first espionage mission in Germany, RNAS Lieutenant Noel Pemberton Billing and his friend Frank Brock entered Switzerland near Belfort. Their mission was to reconnoitre the Zeppelin factory at Friedrichshafen in Southern Germany. Zeppelins had been identified as a threat to bomb England, but two raids on their sheds at Cologne and Dusseldorf had been unsuccessful. A fisherman took Pemberton Billing across Lake Constance and then he spent a day sketching the factory and returned to London. In mid-November, four Avro 504s delivered in crates to a large shed near Belfort were assembled. And then on 21 November they bombed the factory but did not achieve total success. The three raids and one on Nordholz on Christmas Day led German naval commanders to persuade the Kaiser to authorise the bombing of England. An observer on the Nordholz raid was Erskine Childers, the author of *Riddle of the Sands*.

3
East Africa, 1914

During the nineteenth-century European scramble for Africa, Germany acquired several colonies in East Africa and West Africa and supported opposition to the British, notably during the Second Boer War. By 1914, each had a *Schutztruppe* (protection force) of the basic tactical unit of a field company. These usually consisted of three German officers, two German NCOs, a medical officer and 160 African other ranks, known as *askaris* (from the Swahili for soldier), organised into three platoons, two to three machine-gun sections, logistic support that included a military hospital and 250 porters, and a detachment of about 200 armed irregulars known as *ruga rugas*. The colonists also formed reservist *Schutztruppes*.

When war was declared, German Togoland (now Togo and the Volta region of Ghana) was annexed by the British and its naval signalling station seized. British, French and Belgian forces seized Cameroon. The German South-West Africa (modern-day Namibia) *Schutztruppe* of twelve field companies and light artillery was organised into northern and southern commands. The southern command had a camel troop. The colony had a close relationship with the Boers and was of considerable British intelligence interest, particularly with regard to its naval signalling station.

In August 1914 the South African Prime Minister Louis Botha, the former commando leader, informed London that his Union Defence Force had the capability to invade German South-West Africa. A month later, South African troops commanded by General Henry Lukin and Lieutenant-Colonel Manie Maritz mobilised along the border. However, Maritz, a Boer hardliner, took advantage of the situation to proclaim that he was going to free Transvaal, the Orange Free State, Cape Province and Natal of British imperialism. When he was defeated in late October, he sought refuge in German South-West Africa. In late January 1915 Maritz attempted to cross the border into Northern Cape but was defeated by a South African garrison at Uppington, on the banks of the River Orange.

Given that the Boers had formed an intelligence corps during the Second South African War, Botha regarded intelligence as crucial and since maps were limited, he reverted to his practice of using mounted scouts for reconnaissance and intelligence collection. Major Langbaard Grobler and his fifty-strong Scout Corps deployed to Walvis Bay to collect information about Swakopmund and the surrounding area. Other units included 6th Intelligence Unit (Celliers Scouts), 16th Intelligence Unit (Collins Scouts) and Special Intelligence (German South-West Africa), the equivalent of the Security Service Bureau. Since the German authorities had interned suspected opponents and were sympathetic to Maritz's rebellion, human intelligence opportunities were reduced; however, their failure to censor newspapers, letters and telegrams provided intelligence on *Schuztruppe* deployments and intentions. Wireless intelligence intercepts helped to develop orders of battle, supply states and quality of morale. Although the Germans used ciphers, messages were sometimes sent part in code and part in clear speech.

Having landed at Swakopmund a week earlier, Botha issued Operation Order No.1 on 22 January 1915, which included his Intelligence Appreciation:

> The following information as to the enemy's disposition is mainly based upon intercepted wireless telegraph messages and has NOT been verified by actual observation. The information should, therefore, be regarded as the best obtainable but as based mainly on assumption.

1. Our position at Swakopmund has since the arrival of our troops been under close observation by the enemy who occupies a position in contact with our outposts on the East of the towns. In support were reservists available from colonists, shooting clubs, police, postal workers and railway staff.

2. The strength of the forces occupying this position is unknown but as far as can be ascertained no troops other than the 2nd reserve company have been in the position. The peace strength of a mounted company is 120 men which may have been increased to 150 or even more.

3. At Goanikontes, there are apparently the headquarters of the 2nd reserve (Captain Schultetus) and whatever strength of that company is not at any time immediately before Swakopmund, the 5th reserve company (Captain Ohlenschlager), half a battery of mounted artillery and six machine guns.

4. Unless other troops happen to arrive at a time when an attack is made on Goanikontes therefore a liberal estimate of the force of the enemy to be expected there would be 300 mounted men, 2 mounted guns and six machine guns.

5. No information is to hand of the existence of any hostile force at Heigamchab.

6. There is however a force of the enemy at Jackalswater and it is reasonable to assume that some connecting force may be at Heigamchab. The presence of such a force should, therefore, be calculated with and steps

should be taken to guard against its sudden arrival. Nothing is known
about the strength at Jakalswater but from indications it would seem that
about 500 mounted troops, a battery of Field Artillery, and a mounted
Battery may perhaps be there.

7. This is, however, merely assumption on meagre data. In any case no
    reinforcement from Jakalswater could probably reach Goanikontes in less
    than five hours.

During the night of 22–23 February, guides led two South African columns toward
the German capital at Windhoek. Botha commanded the northern column while
Jan Smuts, his fellow commando leader, led the southern one. But guides can be
unreliable or disloyal. One brigade major using his compass to check his line of
march discovered that his guide had deviated. It took time to regain the axis but
his column failed to intercept the enemy force. Although Windhoek was captured
on 5 May, Botha rejected surrender terms and, declaring martial law on 12 May,
formed his force into four columns. Using railways and rivers as axes of advance,
he trapped the *Schuztruppe* at Otavi Junction on 9 July.

Meanwhile, among four intelligence scouts attached to the British South
African Police patrolling the Southern Rhodesia border was Arnold Wienholt,
an Australian and a Boer War veteran who had recently been savaged by a lion in
the Okavango Delta. After the German surrender, the scouts picked up the spoor
of several Germans and renegade Boers who entered Portuguese West Africa
(now Angola) and captured all but eight, who were planning to use camels to
cross Northern Rhodesia and join the *Schutztruppe* in East Africa. Accompanied
by Major Robert Gordon, the head of Rhodesian Intelligence, scouts tracked
the Germans through 135 miles of bush for eight days and captured them in
mid-September.

The 384,000 square miles of German East Africa (now Burundi, Rwanda and
Tanzania) contained about 5,000 settlers, most living in the north-east, and about
8 million Africans. The lush Masai Steppe merges into bush and swamp to the south.
Major H.L. Pritchard described the battlefield in his *History of the Royal Engineers*:

Imagine a country three times the size of Germany, most covered by dense bush,
with no roads and only two railways, and either sweltering under a tropical sun or
swept by torrential rain which makes the friable soil impassable to wheeled traffic,
a country with occasional wide and swampy areas interspersed with arid areas
where water is often more precious than gold, in which man rots with malaria
and suffers torments from insect pests; in which animals die wholesale from the
ravages of the tsetse fly; where crocodiles and lions seize unwary pets, giraffes
destroy telegraph lines, elephants damage tracks, hippopotami attack boats,
rhinoceroses charge troops on the attack and bees put whole battalions to flight.

The central railway ran between Dar-es-Salaam and Lake Victoria while the Usmabara Railway connected Tanga and Arusha, south-west of the forested slopes of Mount Kilimanjaro and the border with British East Africa. Governors Heinrich Schnee and Sir Henry Conway Bellfied had agreed that in the event of hostilities in Europe, their colonies would maintain a stance of neutrality, as agreed in the 1885 Berlin Agreement. When the German East African Expeditionary Force had first secured German East Africa, its commander, the explorer Hermann Wissmann, believed, as the British did, that Africans were the best troops to fight in Africa. He therefore formed a *Schutztruppe* from Sudanese men and Zulus discharged from the British army. He developed a culture of loyalty by paying the *askaris* well, financing the transfer of families to their husbands' bases, and organised an efficient welfare system. The British equivalent was the King's African Rifles, raised in 1902, except that the NCOs were Africans. When Lieutenant-Colonel Paul Lettow-Vorbeck took command of the East Africa *Schutztruppe* in January 1914, it was spread between fourteen garrisons; although he was restricted by the General Staff East African defence plan to maintain neutrality, he prepared contingency plans for offensive operations using guerrilla tactics. Noting that his *askaris* were issued with Mauser Model 1871 bolt-action rifles that used black powder cartridges, he changed tactics of surprise to charging through the smoke that the rifles produced.

The British regarded German East Africa as a threat to the Indian lines of communications, the security of the Suez Canal and the coal bunkers, and the Admiralty signalling station at Aden settlement, particularly when two cruisers, the *Emden* and *Königsberg*, based in Dar-es-Salaam, arrived in the region. When, on 31 July 1914, the *Königsberg* escaped the attention of the Royal Navy Cape Squadron and began attacking British merchant ships on the outbreak of war, the neutrality agreement was shelved and the Cape Squadron bombarded the Dar-es-Salaam wireless transmitter. There were clashes on Lakes Victoria, Tanganyika and Nyasa. Lettow-Vorbeck mobilised four companies and then deployed seventeen field companies to the border from where they raided British East Africa and attacked the railway to Mombasa. With two companies protecting the central railway, 17th Field Company at Tanga patrolled the coast.

On 4 August, Governor Belfield declared martial law and established a headquarters in Nairobi. As intelligence flowed in from the border district commissioners at Taveta and Vanga, Lieutenant-Colonel J.D. Mackay (Middlesex Regiment), a former ranker, who had spent thirteen years in British East Africa and had commanded 3rd King's African Rifles, was appointed head of intelligence. Enlisted into the Intelligence Section was Lieutenant Andrew Russell, who farmed near Mount Kilimanjaro and had escaped from Dar-es-Salaam when war broke out. Lord Delamere and District Commissioner R.W. Hemstead raised, respectively, the Masai Scouts and a Defence Force raised from Magadi Soda Company. The East Africa Mechanical Transport Corps organised a motorcycle dispatch service that eased communications. Imposing censorship, Belfield was confident that he could defeat the Germans; indeed, his confidence became infectious. When several hundred colonists emerged from their farms in the bush, they accounted for a third of the defenders of the colony, but Bellfield refused to release any civil servants, except for those with medical, veterinary and intelligence skills. He then convinced the Joint Naval and Military Committee for the Consideration of Combined Operations in Foreign Territory to instruct the commander-in-chief of India to despatch reinforcements.

The Indian army was divided into the Northern Army, covering from the North-West Frontier to Bengal, and the Southern Army, covering from Baluchistan to southern India. The constituents were regular soldiers, Imperial Service Brigades financed by the princely states, and the auxiliary force of European volunteers. Divisions of one cavalry and three infantry brigades were smaller than British ones. GHQ was located in Delhi. The commander-in-chief was General Sir Beauchamp Duff of the Indian army, and the chief of the General Staff was Lieutenant-General Sir Percy Lake, British army officer. The Indian army had created a General Staff in 1905 with MO2(b) controlling events in the Turkish Empire while MO2(h) controlled India, Tibet, Afghanistan and Persia. A year later, the area to the south of a line drawn from Aqaba to Basra came under the control of the Indian army. The head of intelligence was Lieutenant-Colonel Wilfred Malleson. The intelligence responsibility for the rest of the region, which became known as the Middle East, was controlled by MO2 at the War Office, then managed by Colonel 'Wully' Robertson. There was another reorganisation when MO2 transferred Middle East to MO3.

On 1 September 1914, IEF C of the 29th Punjabis and the equivalent of two Imperial Service battalions, commanded by Brigadier-General James Stewart, arrived in Mombasa. Most Imperial Service troops had just received Short Magazine Lee Enfield rifles and not every company had machine-gun sections. The force intelligence officer was Captain J.G. Cadel (45th Sikhs) who, with Governor Belfield, assessed that an invasion of East Africa would not meet strong resistance. However, detailed information about the *Schutztruppe* was minimal because of the neutrality agreement and therefore the order of battle and location was not known. Tension rose markedly ten days later when the German cruiser *Königsberg* sank the cruiser HMS *Pegasus* in Zanzibar.

Meanwhile, IEF B was en route from India with orders to capture German East Africa. The force consisted of 27th (Bangalore) Brigade, which included the British 2nd Loyal North Lancashires, and the Imperial Service Brigade. Most of the Indian soldiers filing onto the crowded ships had never seen the sea. The force commander, Major-General Arthur Aitken, had last seen action thirty years earlier in Sudan. Shortly before he embarked, he held his only officers' conference, in the Bombay Yacht Club, but did not issue preliminary orders, largely because

GHQ India had not worked up contingency plans for East Africa. However, he insisted he would not tolerate the 'sloppy' uniform code adopted in the Boer War. Captain Richard Meinertzhagen (Royal Fusiliers), who had been seconded to the King's African Rifles in the mid-1900s as the intelligence officer, had just passed the Indian Army Staff College course and joined IEF B in August as its GSO3 (Intelligence). He later became a popular source of First World War intelligence for historians and academics, until 2007 when the American author, Brian Garfield, published *The Meinertzhagen Mystery: The Life and Legend of a Colossal Fraud*. It is not the intention of this book to challenge his analysis; however, some exploits attributed to Meinertzhagen will be treated here as 'claims'.

At a meeting at Mombasa on 30 October, Stewart and Aitken planned to land IEF B at the port of Tanga and then use the Usambara Railway as an axis to lance the German boil harassing British East Africa between it and IEF C advancing from the north. The railway that terminated near the Customs House divided Tanga into European and African quarters. Of the 900 buildings, about eighty were stone, including the Deutscher Kaiser Hotel. The anchorage was shallow and sheltered by Tanga Island. Mackay believed the port to be lightly defended. Major Norman King, the former British consul in Dar-es-Salaam and now political adviser to Governor Bellfield, believed that the German colonists preferred neutrality; however, their treatment of Africans had created opportunities for the British to engineer a rebellion. He believed that the deployment of the *Schutztruppe* to the border meant that it would not defend the coast. King had also prepared a handbook on German East Africa. But his views were not shared by Meinertzhagen in his Intelligence Appreciation: 'From reliable information received it appears improbable that the enemy will not actively oppose our landing. Opposition may, however, be met with anywhere inland, and a considerable force of the enemy is reported to be in the vicinity of Vanga.' Vanga is about 10 miles north of Tanga.

Commander Francis Caulfield, the senior naval officer commanding the cruiser HMS *Fox*, insisted that in accordance with the principles of neutrality, the authorities in Tanga should be notified of British intentions, a proposal rejected by Lieutenant-Colonel Seymour Sheppard, the IEF B chief of staff, citing that the Germans would have advanced warning. When Aitken was briefed that the *Schutztruppe* on the border could reassemble in Tanga within thirty hours, he was confident he could 'thrash the German before Xmas'. Sheppard remarked, 'This campaign will either be a walk-over or a tragedy.'

Although his troops had been on board ships for three weeks, Aitken dismissed a suggestion that they should land to recuperate. On the same day, the Royal Navy found the *Königsberg* in the Rufiji River delta, about 100 miles south of Dar-es-Salaam. Meanwhile, Lettow-Vorbeck had received intelligence from traders and intercepted letters that IEF B would land at Tanga and was confident that 17th Field

Company could contain the landing until it could be reinforced. Eighty-four days after taking command, Major-General Aitken eventually issued Operation Order No.1 from his headquarters on the SS *Karmala* for a landing scheduled within twenty-four hours and selected three beaches in the vicinity of the promentary known as Ras Kanone, west of the town. They were Assault Beach A, which was a small muddy beach on the eastern side of the Ras Kanone headland with cliffs on the one side and mangrove swamps on the ocean side, having above it a red house which was suitable as a navigation marker; Reserve Beach B, which was near the signal station and north of Assault Beach A; and Reserve Beach C, 700 yards south of Beach B and about a mile from the town.

When Aitken learnt that the ageing battleship HMS *Goliath*, which he expected to provide naval gunfire support, had broken down, he ordered 28 Mountain Battery to provide naval gunfire support from a ship.

While Mackay and King saw no reason to change their intelligence assessment, Atkins was displeased that Mackay had no current intelligence on *Schutztruppe* locations in Tanga and during the night of 1–2 November, he sent Lieutenant Russell ashore to reconnoitre for enemy positions between Beach A and Tanga. Shortly before he left, Russell was joined by Second-Lieutenant Henry Ishmael, who had been a plantation manager in Tanga, but who had no military experience. He was, however, smartly turned out in his service dress and Sam Browne belt.

Landing near the red house, they split up. Russell, in civilian clothes, walked through the rubber plantation east of Tanga and entered the town, which was very quiet, and saw police patrols. Making his way towards the Customs House, he nearly walked into a *Schutztruppe* position behind the railway embankment. After a burst of firing from Beach B, he took cover in a field and knocked on the door of a small house. Its resident, an African, said that there was a company of *askaris* commanded by about four German officers in the town and it was common knowledge more were expected very soon. After the African had taken him to another house, whose occupant confirmed the information, Russell thanked them and returned to Beach A at about 3 a.m. to wait for Ishmael, but he did not appear. He was unaware that Ishmael had walked into a German position and was mortally wounded and died in the German hospital.

Shortly before dawn, Russell signalled for a boat and, on returning to the *Karmala*, reported his findings to Major King, noting in particular that there were no German troops between Beach A and Tanga. King asked Russell to go ashore the next night and gave him an escort of three 13th (Imperial Service) Rajputs; however, as they approached Beach A they came under fire, which wounded the boatman, who then rowed to the beach below the red house. Leaving his escorts in the mangroves, Russell again moved through the rubber plantation and again met the first African, who told him no more Germans had arrived in Tanga. Checking the red house, he found several useful photographs and, returning to *Karmala* at about 2 a.m., reported to King that there had been no change in Tanga, 'except for the blighters who had fired at us'.

Captain C.R.F. Seymour (13th Rajputs) also led a patrol that night which reached the railway cutting and reported two enemy machine guns, but his report was ignored by force headquarters. The Imperial Service Infantry Brigade Scouts commanded by Lieutenant J. Ferguson appear to have been misused during the operation.

By dawn on 3 November, the fourteen ships carrying IEF B were hovering off Tanga; however, it was not until 7.30 a.m. that Commander Caulfield personally informed the Tanga District Commissioner, Dr Auracher, that since the neutrality agreement was invalid, he had two hours to surrender or HMS *Fox* would bombard the town. When Caulfield then compromised British intentions by asking if the harbour was mined, Auracher reinforced his belief that it was by returning to the jetty using a circuitous route. In an exchange of telegrams, Lieutenant-Colonel Lettow-Vorbeck told Auracher to expect reinforcements from the border and he was not to surrender. Ordering non-combatants to leave Tanga, Auracher then joined 17 Field Company as a reserve lieutenant. With no response to his demands, Caulfield instructed a tug to sweep the harbour for mines, during which HMS *Fox*, loitering off Beach C, and 17th Field Company exchanged fire. On the border, Brigadier-General Stewart expected to encounter 200 *Schutztruppe* as he advanced; instead, in the misty dawn of 3 November, IEF C was stopped by 600 infantry and eighty-six irregular cavalry.

Shortly after midnight on 4 November, the assault wave from the 13th Rajputs encountered a coral reef about 500 yards from Beach A and the troops were compelled to wade through chest-high and muddy water in the darkness, something most had never done. The following morning two Imperial Service battalions advanced through cocoa and maize plantations flanking the hospital and dense bush on the left. Both battalions came under fire from 17th Field Company and were then driven back towards Beach A by a fierce bayonet charge from 6th Field Company, which had just arrived by train from the border and after a 4-mile night speed march from the *Schutztruppe* camp at Moshi.

Aitken delayed the advance until 2 p.m. so the troops could have breakfast. IEF C advanced from Beach A, the Imperial Brigade through the plantations and bush on the right and 27th Brigade on the left through the rubber plantation. By 3 p.m., the two Kashmir Rifle battalions on the left and 2nd Loyal North Lancashires in the centre became engaged in fierce house-to-house fighting. Meanwhile, the arrival of reinforcements enabled Lettow-Vorbeck to counter-attack against 27th Brigade. One of its battalions quickly folded and ran back through 98th Infantry, in reserve, being attacked by swarms of angry bees spilling from damaged treetop beehives. British propaganda exploited this by portraying it as a fiendish German plot. Lettow-Vorbeck took advantage of the gap and drove into the 10th Grenadiers advancing toward the railway workshops. In spite of fighting hard, the British left flank began to fold and both brigades began withdrawing toward Ras Kanone at about 4 p.m. There was confusion in Tanga when a *Schuzttruppe* officer ordered his bugler to sound 'Pursue the enemy!' but instead he blew 'Assemble!', which led to the field companies disengaging until Lettow-Vorbeck quickly countermanded the order. Since most troops were withdrawing to Muhesa railway station, about 10 miles west of Tanga, he had no troops to pursue the British. Indeed, when Captain Meinertzhagen entered Tanga after dark with a reconnaissance, he found the town 'there for the taking'; however, Aitken lacked the confidence to order an advance and next day, IEF C re-embarked, leaving behind heavy stores, 600,000 rounds of ammunition, rifles discarded on the battlefield and also machine guns which the Royal Navy refused to take, in case they damaged their boats. During the evening of 5 November, Meinertzhagen entered Tanga under a flag of truce to negotiate the evacuation of IEF wounded and several medical orderlies from the field hospital at the red house, and to take an apology from Aitken for the accidental shelling of the hospital by HMS *Fox*. It was only then that the Germans realised IEF C had withdrawn into its beachhead.

As noted in the *Official History of the War*, the Battle of Tanga was 'one of the most notable failures in British military history'. Aitken had disregarded just about every basic principle of warfare. He ignored credible intelligence about the competency of the *Schutztruppe* and was the first Indian army commander to realise that the Germans could not be defeated by using tactics employed in colonial campaigns. Lettow-Vorbeck's victory enabled him to apply his principal strategy of forcing the British to commit troops to East Africa at the expense of diverting troops from Europe. The battle had cost 360 killed and 487 wounded and against sixteen Germans and fifty-five *askaris* killed and seventy-six wounded. The Germans later released wounded officers and those paroled not to fight in the war again. IEF B returned to Mombasa in near disgrace from a population fearful of a German invasion and bombardments of its ports. Aitken was dismissed and replaced by Brigadier-General Richard Wapshare, who had commanded 27th Brigade.

A week after the Battle of Tanga, in an operation conceived by the chief of the General Staff (India) but not immediately shared with the War Office, IEF F, en route from Bombay and Madras to Egypt to defend the Suez Canal, agreed to a request from HQ Aden Brigade to destroy four 6in guns at Fort Turba, near the village of Sheikh Sa'id in the Turkish province of Yemen at the southern mouth of the Red Sea. A brigade intelligence assessment had suggested that the nearby British coaling station and outpost on the nearby Perim Island was within range of the guns. The task was given to 29th Indian Infantry Brigade; however, it was not permitted to take the Aden Brigade Arab-speaking political officer, Lieutenant-Colonel Jacob, because of strict 'need-to-know' principles. The assault force arrived off Fort Turba early on 10 November, but strong winds led to the landing being switched to a sheltered cove almost underneath the fort. At dawn, as a battleship shelled the fort, the first assault wave of two battalions in ship's boats were towed ashore by three tugs, but rough seas, the unreliability of the tugs and shallow water meant that it took four hours to land the task force of 3,000 men. The capture of the fort cost four killed and sixteen wounded. After demolition parties destroyed the guns and an ammunition dump, the troops re-embarked during the afternoon.

GHQ Egypt was focused on defending the Suez Canal and preserving the internal security of Egypt and Sudan. The intelligence function was thus split between the strategic demands of the sirdar (governor) of Sudan in Khartoum, namely General Sir Reginald Wingate, and the high commissioner of Egypt, Sir Henry MacMahon. General Sir John Maxwell, GOC Egypt, was based in Cairo. His head of intelligence was Lieutenant-Colonel Gilbert Clayton, a former gunner who then became a colonial administrator in Egypt and Sudan. In 1915, the Intelligence Department was divided into:

Military Intelligence Branch

I(a)   Operational Intelligence with sections covering Ismalia, Suez and Sudan

I(b)   Secret Service Bureau

I(c)   Topographical Intelligence through GHQ Survey Unit RE and Survey of Egypt

I(e)   Wireless Intelligence

International Communication Censorship

Canal Defence

Intelligence, Canal Defence

Naval Intelligence

Intelligence Office with links to Naval Intelligence, French Naval Air Squadron, Blockade Control and 3 RNAS

30 Squadron RFC

I(b)   Port Said

In early January 1915, Djemel Pasha, the Turkish governor of Syria and Palestine and commander of the Fourth Army, and the German military mission chief of staff Colonel Baron Kress von Kressenstein planned to attack the Suez Canal. Reports from reliable agents and informants in Syria indicated an estimated 70,000 Turks mobilising. The Bedouin tripwire across the Sinai Desert reported an estimated seven divisions concentrating at El-Arish and El-Qussaima. But lack of corroboration and stormy weather grounding aircraft confused the intelligence picture until a window in the middle of the month allowed air reconnaissance.

In mid-January, Captain Lewen Weldon (Intelligence Corps) was instructed by Colonel P.G. Elgood, the Port Said base commandant, to join the *Aenna Rickmers*, a former 4,000-ton cargo ship seized from the Germans, as the ship's military intelligence officer. Employed by the Egyptian Survey Department, he was in England on his biannual leave when war broke out and had been offered a commission as an infantry officer. He was then summoned to return to Cairo where he joined GHQ MO4 (Maps) as the map officer with instructions to establish a central map store.

The ship had been converted to carry two Nieuport mono-seaplanes on its after hatches. The aircrew were French pilots and British observers. While the Royal Navy, Royal Marines, French aviation mechanics and Greek crew were commanded by a Merchant Navy captain, reputed to have been a smuggler, Weldon had overall control of operations and was expected to send reports to GHQ. Air reconnaissance reported an estimated 20,000 troops, some advancing towards El Arish, in Sinai, while others were in large tented camps on routes from Beersheba, including in Gaza. Weldon made it his practice to encipher the observer reports and send them by wireless to GHQ Intelligence. However, the monoplanes were flimsy and crashes were common. One crew managed to reach the shore after ditching but were shot by Indian troops as they walked back to British lines along the Suez Canal. The notes of the observer, a British officer in the Ceylon contingent, were found in the wreckage. Land-based aircraft flew sorties in the vicinity of the canal.

Welford also perfected his methods of operations for clandestine landings to land agents. Generally, the nights picked were moonless and the sea conditions reasonably fair, although rough seas did not preclude attempts. The three-day Coptic gales of the eastern Mediterranean between late September and the end of April were predictable. Sometimes, a small steamboat would tow its local surf boat close to the shore. Once the boat was caught by the surf, there was little its occupants could do except steer as best as possible, the greatest dangers being capsizing and Turkish patrols. Weldon described it as 'taking a high dive without knowing whether there was water or a cement floor below'. Many of the people he delivered were couriers tasked to take messages to contacts or to guide them to the beach to be debriefed by Welford.

When hospitals in Palestine were reported to have been warned to receive wounded with effect from 27 January, this gave Maxwell reasonable confirmation of an attack on the Suez Canal; however, poor weather again grounded aircraft. One agent he had sent to Gaza signalled with a light, but failed to make the rendezvous, even though Weldon searched the beach. He later learnt that the agent had been captured by Turkish coastguards and hung. On 25 January a weather window enabled air reconnaissance to discover a regiment advancing for the crossing point at Qantara. The following day 6,000 troops were reported 25 miles from the Little Bitter Lake and a smaller group was seen near the southern end of the canal. Over the next two days probes south of Lake Timash and the Great Bitter Lake, apparently aimed at the railway, were contained. It then became clear from interrogations of prisoners and deserters and patrols that Qantara was the objective.

Assisting the defending 22nd Brigade was Captain Aubrey Herbert (Irish Guards), Conservative MP, linguist in seven languages and a diplomat in the Middle East and Japan. Although very short-sighted, he had been wounded, captured and then escaped during the retreat from Mons before being sent to Cairo as an intelligence officer. Herbert had previously learned from a Syrian that an affluent Egyptian family had used Greek sponge fishermen to smuggle in 15,000 rifles for an insurrection in Egypt planned for 27 April. Two Turkish companies crossing the Suez Canal early on 3 February on pontoons were annihilated. By next morning, the Turks were retreating, having lost 1,500 men of whom 716 were prisoners. General Maxwell followed the defensive philosophy of remaining west of the canal and prevented a pursuit. Consequently, within three months, the Turks had occupied a defensive line using the strategically important Wadi el Arish from El Arish on the coast south about 200 miles through the desert to Nekhl, from where they raided the canal several times. To support the line, a narrow-gauge railway was extended from Beersheba in mid-October.

The Turks also attacked the small port of Tor in the Red Sea, which was a quarantine station for pilgrims travelling to the Convent of St Catherine. If the Turks seized Tor, they could disrupt shipping by floating mines into the Red Sea. Colonel Alfred Parker, the governor of Sinai and former intelligence officer, arrived at Tor by warship and found the two defending Egyptian companies were being subjected to Turkish subversion. He signalled Colonel Clayton:

In my opinion the present situation contains very dangerous elements, which can be obviated in two ways:
(a)   the entire abandonment of Tor and the withdrawal of the garrison;
(b)   the sending of a sufficiently strong party of Gurkhas or British to ensure the destruction of the enemy.
The first would entail an incalculable loss of prestige among Egyptians and Muhammadans who know Tor as a pilgrim station, as well as among Russians who regard the Convent and its environs as a holy place […] Unless reinforcements reach enemy, a double company of Gurkhas should be sufficient.

After Parker had discovered from monks that the Turkish camp was in a wadi 5 miles east of the convent, two 2/7 Gurkha Rifles companies landed from a destroyer as reinforcements for the Egyptians and were guided by a sheikh recruited by Parker. By noon, the camp and several other positions had been overrun and 108 prisoners captured, including a Turkish major. On the return journey, the ship arrived in the early morning of 13 February at Abu Senima to investigate reports of two Hungarian saboteurs operating in the Sinai under the direction of the Turks.

4
The Western Front, 1915

As the frenetic autumn of 1914 developed into the characteristic positional warfare, the exposed shell scrapes packed with troops, which included Intelligence Corps, standing shoulder to shoulder in freezing, waterlogged outposts were developing into complex trench systems separated by no-man's-land overlooked by knolls and low ridges. The distances between trenches varied, the minimum theoretically being greater than a grenade throw. They were shielded by barbed wire entanglements about 6ft high and variable in width. Any advances would hinge on the effectiveness of shelling. The Security Duties Section investigated reports that enemy snipers were using coal mine tunnels to infiltrate British lines. Although all had been blocked, reports of spies were common. According to the *Times* on 14 November, an individual captured in the BEF sector dressed in British uniform but wearing a Belgian cap claimed to be an interpreter for a British regiment. A captured German who claimed to have lived most of his life in Great Britain spent the day shooting at his erstwhile colleagues before being shipped to a prisoner holding centre. A letter written by a rifle regiment officer from a once prosperous house a mile behind the front line was published in the *Times* on 9 January:

> We have just had as unpleasant three days and nights as we could want, in trenches which are reputed to be the worst in the front-line. They are 35 yards from the advance German line, and once belonged to the Germans. In one place there was a German's leg still sticking out of the parapet and a Frenchman's body, lying alongside. The trenches are about two to three feet in sloshy clay, and the men had an awful time practically standing up their waists in it the whole time. The German snipers keep a deadly lookout for any movement […] I got wet through up the waist sploshing through our ditches from end to another and am not dry yet. Overcoat absolutely caked with clay, and whole body like a rough cast-clay model.

Another correspondent describes that in the freezing weather, wet boots shrunk by snow, rain and ice had to be cut off and that some soldiers had lost their toes to frostbite.

The development of aircraft had caused a significant evolution in warfare, in particular the security of friendly airspace by preventing penetration by enemy aircraft and the neutralisation of cavalry reconnaissance. In March 1913, the RFC had experimented with air photography, but funds were rare and it was left to a few enthusiasts to develop. No.3 Squadron designed a handheld Pan-Ross type camera fitted with a 6in lens and the ability for the observer to develop the glass plate negatives in the air. Observers leant over the side of their cockpit to take photographs, but wearing heavy gloves against the cold and aircraft vibrations usually meant that the quality of photographs was often poor. When the RFC arrived in France, it had only six cameras on its inventory. The *Times* featured observers on 19 January 1915:

> The really first-rate observer must possess extensive military knowledge in order to know what objects to look for and where to look for them; he must have very good eyesight in order to pick them; he must have the knack of reading a map quickly, in order to mark correctly their positions and to find his way.

In October 1914 the RFC had developed dividing maps with a 'grid' system of letters and numbers to ensure accurate reporting of positions on the ground. Shortly afterwards, a 'clock code' was introduced to give corrections of the fall of artillery shots. In an article titled 'The Value of Aerial Observation', dated 19 January 1915, a *Times* correspondent writes:

> To reconnoitre is not easy even in fine weather; but in driving rain or driving snow, in a temperature perhaps several degrees below zero, when an aeroplane traveling with the wind rocks and sways [...] the difficulties are immense. In these circumstances, and from the altitude at which it is necessary to fly in order to escape the projectiles of anti-aircraft guns, columns of transport or of men are easily missed. Indeed, a first attempt as observer will see nothing which is of military value, for it is only after considerable practise that their eye becomes accustomed to scouring a great stretch of land from above and acquires the power of distinguishing objects upon it [...] Many men are absolutely unfitted by such duty, and even trained observers vary in their powers of reconnaissance.

The article added that observers needed to be cool and able to concentrate, in spite of the distractions of air bursts and rifle whistling past or through the aircraft.

During the autumn of 1914 Lieutenant Charles Darley (Royal Artillery), a No.3 Squadron observer and camera enthusiast, set up a darkroom in the stables of a chateau being used by the squadron. Using a private Aeroplex camera fitted with a 12in lens, he collected sufficient photographic coverage of the German lines in front of IV Corps to create an annotated mosaic. Coincidentally, Field-Marshal French had been shown by the French air photographs and an annotated map of German positions. Also aware of Darley's experiments was Brigadier-General Henderson, who sent Major Geoffrey Salmond, GSO2 HQ RFC, to review French methodologies. Salmond recommended that an experimental air photographic interpretation section be established by First Wing, then commanded by Colonel Hugh Trenchard. The section consisted of Lieutenant John Moore-Brabazon, Lieutenant Charles Campbell (Intelligence Corps), Flight-Sergeant Frederick Laws (Royal Engineers) and 2nd Air Mechanic William Corse. Moore-Brabazon was the first Englishman to make an officially recognised aeroplane flight in England on 2 May 1909 on the Isle of Sheppey; seven months later he proved that pigs could fly by taking one in possibly the first live cargo flight. Laws had experimented with air cameras before the war and was the only person in the RFC able to interpret air photographs. Moore-Brabazon and Campbell designed the handheld Thornton-Pickard Model A Camera, but it was heavy and operating the complicated machinery wearing thick gloves was not easy; consequently the quality of photographs was still poor.

The next challenge was to convince the military hierarchy that air intelligence was an essential element of modern operational planning but, as Moore-Brabazon wrote to Squadron Leader Mayle, School of Photography RAF in November 1959:

> It was exceedingly difficult to get anybody to appreciate what we were trying to do, or use the information we got. In fact Colonel Trenchard carried about with him photographs of the enemy trenches which he pushed before members of the army staff who only viewed them with the mildest interest in spite of the fact that they were planning attacks on the very areas about which we could give them information.

After GHQ had moved to St Omer west of Ypres, the BEF DMI moved into a three-storey house. Houses were used for billets and messes. Communication was by mail, despatch riders, usually on motorcycles, and field and public telephones. Each BEF army was supported by a General Staff of:

Army HQ	GSO1 and GSO2
Corps HQ	GSO2 and GSO3
Divisional HQ	GSO3
Brigade HQ	The brigade major, as the senior operations officer, had responsibility for intelligence. But as the demand became more complex, Brigade HQ intelligence officers became more common.

While the General Staff was slow to adapt to fighting a modern war in an increasingly technological battlefield, tending to act before assessing enemy intentions and paying scant attention to intelligence, regimental intelligence officers were learning fast that knowledge and locations of enemy orders of battle were important. Their duties contained in this 3rd Australian Division, General Staff Circular No.57A, dated 12 September 1917 were as relevant in 1915:

Collects and collates all information, both by personal observation, and by close touch with troops in front line, snipers, scouts, patrols, and observers. He must keep au fait with the military situation, and the intelligence reports promulgated from above; must study enemy methods and action; must be in liaison with our Artillery and Machine Guns, and with neighbouring units in the line. He supervises the distribution of war news and intelligence through the Battalion, and keeps the War Diary.

Intelligence activities included:

- Supervise the Intelligence Section – if one exists
- Responsible for collection and distribution of all info that affects the unit
- Control the map stock
- Maintain the operations map
- Maintain a map showing enemy defences, identifications and dispositions [this might mean accompanying or leading patrols, usually at night, into no-man's-land to check German positions]
- Furnish company commanders with information to optimise patrolling
- Brief patrols and supply a list of essential elements of intelligence required
- Prior to an advance or raid, give an intelligence brief
- Draft daily intelligence reports for the commanding officer and send to Brigade HQ at times ordered
- Be familiar with no-man's-land and reconnoitre as required
- Check observation and listening post log books for information
- Conduct intelligence training of scouts
- Ensure that snipers are constantly employed
- During offensives and attacks, ensure that 'jump off' tapes, usually white, are laid in no-man's-land or provide guides

A four-week intelligence course had been developed by GHQ Home Forces by the end of 1915 at the Intelligence School, first in Belgravia. Subjects included:

- Enemy orders of battle
- Interpretation of captured documents, such as official documents, pocket notebooks and letters
- British army organisation

- Map reading, field sketching and air photographic interpretation
- Interrogation
- Care of carrier pigeons and how to handle and attach messages
- Encoding and decoding code and ciphers
- Military reports and staff duties

By 1917, intelligence officer courses were mandatory with the final exercise a practical interrogation at the prisoner-of-war hospital at Dartford. Delegates numbered about thirty officers, most with front-line experience. Lectures were also given by War Office and BEF intelligence officers. The accommodation was a requisitioned house in which the large rooms were divided into cubicles. The officers began each day with thirty minutes of drill at Wellington Barracks taken by a drill sergeant. Delegates were split into intelligence and counter-intelligence. One problem was that BEF GHQ never published an intelligence policy or procedures manual. In late 1917 the school moved to Kingsley House, Harrow-on-the-Hill, where delegates came from the three services and included Dominion and US delegates. Chief instructors included Major Hunt and Captain Herman de Watteville (Royal Artillery), of Swiss extraction. The Americans later established their own intelligence school at Langres, France.

While the 1917 *British Manual of Trench Warfare* regarded trenches as springboards to 'create a favourable situation for field operations, which the troops must be capable of turning to account', the Germans had studied the Russo-Japanese War and applied the principle of defence in depth, of usually three lines of trenches connected by zigzag communication trenches to reduce the effect of shelling and as a tactical measure to impede attacking troops. To address the low water table in parts of Flanders, where practical, trenches were above ground and reinforced with breastworks of sandbags filled with clay. The flat ground of Flanders meant that hillocks and ridges became focal points of determined struggles, simply because height always gives tactical advantage. Supplies were brought forward, casualties evacuated, signals cables laid and barbed wire repaired after dark.

Sniping in the British army was in its infancy until Major Frederick Crum (King's Royal Rifle Corps) formed the Sniping School at Acq through which intakes of about three officers and sixty men passed. Battalion sniping officers worked closely with their intelligence officer. Since raising your head above the parapet was unwise, trench periscopes were developed. The commercial extendable Duerrs Lifeguard periscope with a lateral view of 100 yards wide out to 400 yards could be folded into a waterproof pouch slotted on to a belt.

The static warfare saw the role of the Intelligence Corps subalterns evolve from dispatch rider to interrogator, examiner of documents and patroller. While units dispatched listening patrols, sometimes known as 'sap-heads', of two or three lightly armed men to creep close to enemy trenches and conceal themselves in a fold in the ground or a shell hole, to warn of an attack, Intelligence Corps Scout Section linguists often patrolled alone and collected intelligence by identifying the origins of units from dialects, or types of unit (for instance, infantry and dismounted cavalry) from terminology. They also listened for signs of an offensive and wiring parties preparing paths through entanglements prior to a raid. Armed with a revolver and a pair of wire cutters, Lieutenant Marshall-Cornwall wormed close to the German trenches on the Messines–Wytschaete ridge and learned that a Saxon battalion had relieved the incumbent Bavarians. On another patrol, he removed the insignia from a dead German and from a ruined cottage on the ridge, used binoculars to see along part of German trenches and read the regimental identification number on the soldiers' epaulettes. On 25 February 1915, in a *Times* article, entitled 'British Officers Adventure', in which two British officers, possibly Intelligence Corps Scouts, are described investigating if an enemy trench was still occupied:

> The first thing they came upon was a dugout with a candle burning and a quantity of German equipment scattered about. Thinking that this might have been captured, they continued their way down the trench, however, taking the precaution to blow out the candle. Presently they came upon a trench running at right angles to the one they were in. No sooner had they entered it than they were challenged in German, a shower of bullets followed, and a race ensued for the exit, both pursuers and pursued floundering in the mud and dodging around the traverses. Fortunately the night was dark and the Englishmen escaped unhurt after several minutes spent in the enemy's fire trenches, surrounded on all sides by Germans.

The section also scoured no-man's-land for document intelligence from dead and wounded Germans, such as pay books, identity 'dog tag' necklaces worn around the neck and letters. Pay books gave substantial information such as regimental number, full name, date and place of birth, next of kin details, date of enlistment and active service, gallantry awards and a general description. German dog tags were metal. When the soldier went on active service, his unit details were added and if he was killed, captured or repatriated, his replacement would be allotted the next number in the system and thus unit losses could be calculated. The study of pay books thus gave an estimated strength of the German army and showed that as the war progressed, increasing numbers of older men were drafted into service. By 1917 the emphasis had switched to conscripting those in their late teens. Letters frequently gave an indication of morale and events at home. It was dangerous work, given that both sides launched raids against the patrols.

Since the miles of trenches meant that it was impossible to infiltrate the enemy lines, the BEF adopted a tactic devised by the recently raised Princess Patricia's Canadian Light Infantry in February 1915 of trench raids to dominate no-man's-land and capture prisoners, documents and equipment for intelligence purposes. Generally, the tactic was to isolate the selected enemy sector and prevent counter-attacks by shelling beyond the front line, while infantry stormed the trench. Eventually, preparatory shelling became an intelligence indicator of a raid, thus giving time to deploy reinforcements. While post-war British analysis concluded the costs outweighed the benefits, advantages included increased vigilance and the promotion of the offensive spirit.

When the French gave Major Kirke fifteen homing pigeons in September 1914 to carry intelligence messages, he was doubtful about their reliability; nevertheless, he arranged for twenty-eight homing pigeons to be smuggled across the Channel to occupied Belgium, twenty-one of which flew to the BEF loft. This led to Kirke asking Second-Lieutenant Alexander Waley, an older-than-average Intelligence Corps recruit with no military experience other than proving himself while serving with the RFC during the retreat from Mons, to develop the use of intelligence pigeons. Waley organised lofts in eight towns and villages and, by March 1915, was also using mobile coops fitted to Type-10 GS wagons. He also regularly collected 'intelligence pigeons' from the trenches. Lieutenant-Colonel Alfred Osman, former president of the Pigeon Association, was asked by the Royal Engineers Signals Service to develop a messenger pigeon service from the front line, and by 1918 the five BEF armies each had a motor mobile pigeon loft, fourteen horse-drawn lofts, three fixed lofts and a total establishment of 20,000 birds and 380 pigeon-fanciers.

In the spring of 1915, General Joffre planned to attack the German salient that stretched west to Compiègne by attacking from Verdun in the French sector to the south and from Arras and Rheims in the British sector. When the French intended to press the German defence of Lille, Field-Marshal French selected the village of Neuve Chapelle, between Bethune and Armentières, as his objective because its capture would pave the way for the French to assault the German-held Aubers Ridge, a mile to the east, barely 20ft high but possessing a commanding view across flatlands criss-crossed by small drainage ditches bordering the River Lys. Field-Marshal French selected IV Corps and the Indian Corps, from the First Army, to lead the attack. A deception plan was devised to suggest that troops leaving the Neuve Chapelle sector involved the Second Army to the north and I Corps near Givenchy to the south, conducting diversionary operations.

By March, the whole British front line had been recorded with large-scale trench maps, except for the Ypres sector, which was being taken over from the French. The General Staff planners were beginning to realise the value of imagery intelligence and in spite of poor weather, eighty-five reconnaissance aircraft conducted extensive oblique and vertical air reconnaissance of Neuve Chapelle from which Royal Engineer surveyors developed annotated photo-maps showing the trenches meandering through wrecked houses, ruined roads and splintered trees. Taking the photos was rudimentary with the observer holding the camera on his knee and then yelling to the pilot to keep the aircraft level. The cameras, by now, were mostly Model-A. This type had a semi-automatic gravity feed for several magazines slotted on top, which enhanced capability by allowing several images to be taken quickly, but it was prone to jamming. The observer then identified the target through a hole in the floor and then placed the camera over it and pressed the trigger. Typically, photographs taken from 10,000ft using a camera with a focal length of 8in could photograph one square mile onto 4 x 5in paper. Prints were exposed in the aircraft by pulling a slide. Magazines were changed manually, not an easy task in the cold. A sortie flown by Lieutenant Wadham and Captain Darley saw new trenches to the north-east of the village. To the south-east of Neuve Chapelle were the untouched trees of Bois de Biez.

The First Army Intelligence Section consisted of two regular intelligence staff officers and three temporary captains who were a diplomat, stockbroker and a barrister. Lieutenant-Colonel Charteris wrote after the battle that:

> The barrister's especial job is studying air reconnaissance, at which he is getting extraordinarily expert; finding out all manner of things, some very important, from them. The Germans can quite easily cover up gun positions and other defences, so that the observers in aeroplanes cannot detect them. It is next to impossible to conceal them from the cameras.

The barrister was Captain Carrol Romer (Royal Engineers), who had been employed by the Egyptian Survey Department for three years from 1905 and was now commanding the First Army Mapping and Printing Section and worked closely with Headquarters First Army. Romer took the grid reference system further by inventing that invaluable aid to calculating grid references for map-reading, the romer, essentially a transparent card on which are several map scales. Chateris noted on 24 February:

> My table is covered with photographs taken from aeroplanes. We have just started this method of reconnaissance which will I think develop into something very important [...] It is very necessary to check on the exaggerated reports and imagination of air observers. The photos cannot tell lies.

In many respects, the opening of the third flank of the air saw the revolutionary change in British military topography. During the fast-moving manoeuvre warfare of the first two months, the BEF had used 1:80,000 scale maps of France and 1:40,000 scale maps of Belgium. As the positional warfare developed, demands grew for large-scale maps for the accurate pinpointing of enemy locations and identification of geographical features on the ground. Fortunately, original drawings of Belgium rescued before Antwerp was captured were of such good quality that the British drew 1:20,000 scale maps. In relation to France, British Ordnance Survey enlarged existing maps to 1:20,000 and 1:40,000 scale. In November 1914 MO4 Geographical Section, General Staff (GSGS) sent the 1st Ranging Section, Royal Engineers, principally to locate German artillery batteries by using theodolites to intersect smoke flares dropped over their positions. In April 1915 the section was formed into the 1st Ranging and Survey Section of three topographical sections, which each included a printing section, originally part of the BEF 1st Printing Company. Among specialist maps were barrage maps and trench maps.

Highly detailed trench maps were compiled from air photographs, interrogations, sketches, captured maps and documents collected during raids. Enemy positions were marked in red and British and Dominion forces in blue, a practice that lasted until 1918 when they were swapped to conform to French practices. The British later reverted to the original system until the 1980s when someone suggested that 'red' equated to the Soviets, the Cold War threat, and it was replaced with orange. Every map had a key matching annotations for features. The British nicknamed some features and places to ease identification for the average British soldier, for instance 'Wipers' for Ypres and 'Plugstreet' for Ploegsteert. Marked British maps were classified 'Secret' and not permitted to be taken forward of brigade HQs in case they were captured. In due course the development of air photographs and survey allowed the Royal Engineers to build large models of objectives to familiarise and train attacking troops.

On 10 March, preceded by a thirty-five-minute artillery bombardment of 342 guns in part directed by the RFC, and armed with detailed intelligence, including 1,500 annotated air photographs distributed to units, IV Corps and the Indian Corps overran the single division of Crown Prince Rupperckt's Sixth Army within four hours. However, the inexperienced General Staff struggled with dispatch riders losing their way in mist and field telephone cables being damaged by shelling, and when the artillery failed to neutralise trenches near Aubers, the attack was cut down by heavy fire. Meanwhile, RFC fighters harassed German reinforcements marching from Lille. Further confusion emerged when a prisoner captured by the Gurkhas to the south of the village told his interrogator that two battalions were in Bois de Biez; it then emerged that the wood was weakly held, and the intelligence was enough for French to order IV Corps to withdraw to the village. The following day Haig ordered another attack, with disastrous results. Charteris noted that air photographs pinpointing German gun positions should be a lesson to the British artillery to conceal themselves. He wrote to his wife on 12 March:

> Our intelligence show was successful, in that we found the Germans exactly as we had located them [...] The plans for the battle were all worked out on maps, brought up to date from air photographs for the first time in war. [...] I am

afraid that England will have to accustom herself far greater than those of Neuve Chapelle before we finally crush the German Army

On 13 March IV Corps repelled a counter-attack and advanced with disastrous results. Although part of the salient had been seized, poor command and control and an intelligence failure had degraded success at the cost of 7,000 British and 4,200 Indians against 1,200 Germans. To some extent, the battle was a turning point as former captain and noted *Daily Mail* journalist Ferdinand Tuohy (Intelligence Corps) later wrote in his *The Secret Corps: A Tale of Intelligence on All Fronts* (1920):

> The General Staff apparently abandoned the theory of surprise in attack was possible in war of positional. The most we could expect to keep would be to keep the hour of attack, and possibly the date, secret. As for the location of the attack, it would be impossible to conceal that from the enemy.

Killed a week after the battle was another of the Original 55. Second-Lieutenant George Fletcher, an Eton Classics master and fluent in German, had been in the Motor-Cycle Section and had adopted a cat which he took into the trenches. In September 1914 he had been attached to 2 Royal Welsh Fusiliers and led listening patrols, no matter how foul the weather; when challenged, he was able to reply in German. He once diverted a German attack by shouting an order that saw several enemy seek shelter in a trench dominated by British machine-gunners and riflemen. His brother, Reginald, also Eton and Balliol, had been killed at the Battle of Gheluvelt during the First Battle of Ypres. George was mentioned in dispatches in mid-February. About two weeks after returning from leave, he failed to convince a sentry during a trench raid in March 1915 and the party beat a hasty retreat to the British trenches. He was best remembered for the recovery of a French flag which the Germans were provocatively displaying on a tree, one officer suggesting he should have either been awarded a VC or been court martialled. On 20 March, he was helping to repair trenches with fascines near Bois Grenier when a sniper shot him in the head.

The air reconnaissance survey was extended by 2 Wing RFC to cover the Second Army tactical area of responsibility then taking over the Ypres salient. Meanwhile, Lieutenant Moore-Brabazon's section continued to improve camera efficiency. In the summer, Thornton-Pickard reduced vibration with its Model-C camera. Captain Darley developed a system that with an aircraft flying at 65mph and the observer taking a photograph every fifteen seconds, 75 per cent three-dimensional (3D) imagery could be produced using a stereoscope by pairing consecutive photographs. Lieutenant Elliot Bingham (RFC), serving with No. 11 Squadron in III Corps Wing supporting the Third Army, constructed a stereoscope capable of providing 3D by modifying a camera and portable viewer he had purchased in

Amiens. Royal Engineers survey sections combined air photographs and ground survey techniques to produce detailed maps.

During heavy fighting around Arras on 5 July, Lieutenant A.J. (Alfred) Evans, one of the Original 55 and an examiner of documents, was sheltering in the cathedral crypt from shelling when it was hit several times. As he extracted himself from the ruins he picked up from the rubble a relatively undamaged plaster statue of the Madonna and child, and after carrying it around for some time one of his NCOs took it back to England for him. Evans later transferred to the RFC. A person with the same initials and name became a well-known serial escaper. The statue lay forgotten in his house until 1972 when he donated it to the Intelligence Corps Museum, where it became part of the First World War display. The Madonna was returned to the cathedral in 2015, as part of the centenary celebrations of the war.

The intercepting and disrupting of enemy communications by capturing or killing couriers and translating messages sent by visual means, such as semaphore, fire beacons, flags, flares and heliograph, had been a fundamental military necessity for centuries. The Royal Navy and the Post Office led the British development of wireless interception with the former establishing Room 40 in the Admiralty Old Building in October 1914. A month later the press demanded that wireless amateurs use their skills to listen for spies transmitting from Great Britain; however, military conservatism was slow to respond to the intercept of battlefield communications because there was little intellectual understanding of the science of wireless communications. Decryption of codes and the capturing of code books and brief theft of code books eases code-breaking. The advent of wireless telegraphy led to traffic analysis by listening to transmissions and the gaining of intelligence from the flow of signals between senders and receivers. One of the 'voluntary interceptors' enrolled by Room 40 was Lieutenant-Colonel Bayntrun Richard Hippisley (North Somerset Yeomanry), who had been intercepting German military traffic since 1912.

To address military weaknesses in wireless intelligence, Lieutenant-Colonel Macdonogh had Captain Henry Round and Lieutenant Charles Franklin seconded from Marconi Wireless Telegraph Company to investigate the feasibility of pinpointing enemy locations from their wireless transmissions. After conducting experiments near Devizes in late December 1914, they erected a 70ft mast near Abbeville and pinpointed enemy wirelesses and ensured the destruction of twelve artillery-spotting aircraft. The intercept baseline was then moved to cover the BEF sector between Calais and Amiens. Round later helped Room 40 to establish several direction-finding and intercept stations around the British Isles and a clandestine one in Bergen. At the same time, Captain Rupert Stanley RN had developed a device capable of intercepting enemy conversations for use in the trenches up to a distance of 100 yards.

Although BEF HQ emphasised the need for communication security, some officers treated field telephones as though they were at home and were careless when discussing operational matters. The British used ten-line Enfield switchboards and, at battalion level, four-line exchanges incorporating a Morse key connected to standard D-3 field telephones. Each was fitted with a 'buzzer', which was an electro-mechanical device in which the pulses of speech or Morse were earthed by a ground spike or bayonet. When the Life Guards took over from a French regiment in mid-1915 in such secrecy that they removed their insignia, the Germans threw a bottle into their front line containing the message 'Welcome to the English cavalry'. Suspicions that the Germans were intercepting enemy communications first emerged from Ruhleben Internment Camp when a British civilian, on being debriefed after repatriation, overheard German medical orderlies discussing an 'apparatus which was securing them valuable information'. In mid-1915, a French patrol captured a device in no-man's-land which was evaluated to be a German Moritz trench listening device operated by army and corps-level specialist telephone troops. The system consisted of induction coils that collected the pulses of telephone conversations from earthing devices up to a distance of 3,000 yards. The Germans had also developed counter-measures to minimise interception. Since the British had no technical counter-measures and there was little communications discipline, there was little the director of BEF Signals could do except warn that the Germans could intercept field telephone conversations and instruct that no written messages were to be passed by 'buzzer' within 1,500 yards of the front line. Call signs were later issued to minimise identifying units.

By April 1915, the value of the discreet interception of telegrams, letters and parcels had been recognised as a valuable intelligence collection tool and a counter-intelligence asset. In his book *German Spies at Bay* (1920), S.T. Felstead wrote that 'censorship probably detected most of the German spy network in the UK at the beginning of the war and the detection of later attempts to establish networks'. In matters affecting national security, this was mainly conducted by MO5 (Special Intelligence) intercepting communications by suspected agents and sympathisers. By 1917, approximately 15 million letters and cables were being examined with the censorship of letters and parcels with MO5(h) (Postal Censorship) being the most important bureau employing nearly 5,000 people. Given the need for foreign languages, the Intelligence Corps recruited men who could speak 'uncommon languages' such as Chinese, Arabic and Maltese. Mail between neutral countries was examined on the grounds that German intelligence flourished in Scandinavia and Holland with correspondence from Gothenburg, Stockholm and Flushing found to contain letters addressed to *Abteiling IIIb*, the German Intelligence HQ in Berlin. When ships from the USA and Scandinavia docked at British ports, such as Falmouth, censors clandestinely removed the mail sacks, sent them by train to London where they were examined by MO5(h) before being sent to Dover to meet up with their ship. Censorship of letters sent by service personnel was conducted by unit officers using the criteria 'not permitted to send letters criticising operations, superior officers, allied troops or any statement calculated to bring the Army or individuals into disrepute'. Many officers found the task boring; nevertheless, so wide was the mandate that censorship varied from unit to unit and some were taken aback that soldiers could write such passionate letters to wives and girlfriends.

When veteran *Times* reporter Arthur Moore filed the 'Amiens Despatch' during the retreat from Mons on 23 August 1914 describing a 'terrible defeat' and British falling back in disarray towards Paris, it challenged the official War Office accounts and the perception of a short, victorious war. His editors sent the draft to the War Office Press Bureau, a body established by Frederick Smith (later Lord Beaverbrook) to censor press reports. To Moore's astonishment, he was asked to replace some content with a clarion cry for more troops. The article was published on 30 August under the headline 'Broken British Regiments, Untarnished Honour of Our Troops' and 'More Men Needed' and while the *Times* was accused of being unpatriotic and defeatist, it hinted that the war would not be over by Christmas. The War Office then appointed Colonel Earnest Swinton and Henry Tomlinson to be the BEF official war correspondents with their articles vetted by Lord Kitchener. In due course, more war correspondents were accredited on the proviso they wrote what they believed to be true, and not what was true. Positive propaganda to maintain morale was important. 'Old Bill' was an elderly, grumbling 'Tommy' with a walrus moustache and battered steel helmet created by Lieutenant Bruce Bairnsfather (Royal Warwicks) in 1915 for the magazine *Bystander* as a morale booster for those in the front line and those at home. His younger mate was 'Bert'. Suffering from shell shock and hearing damage after the Second Battle of Ypres in 1916, Bairnsfather was posted to Military Intelligence 7 as the official cartoonist.

To counter German propaganda, David Lloyd George, then Chancellor of the Exchequer, persuaded Frederick Smith in August 1914 to be Minister of Information; the latter asked Mr Clive Masterman, a fellow Liberal MP and a successful author, to head a new propaganda organisation. Masterman selected several authors, including Arthur Conan Doyle, John Masefield, G.K. Chesterton, Thomas Hardy and Rudyard Kipling to draft responses and claims. Second-Lieutenant John Buchan (Intelligence Corps), the author of spy novels such as *The 39 Steps*, was the Secret Service Bureau press liaison officer. When he was promoted to lieutenant-colonel and head of intelligence for the Ministry of Information in 1917, he requested to wear the red insignia of the General Staff and not the green of intelligence staff officers, on the grounds that it 'would facilitate my work in London', but this was refused.

During its invasion of Belgium, Germany claimed that its forces had been attacked by *francs-tireurs* and sabotage groups; it had therefore retaliated with collective punishment, imprisonment, executions and the destruction of historic buildings. *Francs-tireurs* emerged from French rifle clubs and unofficial military societies during the 1867 Luxembourg crisis and, in the event of war, mobilised as militia light infantry, but not wearing military uniform. When the British government published the Bryce Committee 'Alleged German Outrage' report in May 1915 detailing the invasion of Belgium from diary extracts and letters found on captured German soldiers, Germany responded with accounts of atrocities against German soldiers by Belgian civilians. Probably the most effective propaganda concerned the nurse Edith Cavell.

There had always been a close connection between intelligence and prisoners in terms of prison camps as depositories of information and aiding escapes. By the beginning of 1915, most of Belgium was occupied with Ypres, in the the province of Flanders, the scene of heavy fighting. Compared to the Second World War, the story of the approximately 170,000 British and Dominion soldiers captured on the Western Front is largely unknown. Signatories of the 1899 Laws and Customs of War on Land, Article 4, Chapter 2 (On Prisoners of War) stated that: 'Prisoners of war are in the power of the hostile Government, but not in that of the individuals or corps who captured them [...] They must be humanely treated [...] All their personal belongings, except arms, horses, and military papers remain their property.'

Nevertheless, about 5.2 per cent of the captured British and Dominion troops died from disease, starvation and murder. British and Dominian soldiers were given rudimentary training in resistance to interrogation training, such as not to discuss military matters with anyone, including those in British uniforms, and this seems to have been effective. As the culture of the age demanded, the upper- and middle-class officers were generally held in relative comfort. Perhaps the etiquette of the age is best illustrated by Captain Robert Cameron (East Surreys) honouring fourteen days' parole from the Kaiser so that he could visit his dying mother. After his capture on 27 August 1914 near Fresnoy, Second-Lieutenant Le Grand described his two years of captivity as varying from fairly brutal to courteous as he passed through five prison camps, including Sennelager and Gütersloh, until his apparent repatriation in May 1916. The most courteous man he met was Prince Maximilian of Baden, who gave up his appointment as a staff officer to join the German Red Cross to improve the welfare of prisoners. He arranged for some officers to be repatriated from Konstanz through Switzerland.

The lower class of other ranks were usually confined to work camps where the fight continued with sabotage and arson in factories, labour disputes and ruining crops in a country that eventually suffered badly from a blockade. About 10,000 escapes were made with 573 successful 'home runs'. RFC Second-Lieutenant Harold Medlicott escaped fourteen times but seems to have been executed after his fifteenth escape in May 1918. Many returned ashamed of having let the side down and post-war suicides were not unknown. Private Arthur Sheppard, of the 16th Rifle Brigade, who lived in Mark, Somerset, was captured in 1917 after just nine days in the front line and shot himself in 1924 as a direct consequence of his wartime experiences.

In retreats, the situation for troops can be chaotic, as men and units become separated and are cut off. Some are captured and others evade. As the front line stabilised, the principal escape routes were either to Switzerland and Holland, both neutral countries where internment was a risk. Lieutenant-Colonel Dudley Boger and Sergeant-Major Frank Meachin, of 1 Cheshires, were both wounded and captured during the action at Elouges and were admitted to a German general hospital in a convent at Wiheries. Boger led an escape in which six other prisoners scaled the walls and reached a wood where they split into pairs and stole clothes and food as they moved through villages. Boger and Meachin reached Brussels on 1 November and were put in touch with Edith Cavell, who organised their escape to the Dutch border. Boger was recaptured and spent the rest of the war in prison camps. Meachin reached England.

Edith Cavell was born near Norwich and was aged 50 years in 1914. She had lived in Brussels before training as a nurse at the London Hospital. She was then appointed matron of the newly established nurse training Berendael Medical Institute in 1907 and was visiting her widowed mother in England when war broke out. She immediately returned to Brussels to find that the institute had been requisitioned by the Red Cross. An early visitor was Princess Marie of Croy, an old friend, who was already using her chateau as a safe house for soldiers left behind during the retreat from Mons and for refugees. She had established a network of six guides, all poachers and smugglers, in groups of three spread between Mons, Brussels and the Dutch border. Her husband prepared false papers. Would Edith help? Cavell readily agreed to do so. Thereafter, a steady stream of British and escapers and stragglers and young Belgians passed through her chain. She employed them as orderlies in her hospital while they were waiting.

German counter-intelligence intercepted several postcards from British evaders thanking Cavell and on 5 September 1915 she was quietly arrested, as was the princess and thirty-five members of her network. The US Legation heard about the arrests on 12 September but could not apply to see her until the sentence was announced. At her trial held on 7 and 8 October Cavell admitted that she had breached Section 58 of German Military Code by aiding a hostile power and causing harm to German and allied troops by 'conducting soldiers to the enemy'. She also admitted that under Section 90, she had concealed British and French soldiers and Belgians of military age and had facilitated their escape to the Dutch frontier by providing money and guides. Although convicted of helping sixty British and fifteen French soldiers and about 100 Belgians, the actual figure is probably larger. The sentence, which was announced to her in her cell, was that she would be shot.

Mr Hugh Gibson, the secretary of the US Legation, appealed for clemency by reminding German officials that others convicted of helping Allied soldiers had been sent to prisons on Germany and Cavell had treated Germans wounded during the invasion of Belgium. He also warned them her execution would rank alongside the needless burning of Louvain in 1914 and the torpedoing of the *Lusitania* in May 1915. But the opinion of Lieutenant-Colonel Count Franz van Harrach, who had been the chief bodyguard of Archduke Franz Ferdinand when he was assassinated in Sarajevo, was that he would rather see 'three to four old English women shot' rather than see the humblest German soldier harmed; and his opinion prevailed. Taking Holy Communion the night before her execution on 12 October, Cavell told the Reverend Stirling Gahan, the Anglican chaplain, that 'patriotism is not enough. I must have no hatred or bitterness towards anyone', words that are inscribed on her statue in St Martin's Place, near Trafalgar Square in London. The British government exploited her execution as a major weapon in the propaganda war against Germany and as a means of persuading men to enlist. In 1919, Cavell was given a state funeral in London. Anne-Marie L'Hotellier, a hospital manager in Cambrai, was sentenced, in August 1916, to ten years' imprisonment for assisting wounded prisoners to escape.

Resistance to occupation throughout Europe was not new. Margriet Ballegeer was so incensed about German behaviour during the invasion of Belgium that she and Abbé Felix Moons, a family friend, smuggled people across the Dutch border. Since her father was a senior police officer in a village near Antwerp, she could acquire permit applications and identity cards. She used her employment in a shop to cover her role as a courier. When the Abbé was suspected by the Belgian police, he hid with the Ballegeers until Margriet and her father were arrested in 1915, convicted of forgery and sentenced to one and six years' imprisonment respectively.

As the resistance in Belgium developed into functional organisations, so did methods to pass intelligence. Initially, couriers crossing the Dutch border carried messages written on rice paper or silk concealed, for instance, in walking sticks, stems of tobacco pipes and clothing; however, this avenue was undermined in 1915 when the Germans erected two electrified fences along the 125 miles from Aix-Le-Chapelle to the River Scheldt and warned that anyone found within half a mile of them was liable to summary execution. An estimated 2,500 Belgians died in the militarised zone. Nevertheless, couriers stuffed messages into turnips and threw them over the fence at agreed spots at agreed times. In one place, an agent contracted to launder the clothing of German border guards hung out washing to signify he had thrown a message over the fence. While secret writing and codes were used, the sheer pressure of compiling messages in an occupied country meant that mistakes were inevitable.

A role of the BEF Intelligence Section was to collect information from inside German-occupied Europe while the Secret Service Bureau (Foreign Intelligence) focused elsewhere. Newspapers and periodicals provided open source intelligence, but there was always the risk of them being tainted with propaganda or disinformation (the deliberate spreading of false information). In the autumn of 1914, Major Kirke used the absence of Smith-Cumming, on sick leave after losing his leg, to rationalise espionage by assigning Holland and Switzerland to Foreign Intelligence while BEF I(b) (Secret Service) took control of occupied Belgium, France and Luxembourg.

Before and during the First World War, travellers to foreign countries applied for a permit, essentially a modern visa, issued by consular officials. It was not until the 1920s that passports, including a photograph and brief description, were introduced. So far as the British were concerned, some consuls were acting in an honorary capacity and not all were British, which made them not entirely trustworthy. Kirke believed that the consular system in Europe gave the Germans avenues to infiltrate spies into Great Britain and he proposed the establishment of permit offices staffed by military intelligence officers masquerading as consular officials, in order to vet applicants taking an undue interest in Allied activity. They would be in a position to collect information from travellers and to talent-spot individuals suitable for infiltration into Germany and occupied Europe. Kirke therefore established a network of permit offices at ports, such as Boulogne, Calais, Dunkirk, Dieppe and in towns in the BEF sector including Abbeville, Amiens and Rouen. An office in Marseilles vetted passengers and travellers arriving from the Mediterranean, central Europe, the Middle East and Far East.

Persuading Allied intelligence chiefs to bury the distrust that frequently blights intelligence organisations, Kirke and his French and Belgian counterparts had established the *Bureau Central Interallie* (BCI) at 9 The Parade, Folkestone in November 1914. Kirke appointed Major Cecil Cameron (Royal Artillery) to be the BEF representative in Folkestone, codenamed CF. Cameron was the son of a man awarded the Victoria Cross during the 1857 Indian Mutiny. While in India his wife, Ruby, had become addicted to morphine during treatment for a serious tropical illness. Both were jailed in May 1911 for fraud over an insurance claim for an expensive necklace, supposedly snatched from her in the street. Although Cameron was cashiered, most officers believed him to be guilty only of loyalty to his wife. On being released after three years, in June 1914, his friend Smith-Cumming recruited him for the Secret Service Bureau office in Brussels, but the German invasion forced him to move to Givet in northern France where he came to the notice of Kirke. Arranging for Cameron to be pardoned and recommissioned, Kirke instructed him to reactivate his networks in western Belgium and to focus on the railway junction at Liège.

In December 1914, Lieutenant Stanley Woolrych (Intelligence Corps) was on the Rotterdam to Folkestone ferry when he met a Belgian named M. Lorphevre, who volunteered to act as an agent for the British. Aged 19 years in October 1914, Woolrych had applied to join the Royal Fusiliers but when he was rejected with a slight medical problem, his fluency in French and German saw him commissioned into the General Service Corps and attached to the Intelligence Corps. Arriving in France in early December, he was sent to HQ 7th Division as a scout and was directed to the Divisional Laundry. When Lorphevre supplied a detailed report on German use of trains in the Brussels and Charleroi areas, Woolrych forwarded the report to GHQ and was told to develop the source. Several agents were recruited and after being given basic instruction in tradecraft and codes, a train-watching network covering thirteen railway lines in the Charleroi district was developed, the first of several that covered Belgium and Luxembourg. Reports from Charleroi often arrived in Folkestone within four days. Train-watching became a most valuable intelligence source for monitoring the use of railways to help identify enemy intentions, for plotting troop movement as a collation aid, for calculating orders of battle and for identifying units.

According to the January 1917 *Handbook of the German Army*, railway troops were part of the Communications Directorate, along with Mechanical Transport, and they were organised into construction and railway traffic companies, each affiliated to a railway regiment identifiable by number in Roman numerals on uniform epaulettes. The directorate was split into the Western Theatre Director-General at Brussels, Military Railway Directorates at Lille, Sedan and Charleroi and the Eastern Theatre of seven directorates. Principal railway junctions were controlled from railway traffic offices. An infantry division initially required fifty-two trains, although this was reduced to forty in March 1917 as casualties took their toll. Officers travelled in coaches while other ranks travelled in cattle trucks and goods wagons. Flat trucks were for horses, artillery and other war stores. Of particular importance to GHQ were 'constituted' or formed units.

Train-watching circuits generally consisted of controllers managing networks of couriers and observers, some living alongside railways and others able to mingle with soldiers in station bars and with conductors, drivers and coalmen. The leader of a circuit of railway employees was a one-legged former miner named Visser with a body odour problem, who worked on a barge and regularly crossed the German border. He built the MS circuit at Hasselt covering the area between Courtrai and Ghent and by 1918 was passing 130 weekly reports. Counting methods varied. M. Lorphevre used cheeses, for instance: *Gruyere* meaning passenger coaches containing troops, *Chester* meaning coaches containing wounded; and *Port Salut* meaning wagons containing horses. One woman living in a house overlooking a railway in Luxembourg used knitting patterns in local newspapers, using, for example, plain stitch to mean a carriage carrying troops and purl stitch to mean horses. Train-watchers were expected to report and not to speculate.

In the spring of 1915, Kirke established an office at 7 Lincoln House, Basil Street, Knightsbridge, London (code-named WL) and recruited Captain Ernest Wallinger (Royal Field Artillery) to run it. Wallinger had lost a leg during the Battle of Aisne, had previously been at the BCI and lived in style in a flat above the office. His brother, John, was formerly head of Indian Political Intelligence in Bombay. Kirke recruited Captain Sigismund Payne-Best to work with Wallinger and to meet the Rotterdam–Tilbury ferry to collect intelligence passengers and crew, vet the passenger list for enemy infiltration and talent-spot anyone willing to return to occupied Europe as agents. As soon as passengers arrived, they were required to apply for identity card and passes to travel inland. Ernest scored a coup in 1916 in Rotterdam when a German walked into his office clutching a prized but charred German *Field Post Office Book* he had rescued when some documents were being destroyed. A copy of the book was held in the few head post offices. The German had asked for the location of the Rotterdam office by asking a policeman.

After twice being wounded at Gallipoli in 1915, once by friendly fire, Major Ivone Kirkpatrick (Royal Inniskilling Fusiliers) joined Wallinger in London to vet the Rotterdam–Gravesend ferry. In 1917, aged 20 years, he replaced Captain Best in Rotterdam and set up the *Felix* network of Belgian prostitutes in Rotterdam collecting information from their German clients. When the Germans heard in 1918 that he wanted another *Field Post Office Book*, they sold him a fake.

Kirke also established subsidiary offices in Lanakon, Belgium, and Geneva in Switzerland, under the control of Captain Lewis Campbell, and allowed the French to set up a permit office in London. The permit offices proved their worth and were later turned into passport control offices which were continued during the Second World War, most of them run by Intelligence Corps officers attached to MI5 or MI6.

At the same time, Captain Vernon Kell established Secret Service (Foreign Bureau) offices in Great Britain, including Folkestone, Southampton and Tilbury, and in Bergen in Norway. Major Laurence Oppenheim (Northamptonshires), the military attaché in Amsterdam and a career soldier, controlled the collection of intelligence in Holland and was at the heart of operations in Belgium, but he was often at odds with Richard Tinsley, a former Cunard merchant seaman and Royal Navy reservist, who ran an effective operation in Holland and Germany from a commercial premises in Rotterdam. His counter-intelligence operations led to five spies being arrested as they entered England and he survived compromise by German counter-intelligence in May 1916. Nevertheless, rivalry emerged between the offices, which led to duplication of reports, false collateral and recruiting each other's agents.

5
Aden, Egypt and Mesopotamia

When, on 28 July 1914, First Lord of the Admiralty Churchill ordered two Turkish battleships being built in Great Britain to be requisitioned, this outraged Turkey because the money for them had had been raised by public subscription. On 10 August, two German warships eluded the British Mediterranean Squadron and, anchoring off Constantinople, went through the charade of being sold to the Turks. Despite British attempts to keep Turkey neutral, a Turkish squadron, including the two ships, bombarded Russian Black Sea ports, which then led to Churchill ordering the Dardanelles Squadron to commence hostilities against Turkey.

Politically, the Aden settlement was important because its port gave pilgrims from south-east Asia and the Persian Gulf use of the Sacred Road north to Mecca, even if they were at risk of robbery and extortion from bandits in the Radfan. Strategically, the colony guarded access to the Red Sea and the Suez Canal. The landward defence relied on loyalist desert rulers defending their states, the most important being the Amir of Dhala, but since Aden Brigade did not have an intelligence section, analysis of Turkish military activity and intentions was patchy.

On 23 December 1914, Lieutenant-General Lake, in India, suggested that a field telephone connect Brigade HQ with Lahei, a hilltop town 25 miles from Aden, and that the three main tracks north be improved. On Christmas Day, after the Amir reported that five Turkish battalions and five guns had deployed to Qataba, Brigadier-General David Shaw, the brigade commander, selected the government well at Ath Thalub as his main defensive position. When two officers checking the eastern track from Bir Salim to Bir Amir reported deep sand 3 miles south of Lahej and that camels would be needed to tow artillery, 1/23rd Sikh Pioneers, which had been left behind by EIF F, spent six weeks improving it. Shaw reformed the Aden movable column and reinforced it with an enlarged infantry company and a 15-pdr field artillery battery to be based at either Nobat Dakim or Lahej.

In January 1915, HQ Aden Brigade assessed that 1st Brecknockshires (TF) needed more training. The battalion was one of several reservist units sent to India to replace the IEFs. In mid-February, Colonel William Walton (Royal Scots Fusiliers) arrived as deputy commander from commanding 9th Royal Berkshires in Flanders. He had served in the intelligence division from 1903 for three years and had recommended to GHQ India that dhows taking mail and money from Jeddah to the HQ VII (Yemen) Corps in Sanaa be intercepted. Reports from Perim Island then suggested that 3,500 Arabs were planning to land added credibility to intelligence on Turkish intentions that an attack on Aden was likely; however, Lieutenant-General Nixon, then commanding the Southern Army, instructed that offensive operations were not to be conducted north of Sheikh Othman, that is outside Aden settlement, except in a 'grave emergency' and only after agreement from the GHQ.

By early May the fighting in Gallipoli had enhanced Turkish military confidence. The next objective must surely be Aden. After a visit to the Sultan of Lahej, Lieutenant-Colonel Jacob, the brigade political officer, and Captain Paige, the brigade intelligence officer, suggested to Brigadier-General Shaw that friendly Arabs should be armed as a counter-measure to Turkish subversion. In mid-May, Brigade HQ instructed the camel troop to rejoin the Aden troop at Lahej and that Captain Norbury, who commanded it, should replace Captain Paige as the brigade intelligence officer. A week later, HQ Southern Army complained to Brigadier-General Shaw that the quality of intelligence from Aden was poor, which was hardly surprising. Brigade HQ lacked an intelligence section, there were no Turkish linguists to interrogate prisoners and translate documents and there was no air reconnaissance capability. The brigade relied almost entirely on Lieutenant-Colonel Jacobs for its principal source of human intelligence. When reports suggested that VII (Yemen) Corps was preparing to attack Lahej and that the Sultan of Haushabi had defected, Jacobs doubted their validity; nevertheless, Brigadier-General Shaw confirmed with Lieutenant-General Lake that 'grave emergency' included a Turkish advance to Lahej. The reported defection was significant because it gave the Turks the ability to attack Lahej either from the mountainous Radfan or direct access to Aden from the east coast or both.

When an intelligence report dated 11 June indicating that Turks had reached Mauia was confirmed by the sultan, the Aden camel troop patrolled the caravan routes to Dhala; however, summer midday haze restricted heliograph communications to the station on Jebel Shamshan in Aden. An attempted landing on Perim was defeated, even though nationalist discontent within the Indian army had led to telephone lines between the outpost HQ and the gun battery being cut. In February, a mutiny by the 5th Native Light Infantry, which was incited by Indian revolutionaries of the US-based *Ghadar* (Mutiny) Party, was undermined within the week by a British counter-intelligence operation. The Ghadrites believed they could persuade Indian soldiers posted overseas to mutiny against the British. In late March, eight sepoys of the Perim outpost fired at their officers and a sapper murdered two Indian officers in their sleep.

When reports emerged that the 39th (Turkish) Infantry Division, from VII (Yemen) Corps, had crossed the border at Ad Daraj, Shaw appointed Lieutenant-Colonel Pearson, the commanding officer of 23rd Sikh Pioneers, to command the

Aden movable column and provided him with a pack wireless detachment. Pearson's adjutant, Captain Francis Squires, would be the column staff officer at Brigade HQ. The rest of Aden Brigade would be the main body. The lack of hard intelligence was alleviated the next day when an agent living in Sheikh Sa'id reported to Captain Nicholas, on Perim Island, that the Turkish division intended to attack Lahej in three columns from the general direction of Dhala. That evening, Jacob learnt from the sultan that its advance guard had reached Al-Milah, about 5 miles north-east of Nobat Dakin, but he did not believe it would attack Lahej. But camel troop reports the following day suggested that the enemy would soon reach the town. Shaw therefore instructed Pearson to reinforce the defence of Lahej on 1 July.

Next day, Aden Brigade began its march, but unusual searing heat and lack of water took its toll, particularly among the 1st Brecknockshires, and the timetable slipped. As Pearson entered Lahej late in the afternoon of 4 July, shelling was wreaking havoc and confusion was rife as 39th Division advanced across fertile fields and through orchards towards the northern fringes of the town. The sultan was then fatally wounded by friendly fire as he galloped into the town to meet Pearson; he died in Aden on 13 July. When he realised that he would not reach Lahej, Shaw sent a dispatch rider with orders for Pearson to withdraw to Bir Nasir; however, the galloper was unable to reach the town. Squires successfully reached Lahej and, reverting to his role of intelligence officer, kept Pearson informed of the battle. With no sign of Shaw and amid confusing reports, at 11 p.m. Pearson decided to withdraw south to the government guesthouse and the hospital. Squires was severely wounded clearing houses along the route during which a Turkish machine-gun section was captured, not that there were any Turkish linguists in Aden. Brigadier-General Shaw later reported:

> During the night, hostile attacks from the West were beaten off, some hand to hand fighting taking place. But some parties of the enemy, who had penetrated Lahej from the north, continued practically throughout the night to attack with shell and rifle fire our troops and the hospital which was situated in a garden to the south of the town [...] The remaining British and Indian troops who, owing to want of water, had been unable to reach Lahej, were collected to cover the 15-pdr battery which in consequence of the deep sand and lack of extra camel transport had found it impossible to advance by 7 p.m. beyond a point about four and a half miles South of Lahej. At midnight this supporting force was withdrawn to cover the water supply at Bir Nasr two miles further South [...] Having been informed that, owing to the desertion of all transport and camelmen, and the treachery of our Arab friendlies, the troops in Lahej were no longer able to maintain their position in face of and under shell fire of the superior forces of Turks and Arabs, I ordered this force to use all available transport for the removal of sick and wounded, and to withdraw to the water at Bir Nasr. Using the only

available means of transport for carrying the wounded and sick, three–quarters of the ammunition, all kits and equipment together with two 10–pdr guns and some .450 machine guns were abandoned at Lahej. I left Bir Nasr at 9.30 a.m. and, in view of the fact that our troops were suffering very severely from great shortness of water and food, withdrew the force to the next water supply at Bir Amr. The enemy did not follow up and the retirement was continued at 4 p.m., Sheikh Othman being reached at 9 a.m. on 6 July.

Believing that Sheikh Othman could not be held without exposing Aden, which he regarded of 'imperial importance', as he did about the Admiralty wireless station at Steamer Point, Shaw withdrew to a defensive line across the Khormaksar isthmus which allowed the Turks to capture the village and cut the settlement's water supply. Captain Squires died of his wounds on 7 July.

While HQ Southern Army and the Secretary of State (India) in London blamed the defeat on poor logistic planning and the effects of heat, the director of military operations, HQ Southern Army drew up plans to reinforce Aden Brigade. Lord Kitchener sent the 28th Indian Infantry Brigade, then in Egypt, and two artillery batteries to Aden. Meanwhile, a prisoner had volunteered that the Turkish division consisted of five weak battalions of about 350 men each, a mounted infantry squadron, ten mountain guns and about 400 Arab irregulars. Welcome intelligence was received on 14 July that the Turks would not attack during Ramadan. Brigadier-General Younghusband, who commanded 28th Brigade, regarded Aden a sideshow to operations in Mesopotamia and rejecting views that Lahej should be recaptured to maintain British regional prestige, he assured HQ Southern Army:

> There is no cause for any alarm or despondency in situation here. It is practically impossible for any hostile forces which could be brought against Aden to take it. I consider arrangements [by Shaw] quite secure and suitable but as soon as troops arrive from Egypt. I shall occupy Sheikh Othman as a detached post, strongly entrenching around water supply. I do not recommend any further military operations in this season.

A week later, 28th Brigade recaptured Sheikh Othman and then drove the Turks to within 5 miles of Lahej until heat and sand forced Younghusband to abandon the pursuit. For the next three years, both sides settled into a pattern of skirmishing in the spring, patrolling and intelligence-gathering in the summer and combat operations in the cool of the autumn and winter. During this period, Captain Morice Lake (109 Indian Infantry) assembled 600 men from the Arab Legion defending the Suez Canal and the Arab Labour Corps building the Sheikh Othman defence line into the irregular 1st Yemen Regiment to collect intelligence and dominate the desert between Sheikh Othman and Lahej. The British air presence in Aden began in June 1917 when RNAS seaplanes flying from the carrier HMS *Raven II* bombed Turkish positions. An airstrip for the RFC was then built at Khormaksar.

The Turks did not expect any major offensives in Mesopotamia and although there were troops from 38th Division at Shatt-al-Arab, the majority were at Basra. Divisional HQ lacked maps of the region. But the British had other ideas. The Anglo-Persian Oil Company had exclusive rights to petroleum deposits throughout most of Persia and in Kuwait and on 6 November IEF D captured the battery in the small fort at Fao, which overlooked Shatt-al-Arab. Subsequent amphibious operations in the area were exasperated by the lack of barges and tugs.

The IEF D Intelligence Department was commanded by Major William Beach (Bengal Sappers and Miners) and consisted of:

I(a)   Tactical section: Turkish Sixth Army
        Strategic section: Middle East and Near East regional intelligence
I(c)   Topographical section: twenty-three Indian sappers faced the mammoth
        task of surveying huge areas of desert

Instead of an Intelligence Corps (Mesopotamia), about ten Special Service Officers were assembled with the same remit of supporting General Staff intelligence officers and as interrogators and military counter-intelligence support. Of the force interpreter establishment of 500, few could speak Arabic sufficiently well for human intelligence operations. There was almost a complete lack of German and Turkish linguists. The one Turkish linguist was also the cryptographic officer and the one German linguist was involved in other duties. The passage of strategic information was complex. GHQ Egypt and the Russians passed intelligence to the War Office which then transferred relevant items to IEF C. The passage was partly resolved when Major Frank Marsh, a former military attaché in Meshed, was appointed the Caucasus military attaché to the Russians.

Agent networks behind Turkish lines were unreliable, largely because communication was slow. The Indian army possessed a wireless intelligence capability but it was directed at diplomatic intercepts of the international telegram lines passing through India to places such as Russia and China. A problem in calculating Turkish orders of battle was the flexible nature of unit titles. Most Turkish other ranks were illiterate and units were therefore named after their commanding officers, who changed. The British faced the same problem fighting the Japanese in Burma during the Second World War. Nevertheless, a weekly intelligence summary was circulated to senior commanders and the Special Service officers.

After a delegation told Lieutenant-General Sir Arthur Barrett, commanding IEF D, that the Turks had abandoned Basra, the British entered the city in mid-November. Ten days later, Barratt dispatched a combined army and naval force to Qurna at the junction of the Rivers Euphrates and Tigris with the intention of consolidating the approaches to Basra. The junction formed the legendary site of the Garden of Eden. After a stiff fight, the surviving Turks surrendered in early December. London and Delhi agreed Barratt should go firm, but Lord Crewe, the Secretary of State for India, rejected the notion on the grounds that the *Entente Cordiale* had agreed to no acquisition of territory until the end of hostilities. Sixth Division was reinforced with the 12th Indian Division to form II (Indian Corps), but the latter was weak in artillery. Lieutenant-General Nixon, recently commander of the Northern Army, arrived on 9 April 1915 to take overall command with the remit to 'consider a plan for an advance to Baghdad'. General Sir John Murray, the CIGS, disagreed because he believed it would be difficult to support the force, but Lord Kitchener overruled him.

While Enver Pasha commanded the Turkish Sixth Army in Mesopotamia, Colonel Ibrahim Nu-red-din, the former commander of Iraq Area Command, controlled ground operations. When several thousand Turks negotiated the flooded marshes west of Basra and attacked 30th Brigade, from 12th Division, at Shabia on 10 April, strategic intelligence estimated them to be 16,000 strong; in fact they numbered 23,000, of which 10,000 were Arab irregulars. But the War Office estimated the Turks to number 65,000, which led to General Nixon not trusting its intelligence. Confident that Basra was secure and that his tactical intelligence would give early warning of Turkish intentions, Nixon advanced towards Kut-al-Amara on 22 April. The following day ill health forced Lieutenant-General Barratt to hand command to Nixon. In turn, Lieutenant-General Charles Townshend (late Royal Marine Light Infantry) took command of 6th Division. In the oppressive heat of early summer, Townshend used anything that floated to move troops and equipment. Responding to an Indian request for air support, the Australian Flying Corps formed the Mesopotamian Half-Flight of four pilots and forty-one ground crews to support three aircraft supplied by the Indian army. The half-flight arrived in Basra on 26 May and was joined by two RFC (India) pilots and a New Zealander, Captain H. Reilly. Ten days later it supported British forces using rivercraft and surprised Turkish forces on islands around Al-Quma with air reconnaissance, converting the retreat into a rout with bombing and machine-gunning. The naval launch HMS *Shaitan* chased the Turks the 50 miles to Al-Amara and induced the 2,000 defenders to withdraw on 2 June. However, the underpowered aircraft struggled with thin desert atmospherics, heat, lack of water and spare parts until the arrival of two Caudrons helped alleviate the situation. In spite of assurances to Prime Minister Herbert Asquith's new coalition in London that there would be no further advance, Nixon was mesmerised by the capture of Baghdad and was instructed by Lord Hardinge, viceroy of India, to continue, after the latter's request to London for authorisation was not answered.

In early July, 12th Division was checked south of Nasiriyeh on the River Euphrates by an enemy reported to number 2,000 defenders, but was actually 5,000; the first indication of strengthening Turkish resistance. During the fighting, the engine of the Caudron crewed by Reilly and his observer lost power and although they landed in floodwaters behind enemy lines, they were helped by friendly Arabs. Two New Zealanders were killed when their aircraft force-landed among hostile Arabs, but it cost the attackers one dead and five wounded. The badly damaged aircraft was later recovered. Although malaria was ravaging II Corps, after a pilot had sketched the water-logged terrain, Nixon used boats to capture the town towards the end of July. He then persuaded Hardinge and Duff that he should advance to Kut-al-Amara, 90 miles to the north and 180 miles from Basra, and seize control of Shatt al-Hayy where an ancient canal links the two rivers; however, London was uneasy. Tactical intelligence, largely from prisoners, estimated the enemy strength at Kut to be low. Major Leachman was liaising with tribal leaders as the corps advanced. Major Gerald Leachman (Royal Sussex Regiment) had spent five years in the desert as a political officer interceding in inter-tribal disputes and battling with German agents for the loyalty of the tribes. Whereas Lawrence of Arabia adopted the clothing of a Bedouin noble, Leachman dressed as an ordinary tribesman, sometimes shoeless. His swarthy appearance and an expertise with camels allowed him to masquerade as an Arab.

When air reconaissance and cavalry patrols discovered a dry approach and Major Reilly sketched the enemy positions, interrogations suggested the Anatolian backbone of the Turkish army was demoralised and that Nur-ud-Din was unpopular. Townshend built a dummy camp on the Turkish right, feinted against the enemy centre on 27 September and then hit the left flank hard. In a period of doom and gloom from the Western Front and Gallipoli, the victories in Mesopotamia were a blessing. The viceroy of India also badly needed a victory to keep the Indian population on side.

As II Corps went firm at Aziziyah on 3 October, Nixon considered his next moves. The intelligence suggested that 8,500 infantry, of whom 3,000 were in front-line positions, and 600 cavalry were defending Baghdad. Further intelligence then emerged from Major Marsh at the end of December that 30,000 Turkish reinforcements were being diverted from the Caucasus to Mesopotamia under command of Pasha Khalil and that Field Marshal von der Golz was being sent to the theatre. A British employee of the Anglo-Persian oil company reported being impressed by Turkish troops and the British Embassy in Sofia reported substantial troops deploying from Constantinople to Baghdad. The principal German agent with orders to raise *jihad* narrowly escaped capture. The reports were backed up by Secret Service Bureau (Foreign Intelligence) from London reporting significant troop movement towards Mesopotamia; however, the inaccuracies of War Office intelligence before the Battle of Shaiba led to Nixon rejecting the assessments, particularly as prisoner intelligence and air reconnaissance were not suggesting fresh troops. While the Committee for Imperial Defence recognised the political and military significance of capturing the city, the decision was passed to him as the man on the spot.

Although Major-General Townshend advised Nixon's chief of staff, Major-General G.V. Kimball, that II Corps should halt at Kut, Kimball replied that Nixon intended to advance because he was confident that tactical intelligence would give him a four-week warning of enemy intentions, even though a Turkish screen was hindering the collection of information. When an Indian Political Service report suggested a large force was assembling 8 miles north of Qurna and at Nasiriyeh, about 110 miles up the River Euphrates, a strong reconnaissance found the Tigris blocked and Turks in defensive position south of the town.

When No.30 Squadron RFC, commanded by Major J.E. Tennant (Scots Guards), arrived from Egypt with four aircraft in July, he created A (Mesopotamian Half-Flight) Flight and B (RFC) Flight. Three RNAS Short seaplanes sent from East Africa but unable to operate from the River Tigris were converted into land-based aircraft. However, one RFC aircraft was lost when it crashed at the advanced landing ground at Sanniyat. The following day the Turkish positions were photographed, but the photographic paper was so poor that the product images were practically useless. On 22 October Captain White and Captain Francis Yeats-Brown were flying over Turkish entrenchments at Zeur when they were forced to land behind enemy lines with engine malfunctions; however, the engine was ticking over and they taxied 17 miles and found a gap in the Turkish front-line entanglements. The engine then picked up and they took off. In probably the first instance of downed airmen being rescued, Captain T.W. White was tasked to search for a Short seaplane piloted by Major Gordon and his passenger, Major-General Kemball. Seeing the aircraft on the ground near a hostile Arab camp, he landed and, handing the general a rifle, hustled him to his plane and took off. Gordon was rescued by an Indian cavalry patrol.

Although the ethnic shift of Turkish divisions had shifted from Arab to Anatolian, Turkish commanders were still concerned about the hitherto inadequate fighting record of Turkish troops in Mesopotamia. On 5 October Major Reilly, flying up the river near Aziziya, discovered a formidable defensive position at Ctesiphon but was then shot down. As the British approached, Turkish subversion reminded Muslims in the Indian army that Ctesiphon was the burial place of Prophet Muhammad's best-loved companion, Salman Pak. Although British officers attempted to intercept bundles of subversive pamphlets left on barbed wire calling on Indians to murder their British officers and swap sides, there were desertions.

On 22 November, 6th Division assaulted Ctesiphon but met resolute Turkish defence and after a savage battle, in which he lost half of his strength, Townshend abandoned equipment and stores including wirelesses because of insufficient pack mules, and retreated towards Kut. The next day Captains White and Yeats-Brown were captured while they were cutting telegraph wires near Baghdad; their engine lacked insufficient power to take off. With No.30 Squadron reduced to one aircraft and one pilot, air superiority had been lost and consequently Nixon was forced to restrict air reconnaissance. Townshend reached Kut on 7 December, but he was not unduly concerned because the town sat in a loop of the river, he had sixty days of supplies and was supported by the Royal Navy rivercraft. The Turks launched their first major attack two days later. Field-Marshal Goltz then took charge of the siege three days later and invested Kut using two corps. Nevertheless, Leachman organised the escape of the cavalry through the stranglehold to British lines.

In early December Lieutenant-General Sir Fenton Aylmer VC, the adjutant-general (India), formed the Tigris Corps from 12th Division, two Indian divisions sent from France and 28th Brigade from Aden and between January and March he launched four co-ordinated attacks with Townshend but failed to break the siege. By mid-January 1916, Colonel Khalil, an uncle of Enver Pasha, had replaced Nur-ud-din. In March, Major Leachman sneaked into the Turkish redoubt at Dujaila and discovering that it was occupied by about forty soldiers, informed Brigadier-General Kemball-Aylmer, who was about to assault the redoubt in an attempt to lift the siege. But he refused to cancel a preparatory artillery bombardment and when the Turks realised an attack was underway they quickly reinforced the defence and repulsed the assault with heavy loss to the British. As supplies ran short, the RFC dropped 19,000lb of stores in 140 flights, the first time that the army was supported from the air.

In April, after GHQ India ceded command to the War Office, a Cairo Intelligence Department suggestion that an intelligence officer be sent to Basra to raise a 'fifth column' in exchange for the possibility of Arab independence was rejected by the French protecting their regional aspirations on the grounds that Arab alliances in Turkish-occupied Mesopotamia could not be guaranteed. The next suggestion was to bribe Colonel Khalil.

After being evacuated from Gallipoli in December, Captain Aubrey Herbert and the diminutive Lieutenant Thomas Lawrence (Royal Engineers), from Cairo Intelligence Department Military Intelligence 4 (Topographical), and an Arab linguist arrived at Shatt al-Arab in mid-April as part of a fact-finding mission. Although Lawrence's height of 5ft 3ins meant he was below the recruiting standard, his mentor at Oxford University, Major Stewart Newcombe, now an intelligence officer, had supported his commission when war broke out.

Herbert noted that Indian army officers were treating the fighting as if it was a North-West Frontier campaign. Their interrogations of prisoners provided little information, except that the Turks were confident of victory. One Kurdish prisoner nicknamed 'Blackbeard' by Herbert said that he was a schoolmaster and added, 'you have failed at Gallipoli. We hold you up in Salonika and you are only visitors at Basra. I do not mind how much I tell you because we are going to win.'

After a further attempt to relieve Kut took place on 22 April, Townshend cabled General Lake:

> The Turks have no money to pay for my force in captivity. The force would all perish from weakness or be shot by the Arabs if they had to march to Baghdad, and the Turks have no ships to carry us there. Let the parole be given, not to fight the Turks only. During negotiations no doubt the Turks would permit of your sending up ships with food. The men will be so weak in 3 or 4 days' time that they will be incapable of all exertion, and the stenches in Kut are such that I am afraid pestilence may break out any time. Money might easily settle the question of getting us off without parole being given and it would be a great thing. The defence has been spoken to me by Khaled in the highest terms. Your decisions must reach me if you act quickly. It would take me three days to destroy the guns.

Four days later, General Townshend negotiated a six-day truce to resupply the garrison and met Khalil, who demanded unconditional surrender. He refused gold but suggested terms might be possible. Lake then instructed Townshend to offer fifty guns, an assurance that the garrison would be paroled not to fight the Turks and £1 million in sterling, but with German officers demanding unconditional surrender Khalil rejected the offer, as he did £2 million, on the instructions of Enver Pasha. And thus on 29 April, after a siege of 147 days, Townshend surrendered. Of the combatants, about 280 British and 205 Indian officers and 2,590 British and 7,000 Indian other ranks were captured, together with 3,250 Indian non-combatants. During the day, Lieutenant-Colonel Leachman guided Herbert and Lawrence across the lines and they were taken, blindfolded, to Khalil in his tented command post to negotiate the surrender and an exchange of sick and wounded. Of 1,456 sick and wounded, 1,136 were exchanged: 345 were sent to Baghdad and were exchanged three months later. Khalil undertook to refer the parole issue to Enver Pasha and Constantinople, but he was not hopeful. When he then suggested that the British rivercraft transfer the prisoners to Baghdad, Beach vetoed the proposal because he wanted to avoid admitting how short the British were of craft. The success of the negotiations was degraded after Townshend had ordered his artillery to be destroyed. The three British officers spent the night in the Turkish camp before returning to the British lines next day. On 1 May, a British ship towing food barges reached Shumran. Three days later, the first echelon of officer prisoners left for Baghdad by tug. Throughout the truce, Herbert and Turkish officers investigated outbreaks of shooting, until 9 May, the last day.

The surrender was the only mass surrender of British forces in the First World War and the first since Yorktown in 1781 and yet the humiliation is rarely discussed. Causes of the disaster included intelligence errors by General Nixon, a former senior intelligence officer, failing to recognise that the Turkish army was not a North-West Frontier tribe and that it was highly motivated by its victory at Gallipoli. His judgement was also affected by the glory of capturing Baghdad.

As one would expect of the age, the status of the captured officers ensured they could pay for food and a donkey and cart for transport. However, it was a different story for the other ranks, who endured a ghastly 1,200-mile march to Anatolia and nearly twenty months of captivity during which about 70 per cent died either on the march or in prison and work camps from murder, starvation, thirst, disease and exhaustion, some working on building the Taurus Railway. The statistic is greater than those Allied service personnel who died in Japanese captivity during the Second World War. There was no excuse for the official denial of their plight because the US Embassy in Constantinople and in Berlin and the US YMCA suggested to Turkish officials that a War Prisoners' Aid scheme similar to that organised for German prisoners in Britain and France be organised; however, Turkish negotiators did not want foreign representatives visiting prison camps. Colonel Spackman, of the Indian Medical Services, wrote in the *History of the First World War*:

> The disaster that befell the British prisoners in Turkey cannot really be blamed on individuals. It stemmed from the inability of the Turkish High Command to foresee the inadequacy of their civil and military administration to feed and transport so large a body of men of whose deteriorated physical condition they had been warned.

Major-General Stanley Maude was appointed to command the new Mesopotamia Expeditionary Force on 28 August 1916. He had commanded 13th Division at Gallipoli where his methodological approach had earned him the nickname, 'Systematic Joe'. General Duff was replaced on 1 October 1916 by a War Office appointee, General Charles Monro, who had commanded the Middle East Expeditionary Force at Gallipoli. Both generals appreciated the onset of industrialised warfare and the importance of matching military requirements with appropriate manpower.

6

Gallipoli and the Aegean

The idea of a twin blow against the Turkish Empire by the simultaneous breaching of the Dardanelles, and therefore reaching Constantinople, and landing at Alexandretta Bay had been first mooted as of interest to the British during the 1904–06 Taba Incident. Alexandretta Bay was typically eastern Mediterranean: a gentle coast seeping into plains entirely suitable for cavalry. A landing would also sever Turkish lines of communication between Anatolia and Syria.

In December 1914, the Eclipse-class light cruiser HMS *Doris* was instructed to map the Turkish-occupied coast from Sinai north to Anatolia and to conduct small-scale raids. On board was a monoplane piloted by a French naval officer and his observer, Major T.R. Herbert of the Egyptian army. Accompanying the operation was Mr Harry Lukarch, secretary of the Cyprus defence committee, who could provide local knowledge, and Captain Weldon. Weldon had missed the departure of the cruiser and was taken in a torpedo boat commanded by a warrant officer. His role was to accompany landing parties and talent-spot individuals who might be prepared to collate military and topographical information on Alexandretta Bay and other landing sites. The appearance of the cruiser had the desired effect of the Turks deploying three divisions in the vicinity of the bay.

At the beginning of March, *Aenna Rickmers* was ordered to the Gulf of Smryna where British and French warships were shelling the forts. Its aircraft, still controlled by Captain Welford, provided naval gunfire support. Early on 11 March a torpedo launched by a Turkish boat hit the ship, but damage control repairs ensured that it remained afloat long enough for the crew to coax it to Mudros on the island of Lemnos where the captain beached it. The harbour was packed with warships, transports and colliers and the land was a mass of camps. On ships carrying Australians and New Zealanders were hung large banners: 'Constantinople or bust! On to the harems! Bring on your Turkish delights!' Since it was going to take several weeks to carry out repairs, the ship's aircraft were transferred to the *Rabenfels*.

By 1915, the war was spreading on a scale not seen since the Napoleonic wars. The new War Cabinet recognised that stalemate was evident on the Western Front with First Lord of the Admiralty Winston Churchill, suspicious of the French commitment to frontal assault, asking, 'Why are we sending our armies to chew barbed wire in Flanders?' He then suggested in early January a naval attack to force the Dardanelles channel and access not only Constantinople but also to the mouth of the River Danube and thus the Austro-Hungarian Empire. Lieutenant-Colonel Maurice Hankey, secretary to the council, later wrote: 'The whole atmosphere changed. Fatigue was forgotten. The War Council turned eagerly from a dreary of a slogging match on the western front to brighter prospects, as they seemed, in the Mediterranean.'

Although Prime Minister Asquith and Lord Kitchener rejected the proposal as not feasible, it had support and Hankey drafted a memorandum that Constantinople should be threatened by a naval attack in order to undermine the power of the Young Turks, divert German attention from the Western Front, encourage Bulgaria and Greece to side with the Allies, and open up the warm-water Black Sea ports to trade with and supply Russia.

After Russia had appealed to Britain for assistance against a Turkish offensive in the Caucasus on 2 January 1915, planning began for a naval demonstration in the Dardanelles in order to divert troops from Caucasia. Admiral Sir John Fisher, the First Sea Lord, proposed that the BEF be replaced by a territorial force army and that it and a Greek force should land on the Dardanelles and then attack Austria–Hungary. Meanwhile, Major-General Caswell suggested that the Eastern Mediterranean Squadron should systematically degrade Turkish defences on the Dardanelles and that troops should seize the forts. In spite of serious reservations from Fisher, the War Council approved the plan on 25 January; however, it was not known that after a naval bombardment on 3 November 1914, the outer, intermediate and inner defence zones of the Dardanelles had switched from static coastal artillery to mobile artillery and that sea mines had been sown as far north as the narrows at Kephez Point.

Defending the Dardanelles on the Gallipoli peninsula and the Asiatic coast opposite was the Fifth Army of 100,000 men formed into III Corps, of two divisions, on the peninsula and XV Corps on the mainland. In overall command at army HQ at Gallipoli was General Otto Liman von Sanders, head of the German Military Mission. Attached to III Corps was the 19th Infantry Division, which was commanded by the inspirational Lieutenant-Colonel Mustapha Kemal, the future Kemal Attaturk and ruler of Turkey and member of the second Young Turk cohort. He defended Gallipoli during the Second Balkan War. With a defensive strategy to absorb the impact of landings and wait for the remainder of Fifth Army, the Turks converted Gallipoli into a militarised zone by strengthening existing fortifications, fortifying buildings, digging trenches, improving roads and improvising mines. Searchlights scanned the narrows by night.

The struggle for the Dardanelles began on 19 February when the Eastern Mediterranean Squadron bombarded the fortifications; although the results were disappointing, several forts were silenced and Royal Marines Light Infantry demolition parties experienced opposition at Kum Kale and Sedd el Bahr. The apparent success led to optimism among the Allies and pessimism in Constantinople. Meanwhile, minesweeping operations of the intermediate defences battling swift currents and continuous fire was restricted to night. Room 40 intercepted a German telegram indicating that the coastal batteries were short of heavy ammunition, and three days later on 15 March, under pressure from Churchill and after Vice Admiral Sackville Carden, commanding the Eastern Mediterranean Squadron, had fallen ill, his deputy, Rear Admiral John de Robeck, agreed to force the Narrows even though he believed the forts could not be silenced by naval bombardment alone.

The attack ended in ignominious defeat when the three battleships ran into a minefield and accurate shore fire. A Russian naval attack from the Black Sea was equally unsuccessful. Not only had air reconnaissance failed to spot the mines in the prevailing heavy seas, Turkish gunners had noted from previous actions that the ships always turned to starboard. Unknown to the Allies, Turkish ammunition stocks had been reduced to twenty-seven shells; indeed, Vice Admiral Johannes Mertens, the German artillery adviser, believed the situation so serious that he contemplated an evacuation. As far as the Allies were concerned, where naval operations had failed, the army could succeed, but lack of progress strengthened the Turkish resolve. Intelligence began to dry up and greater reliance was placed on human intelligence from diplomats, observations from Allied ships and air reconnaissance by seaplanes flying from HMS *Ark Royal*, even though they were hindered by low cloud.

On 12 March, Lord Kitchener summoned his former South African War chief of staff, now General Sir Ian Hamilton, and gave him command of the Mediterranean Expeditionary Force (MEF) of 78,000 men. He instructed Hamilton to support naval operations to breach the Dardanelles and to report direct to him, and not the General Staff. He expected the Turks to abandon Gallipoli immediately after the first 15in naval shell exploded. The MEF was made up of the 29th Division, the Royal Navy Division and the Australian and New Zealand Corps (ANZAC) then being led by Lieutenant-General Sir William Birdwood in Egypt training for deployment to France. Commanding the intelligence section was Major Stephen Butler.

Hamilton was given an outline of a defensive plan developed by the Greek General Staff, which had estimated an assault force of 150,000 men. In the short time available, all that MO2 could do was supply him with an outdated map, a 1903 intelligence report on the Turkish army, a phrase book and a tourist guide for western Turkey and Constantinople. As one writer commented: 'He might have been forgiven for assuming that he was taking 70,000 troops for a spring cruise in the Aegean followed by a pleasant summer holiday overlooking the Golden Horn.' Hamilton later admitted that his 'knowledge of the Dardanelles was nil; of the Turks nil; of the strength of his own forces next to nil'. He later summed it up thus: 'Beyond the ordinary text books, those pigeon holes were drawn blank. The Dardanelles and the Bosphorus might be in the moon for all the military information I have got to go upon.'

In fact, the War Office and the Admiralty possessed considerable intelligence on the Dardanelles, some reaching back to 1807. This included coastal surveys by naval hydrographers, diplomats and seafarers channelling information and sketches to London, and a detailed map highlighting the ground from Gaba Tepe to the Kilbil Bach plateau plotted by a naval officer in 1876. In 1906, Captain Charles Woods, a military attaché, had filed a discreet report on the fortifications with the General Staff and Intelligence, but it had been mislaid. He sent another copy but it was also mislaid. The same year, Lieutenant-Colonel William Robertson, in MO2, had issued a memorandum entitled 'The Possibility of a Joint Naval and Military Attack up the Dardanelles', in which he summarised known intelligence and listed future military options. Other information collated by MO2 in 'The Turks' Coast Defences' in 1908 was regularly updated.

The last military attaché in Constantinople, Major Frederic Cunliffe-Owen, an astute officer who sent regular intelligence reports to London, had surveyed the peninsula listing batteries, minefields, torpedo tubes and smoke canisters and had suggested that Turkish mobilisation plans were inept and failed to adopt modern methods. He had advised London in July 1914 that as part of the Turkish mobilisation, the German Military Mission would remain and some officers had been attached to Turkish formations. He felt the high command lacked the capacity for preparing the army for war. In late August, he concluded that even if sea mines protecting the Narrows were negotiated, the coastal batteries were formidable. Mr Clarence Palmer, the British vice consul at Chanak, a coastal town coast opposite the Narrows, had used fishing trips and picnics to sketch Turkish forts and plot minefields. Rear Admiral Arthur Limpus, who was commanding the British naval mission to Constantinople when war broke out and was now commanding the Malta naval dockyard, provided intelligence, as did Philip Graves, a former *Times* Middle East correspondent and half-brother of the poet Robert Graves. He had also been an adviser to the Turkish Ministries of Finance and the Interior and had been consul general in Crete and Salonika. He had also passed information about the terrain and transportation infrastructure in the Turkish Empire. He described the Turkish army as 'I should say that the military are only moderately trained and composed of tough but slow-witted peasants liable to panic before the unexpected'.

In 1912, MO2 had published the first edition of the *Handbook of the Turkish Army* and had then transferred responsibility for its production to the Intelligence Branch in Cairo, who provisionally updated the second edition in March 1915, in time for the Gallipoli landings. Over the next thirteen months, seven editions would be published as more information became available from Gallipoli and Mesopotamia.

Compared to the BEF, this Intelligence Section was small:

Head of Intelligence	Colonel M.C.P. Ward (Royal Artillery).
GSO1 (Intelligence)	Lieutenant-Colonel Charles Doughty-White (Royal Welch Fusiliers). His last active service had been ten years earlier. He had been involved resolving a border dispute in the Balkans and had spent several years as a diplomat in Turkey.
GSO3I(a) (Intelligence)	Captain George Lloyd (Warwickshire Yeomanry). A Liberal MP. His assessment of the Hejaz Railway in Arabia included a detailed assessment of the local economy. This and his studies of the Turkish economy led to his appointment in January 1907 as a special commissioner to investigate trading prospects around the Persian Gulf.
GSO3I(b) (Secret Service)	Captain Wyndham Deedes (Kings Royal Rifle Corps). Commissioned in 1901, he had been seconded to the Foreign Office and had was a Turkish linguist. Cipher Officer. Captain Edward Keeling. An Army Pay Corps major.

Although a proposal to raise an Intelligence Corps of nineteen officers foundered, several officers were blistered to GHQ to conduct intelligence operations. These included Lieutenant Ian Smith, a former military attaché in the Kurdish city of Van in Eastern Turkey, and the poet Captain Robert Graves (Royal Welch Fusiliers).

Supporting the operation was the Security Service Bureau (Foreign Intelligence) in Athens masquerading as the British Refugee Commission, or the R Organisation, commanded by Major Rhys Samson, a former consul in Adrianople. Using the nomenclature R, his prime roles were intelligence collection and counter-intelligence. At Mytilene on the island of Lesbos the British consul, Captain Clifford Heathcote-Smith, organised train-watching networks and collected information on the coastal batteries at Smyrna. He predicted a Turkish attack in Egypt in 1916. An important counter-intelligence responsibility was to develop and maintain a central blacklist of individuals posing threats to British regional interests. One group was those Greeks who supported the pro-Allies, Eleftherios Venizelos and those loyal to King Constantine I, whose wife was a sister of Kaiser Wilhem, and who was openly pro-German.

Another issue was to tackle the German subversion being spread by a German consul in Persia. Documentary intelligence seized during his arrest including plans to raise *jihad* in Afghanistan and to further subversion of Indian soldiers, as part of a strategy of the Turco-German drive through Mesopotamia into India. In 1914, Kaiser Wilhelm II had hatched a plot to undermine British, Russian and French imperialism by, in his own words, 'inflaming the whole Mohammedan world to wild revolt'. Although Turkey was obliged to help, the subversion was conducted by German diplomats and intelligence officers. Oskar von Niedermayer and Otto von Hentig led an overland mission from Damascus to Kabul to persuade the amir of Afghanistan to allow his country to be used as a springboard to promote *jihad*; however, the wily amir, sandwiched between British India and Czarist Russia, procrastinated for six months. In May 1916, a month after the British surrender at Kut-al-Amara, the mission returned to Damascus, much to the relief of the British and Indian domestic intelligence agencies.

When General Hamilton arrived at Tenedos on 17 March, he had conflicting orders from Churchill and Kitchener. Nevertheless, he and Admiral de Robeck began planning an enterprise about which little was known – an amphibious landing on a hostile shore. Basic principles differed, such as the army preferring a night landing and the navy objecting, citing inaccurate charts and minefields. As Hamilton developed his plan, a deception plan was devised suggesting a landing at Smyrna but it was not accompanied by any discernible activity.

Breaches of operational security emerged. In a newspaper interview, the French General d'Amade discussed several options to breach the Dardanelles. Four British officers openly purchased four tugs and forty-two large lighters in Piraeus. Egyptian newspapers highlighted troops practising landing drills and equipment being repeatedly loaded and unloaded from ships. Locals asked troops embarking in Egyptian ports if they were going to Gallipoli. New jetties at Mudros and the nearby island of Imbros invited intrigue as enemy agents, informants, fishermen, dhow skippers and brothel-owners sympathetic to both sides reported Allied activity.

When Lieutenant-General Birdwood asked for a captive balloon or kite be sent to the Dardanelles, it was not immediately clear how it should be tethered. Since October 1914, RNAS Wing-Commander Clive Maitland Waterlow (Royal Engineers) had been commanding a detachment of captive spherical balloons in Belgium spotting for the monitor HMS *Menelaus* which was bombarding the coast between Nieuport and Coxyde. But they proved unstable in anything more than a light breeze; in January 1915 he inspected a Belgian 28,000 cubic feet Drachen balloon at Alveringheim and, believing it to be suitable, sent Flight-Commander John Mackworth to visit the manufacturers at Chalais-Meudon in France. In February Maitland submitted a detailed review, and, after being given two *Drachens,* sent one to Vickers at Barrow-in-Furness to be duplicated and the other to the Roehampton training school. In March 1915, two 'Type H' Kite Balloons emerged from Vickers and recruitment into the Kite Balloon Service began from Post Office telephone engineers and regular and special policemen with a taste for novelty. The officer vacancies attracted a greater than average number of extroverts, sportsmen and intellectuals. The Admiralty then refitted a requisitioned 3,500-ton steamer, *Manica*, to support balloon operations and increased the establishment of thirty airship ratings with volunteers from the Naval Anti-Aircraft Corps to form No.1 Balloon Section RNAS. After trials off Cape Matapan, the *Manica* arrived at Lemnos on 9 April and within days, Mackworth was spotting for the cruiser HMS *Bacchante* shelling a Turkish camp:

> The enemy were not aware of the presence of the balloon ship, and had taken no special precautions against being overlooked. The consequence was that when Manica put up her balloon, the first sight which greeted the observers was a sleeping camp, neatly arranged in a dip in the ground, out of sight of *Bacchante* but within easy range of her guns. Through their excellent field glasses, they could see an occasional dot moving about, but for the most part the camp was not yet astir. If there were sentries, they doubtless regarded the distant balloon hanging in the sky as a harmless form of amusement for jaded British officers, and saw no connection between it and the long guns of the *Bacchante* which were nuzzling round towards them. But the boom of the cruiser's forward turret opened their eyes and a rude awakening followed when the top of a hillock some hundred yards beyond the camp was hurled into the air. No reveille ever blown commanded so instant a response. Every tent burst into life, and the ground was soon swarming with running specks. A second shot burst on the northernmost fringe of the camp, and a third right in the midst of the tents. *Bacchante* had the range to a nicety, and began to fire salvoes of 6-inch shells. A scene of indescribable confusion followed. Tents were rent to pieces and flung into the air, dust spouted in huge fans and columns, and brightly through the reek could be seen the flashes of bursting shells. Like ants from an overturned nest, the little brown dots swarmed and scattered. Across the plain galloped a few terrified mules, and in an incredibly short time the wreckage was complete. Of the once orderly camp, nothing remained but torn earth and twisted canvas, and when the smoke cleared away, no movement was to be seen. The trial was simple but convincing. *Manica* signalled 'Cease Fire', and lumbered home behind her consort, metaphorically wagging her tail.

In mid-April, in preparation for the landings, Major Charles Villiers-Stuart, the ANZAC GSO2 (Intelligence), persuaded a seaplane pilot to take him for an aerial of the peninsula in which he used a 1:40,000 map to record Turkish positions and guns. This led to Birdwood selecting Z Beach north of Gaba Tepe for his corps. Crucially it had several exits suitable for a mounted breakout.

At midnight on 16 April the submarine E-15, commanded by Lieutenant-Commander Theodore Brodie, left Mudros with orders to infiltrate the Dardanelles and penetrate the Sea of Marmara, but swift current swept it on to a shoal 600 yards from Fort Dardanus where it came under fire that killed Brodie and six crewmen. Among those captured was Lieutenant Clarence Palmer RNVR, previously the vice-consul at Chanak. Under threat of being executed, Palmer admitted knowledge of the landings and suggested they would be on the northern beaches of the peninsula. He survived the war in a Turkish prison camp and the hat that he was wearing when captured is in the Istanbul Military Museum in Istanbul.

During the early hours of 25 April the Dardanelles army landed on five beaches at the south end of the Dardanelles in order to establish a beachhead from which Turkish positions opposite Z Beach could be squeezed. Bernard Freyberg had emigrated with his parents from England to New Zealand, where he qualified as a dentist and developed into a strong swimmer. Joining the New Zealand Territorial Force, he returned to England via the USA and Mexico and was persuaded by Winston Churchill in 1914 to accept a Royal Navy Volunteer Reserve commission in the Royal Navy Division. During the initial landings he swam ashore in the Gulf of Saros, north of the Gallipoli Peninsula, distracted the Turkish defenders with flares, and was awarded the DSO. As the ANZACs approached Z Beach the current swept the boats to a bay about 2 miles to the north, to a beach that is now known as ANZAC Cove. The British landings at V and W Beaches at Cape Hellas ran into fierce resistance while S, X and Y Beaches were found to be lightly defended. When a Turkish prisoner said the area was defended by just 1,000 men, this was interpreted to mean the immediate area. In fact, he meant the area to the south of Gaba Tapa, where weak Turkish resistance had been galvanised by the dynamic leadership of Atta Turk.

At V Beach, the collier converted into an assault ship SS *River Clyde* grounded short of the beach and the first assault wave were rowed ashore while a bridge of lighters designed to hasten the landings was constructed under heavy fire. Few reached the beach unwounded. On board the ship was Lieutenant-Colonel Doughty-Wylie. With two other staff officers, he watched helplessly as the tragedy unfolded during the day. On the Creasy-class cruiser HMS *Euryalus* tasked to support the landings on W Beach was Captain Weldon, as the military intelligence officer, recording on the 'spotting' map the locations of enemy guns, trenches and bodies of troops as targets for naval gunfire.

During the night, after Major-General Aylmer Hunter-Weston issued orders that his 29th Division must establish itself ashore, a difficult battle erupted in the village of Sedd el Bahr. Fed up with being a spectator and armed with his swagger stick, Doughty-White injected some order into the chaos ashore, at one stage leading a bayonet charge with a rifle he had picked up. A bullet removed his red-braided cap. In spite of snipers, he helped clear buildings and by mid-morning the British were reasonably secure in the village. Doughty-White then led a charge up Hill 141, supported by naval gunfire support, and captured its small castle, but as the British were reorganising he was shot dead. He was awarded a posthumous VC for his gallantry, and the road from V Beach to the fort is named after him.

The principal information source throughout the fighting was human intelligence from prisoners, deserters and dead bodies, many putrefying in the heat. Landing on 25th April at Anzac Cove with two Greek interpreters was Captain Aubrey Herbert. He and members of the ANZAC Intelligence Section hacked a dugout in cliffs overlooking the shingled beaches 'like a rookery with ill-made nests'. Landing supplies was slow, water was brackish and the area was frequently shelled; indeed the dugout was struck by shrapnel several times. A blanket was draped across the entrance to reduce the risk of ricochets. Herbert also had a counter-intelligence role, in one instance investigating members of the unarmed Zionist Mule Corps, many of whom were German-speaking immigrants who had escaped to Egypt from Palestine, being accused of espionage. While extracts from Herbert's diary suggest that he welcomed the relaxed Australian and New Zealand approach to discipline, he had to convince them that Greek, Armenian and Arab prisoners generally hated the Turks and were therefore ready providers of intelligence. The Anatolians, who formed the backbone of the Turkish army, were resilient and the Muslims were inspired more by faith than nationality and unit cohesion. Most of the prisoners were transferred to camps in Egypt.

With the Dardanelles army confined to southern Gallipoli and under near-permanent observation, the balloons became crucial for artillery and naval gunfire support and intelligence collection. During the landings, balloons tethered to the *Manica* spotting for the ANZAC landings forced the Turkish battleship *Turgud Reis* seen lurking in the Narrows to retire, although it returned about three hours later to shell anchorage and was again driven off. After nine hours, the balloon was hauled down. The following day, balloonists spotted for HMS *Triumph* and HMS *Queen Elizabeth*, with the latter hitting a magazine at Kojadere. So successful were the balloons in targeting enemy batteries and spotting for warships bombarding the lines of communication junction at Gallipoli town that two more were ordered. An attempt to tether a spherical balloon previously used in the South African War from the tug *Rescue* was unsuccessful. As naval gunfire support improved, the *Manica* came to the attention of Turkish artillery and was bracketed by two howitzers that opened fire simultaneously; as the ship weighed anchor, a fluke that had fouled a submarine cable was cut by an officer firing a rifle at it. German U-boats later sank HMS *Queen Elizabeth* and a torpedo that missed *Manica* hit HMS *Triumph*. In spite of the U-boat threat confining it to the harbours of Mudros and Imbros, except for specific operations, the Admiralty recognised the value of balloons and on 9 July the second balloon-ship, *Hector*, arrived at Mudros. In September, *Manica* was converted into a seaplane carrier and left to support the East Africa Expeditionary Force.

In order to avoid naval gunfire, the Turks dug their trenches close to the British front line. On 7 May, as part of a psychological warfare operation to 'disabuse the Turks of the belief that prisoners were killed', Herbert went to Quinn's Post in the ANZAC sector, shouted across no-man's-land, suggesting that England did not have a quarrel with Turkey and quoting the Turkish proverb 'An old friend cannot be an enemy'; he recommended surrender as an option. The Turks replied by shelling the post. When early on 19 May the Turks launched a major attack against the 400 Plateau feature and it resulted in 10,000 Turkish casualties, Herbert interrogated a captured Turkish officer. But due to the stench of the dead, the suffering of the wounded littering the battlefield and disease affecting both sides, General Birdwood sent Herbert to General Hamilton recommending a truce be negotiated. Hamilton agreed and the next day Herbert was exchanged for a Turkish officer who was guided through the Australian lines by another intelligence officer. Blindfolded, Herbert rode with a senior Turkish officer to a position and after an attempt to interrogate him, he toured the Turkish positions opposite Quinn's Post and noted both sides had fraternised. When he chatted to several Albanian conscripts, one, pointing to a row of graves, remarked, 'that is politics'. Indicating a row of bodies he said, 'that's diplomacy. God pity all of us poor soldiers.'

When the 42nd (East Lancashire) Division landed on 24 May, General Hamilton formed VIII Corps and handed its command to Lieutenant-General Hunter-Weston, who had gained a reputation for applying the strategy of charging positions. He failed to take Krithia in early June; nevertheless, several Germans were captured. When Herbert was sent to Tenedos on sick leave, he found popular support was split between the Allies, Germany and Turkey and that spy mania was rife. He became involved in counter-intelligence and linked up with Captain Compton Mackenzie, the well-known author.

Mackenzie had attempted to enlist on 5 August 1914 on the pretext that he was aged 17 years and had been a 1st Hertfordshires officer-cadet; however, a friend at the War Office advised him to return to Capri, write his novels and keep everyone happy. He tried again in October but he was declared medically unfit, except for service in Egypt. And then in mid-March 1915, a friend wrote to him mentioning that Lieutenant-General Hamilton had read his latest novel and wanted him to join his intelligence branch as a cipher officer. Commissioned into the Royal Marines, Mackenzie assembled most of the accoutrements, except for a uniform, and was compelled to wear an other rank's tunic. He disembarked at Alexandria on 12 May but no one appeared to know where the MEF rear base was until he was told by an Australian major who had been wounded at ANZAC Cove. During his transfer to Tenedos on the troopship *Franconia*, he censored letters sent to the troops. On board a tug towing a lighter loaded with a damaged biplane, he met Major Eustace Twisleton-Wykeham-Fiennes (Queen's Own Oxfordshire Hussars), the naval division intelligence officer, who was interrogating prisoners helped by two interpreters badged as Royal Marines officers 'with the air of men enjoying a jolly talk after a long and tiring day'.

When Mackenzie found GHQ Intelligence Section in the gymnasium of the *Arcadia*, off Imbros, Major Deedes tasked him to collate counter-intelligence reports and transfer information from intelligence summaries into the MEF war diary; it would eventually contribute to the official history of the campaign. Most of the information came from Source 'V', Major Samson in Athens, British military attachés in the Balkans and the French GHQ. Coded information from V was decoded using a small ruler marked in millimetres and a pocket dictionary and then encrypted and transmitted to Special Service Bureau (Foreign Intelligence). V may have been Surgeon-Lieutenant Michael Vlasto, a Greek-speaking veteran of the Battles of Coronel and Falklands in 1914, who had been recruited in early 1915 as an intermediary between a Cretan Greek and the Royal Navy, passing information on Turkish activity on Lesbos. When Mackenzie landed on W Beach on 4 June with General Hamilton and several staff officers to witness a major attack along the entire Turkish line and met several 4th Worcestershires escorting prisoners of war, Colonel Ward asked him to identify their regiment; Mackenzie used his *Handbook on the Turkish Army* and identified them as the 15th Regiment. Captain Deedes interrogated them; Mackenzie stayed ashore until 21 June.

In early June, Herbert noticed that prisoners were claiming their food had improved, ammunition was plentiful and concluded that since morale was intact, the surrender of Gallipoli was unlikely. At the end of the month Herbert went to Walker's Ridge to follow up reports of Turkish wounded in no-man's-land with Major Carew Reynall, of 9th Battalion, and dragged two badly wounded Turks over dead bodies to safety for treatment by a RAMC doctor. Captain Milward, a 29th Division intelligence officer, examined six prisoners captured on 16 June during a pointless raid on a British trench. On 8 July, R Organisation advised HQ MEF that the Turks' morale had dropped after a battle, detailed desertions, and reported that German officers were shooting dispirited Turkish soldiers, and that there were chronic shortages of ammunition.

On 7 August, IX Corps landed on three beaches around Suvla Bay with orders to link up with the ANZAC Corps and drive the Turks from Chunuk Bair; however, 34th Brigade, 10th (Irish) Division lost cohesion largely because the troops were landed in the wrong place and in the wrong order. Air reconnaissance had previously indicated that the nearby salt lake was no longer an obstacle and that the Turks had a redoubt covering A Beach. Excessive operational secrecy also surrounded the landings and thus when the second divisional wave arrived direct from Mitylene, its commander had no idea what was happening and what was expected of him and consequently the division landed on two beaches. As senior commanders prevaricated, communications failed and water ran out, the troops came under intense fire from a few snipers and were then counter-attacked. Nothing was achieved.

No.3 Squadron RNAS at Tenedos was supporting operations with its mix of wheeled Sopwith Tabloids and a seaplane brought from the UK on HMS *Ark Royal*, the world's first aircraft carrier. Some aircraft had arrived in crates and were unserviceable, while others were plagued by mechanical problems and unreliable wirelesses; nevertheless the pilots achieved a reputation for giving as much air support as possible. Ship-borne operations were in their infancy and accidents were not infrequent. While Turkish commanders halted air operations in rain or extensive clouds, Allied aircraft took off. Pilots were given freedom that allowed them to reconnoitre the battlefield, develop the use of air photographic reconnaissance and provide naval gunfire support. A forward airstrip was constructed at Cape Hellas, which gave the aircraft longer time over target. When the RNAS passed under command of the Royal Navy in August, Lieutenant-Colonel Frederic Sykes, in France, was given No.2 Squadron and a Royal Marines commission as a wing-captain and sent to the Aegean to review air operations. He found that No.3 Squadron was woefully disproportionate to manage its tasks. Although lobbied by Samson, he identified the wings had two objectives of winning air superiority and providing tactical intelligence. In his final report to the War Office, General Hamilton highlighted the exploits of the RNAS and Colonel Sykes 'for the nonchalance with which they appear to affront danger and death, when and where they can'.

Herbert returned to Gallipoli in early August and was immediately involved in the evacuation of 300 prisoners, amid the usual shelling. Following an attack the next day he gained a considerable amount of intelligence from two captured Germans. By now, both sides accepted that fighting would continue and with winter approaching the HQ ANZAC Intelligence Section moved to more comfortable lodgings in a former Turkish fort already housing an Indian battery and the survivors of a New Zealand battalion. In mid-October, Herbert experienced another bout of illness and was evacuated for several days.

By mid-October, the impasse at Gallipoli was sucking in troops with little profit. Kitchener had lost faith in Hamilton and on 14 October replaced him with Lieutenant-General Sir Charles Monro with the same instructions that he was to report direct to Kitchener.

When an Armenian deserter crossed into the Australian Light Horse lines in November and was graded as an 'intelligent man who answers without hesitation' he told Herbert that he had surrendered because he was physically weak, had been wounded twice and was not being treated well by the Turks. In April 1915, the Turks had systematically begun to drive the Armenians from their homeland in east Turkey in the Armenian Genocide. He claimed that his unit did not have any underground shelters but did have overhead protection. He denied the Turks had been ordered to snip their cartridges into 'dum dum' bullets. The promise of 'big guns' from Germany had been announced so often during the previous three months that he simply did not believe it any more. A prisoner describing the terrain between Ari Burnu and Gaba Tepe, said that the ground at Gaba Tepe was flat with trees. Two emplaced big guns commanded by a sergeant had not been seriously affected by British artillery. The prisoner claimed that Turkey had sent 200,000 men to Gallipoli, including from three divisions and the 13th, 14th, and 15th Regiments. Germans were controlling guns at Sedd el Bahr. In the prisoner's company, only officers were allowed blankets and there was no preparation for the winter. He believed the Turks had six aeroplanes.

After concluding there was little hope of success because the Turks would always be able to reinforce Gallipoli Peninsula, the War Committee agreed to evacuation. His view was rejected and Monro planned a three-stage evacuation. The preliminary stage would involve the immediate removal of men, animals and stores no longer required straight on to boats from their positions; the Royal Navy believed that 10,000 troops could be lifted each night. The intermediate stage would thin out the troops and artillery over the course of ten nights, leaving a thin defensive crust. The final stage would involve the evacuation of 20,000 troops over two nights.

Deception was critical and ruses were devised to convince the Turks of an air of normality; for instance, the ANZACs no longer fired at night unless their positions were attacked, and supplies were taken from inside piles of dumped stores. Horse- and mule-drawn carts and limbers continued their supply runs, even though loads were non-existent and tents were left in position. Stores to be left behind were set to burn.

During the night of 18–19 December, troops in Suvla Bay and ANZAC Cove and a substantial amount of equipment and horses and mules were evacuated in a flawless withdrawal. When Lieutenant-General Robertson was appointed CIGS in December, no supporter of the campaign and with a firm grip, he ordered Monro to evacuate VIII Corps from Cape Hellas. Deception measures included the deliberate compromise of a fake order instructing VIII Corps to take over from IX Corps. Although the fighting intensified, the deceptions continued. As the trenches emptied, quiet periods were introduced at night and soldiers wore sandbags over hobnailed boots. Catapults threw grenades, and punctured sandbags dribbled sand into tins attached to rifle triggers. Trenches were discreetly filled in to prevent their use by Turks, booby traps were prepared and mines laid. On 1 January 1916, the final evacuation was disrupted by shelling and poor weather, but within eight days only the Turks occupied Gallipoli.

History ascribes a failure of the Allied offensive at Gallipoli in 1915 to inadequate intelligence. Most forget Turkish military resilience. The intelligence existed at the DMI, but until the arrival of Robertson as CIGS the operation was under the control of Kitchener, who largely rejected the concept of the General Staff and its resources.

Hitherto, the intelligence organisation in the Middle East had been dysfunctional, parochial and largely unsuccessful and, in the spring of 1915, Major Eric Holt-Wilson was sent from London to review the organisation.

By mid-1915, sciatica had prevented Captain Mackenzie from further active service and towards of the year he joined Major Samson as a HQ MEFI(b)

(Secret Service) liaison officer. When Samson was warned to move his headquarters to Cairo, in June, Mackenzie formed the Aegean Intelligence Service and sent political intelligence to the British minister in Athens, military intelligence to GHQ Cairo and naval intelligence to the Eastern Mediterranean Squadron at Mudos on Lemons Island. Virtually a free agent with a budget of £5,000 per month, he recruited thirty-nine intelligence officers, purchased a 200-ton Greek 'intelligence' yacht to land agents on enemy territory and developed a personality list of 20,000 names. A principal contact he met in Athens at least twice a week was a Greek bell porter employed in the German Legation, who provided information about the German intelligence organisation in the city. He sent two officers to the port of Volos where, under the cover of permit officers, they organised intelligence collection and counter-intelligence operations in central Greece.

Agents were recruited from inside enemy bases on the Dodecanese Islands. There were disasters. An Englishman living in Smyrna and his Greek couriers sending letters to contacts on the coast were compromised when the cigarette ash from a Turkish censor vetting mail set a letter alight and exposed secret writing. Eight couriers were hanged, as was the Englishman. When Samson left Athens in December, Mackenzie based himself on the island of Siros in order to concentrate on Greece. Another officer focused on enemy air forces. Intelligence collection focused on human intelligence gained issuing at permit offices. One intelligence officer responsible for the permit control and port control of some thirty islands in the Cyclades was Lieutenant Francis Storrs RNVR, an academic and younger brother to the Arabist and colonial administrator Ronald Storrs. While test-firing a deck gun fitted to the 'intelligence' yacht in May 1917, he ignored a warning to remove his pipe and lost two teeth when it recoiled. Mackenzie wrote of Storrs in his book, *Ægean Memories*:

> Without [Storrs], whatever fruits our work in the Cyclades bore could never have been achieved. Virgil and Horace spoke at his summons, and he commanded all the elegance of light verse that is the Cambridge man's prerogative. His conscientiousness was almost excessive. Night after night he would be working on the files of his office until two or three in the morning after a hard day's work of almost incessant worrying interviews. He was a martyr to bad headaches, but I never heard him give way to more than a weary groan of expostulation when human folly or vice was seeming unendurable any longer. I can never repay Francis Storrs in this world for his personal loyalty and devoted service.

As is so often the case with intelligence activities, Mackenzie's unorthodoxy did not set well with his superiors in the new MI6. Assessed to be too close to Prime Minister Venizelos, who had won a general election in 1917 but had been dismissed by King Constantine, Mackenzie was transferred to command the Anglo-French police in Athens, which he did with considerable enthusiasm until he was undermined by allegations that he had attempted to assassinate the king. Moved to Taranto, control of the Aegean Intelligence Service then moved to Switzerland and then Paris in mid-1917, but still targeting the Turkish Empire.

Mackenzie was one of several First World War intelligence officers who cashed in his experiences with his book *Green Memories*, but broke every rule by including secret letters and documents, naming serving MI6 officers, exposing the cover of agents in foreign capitals and revealing the real name of the chief of MI6 – Mansfield Smith-Cumming. An MI6 memorandum stated in 1932 that: 'There is scarcely a page of *Greek Memories* that does not damage the foundation of secrecy upon which the Secret Service is built up.' At a trial partly held in camera, it turned out an agent named by Mackenzie had died ten years earlier, another listed his intelligence work in *Who's Who*, a third had reviewed the book in the *Times* and no one knew that Smith-Cummings had died in 1923. Investigating Special Branch officers stood Mackenzie with several pink gins. Although the book was never published, Mackenzie was convicted and fined at the Old Bailey. A severely edited version was published in 1939. To pay for his costs, Mackenzie wrote a hard-hitting satire about MI6 and its rivalry with MI5.

When Bulgaria threatened Serbia in 1914 and Prime Minsiter Venizelos sought Allied support, a Franco-British force of two brigades landed at Salonika (today Thessalonika) as reinforcements, but were too late to prevent the Serbian defeat. In spite of predictions by Greek General Staff the force would be driven into the sea, most of the subsequent fighting took place around Lake Doiran astride the border with Macedonia.

In late 1917, the Salonika Expeditionary Force of fifty Intelligence Corps officers commanded by a commandant and consisting of five 1st Class, ten 2nd Class and fifteen 3rd Class agents assembled from the nineteen identified from the Dardanelles army and the remainder made up from interpreters from within the Salonika Expeditionary Force. Among the fifty was Captain Robert Graves and Second-Lieutenant A. Williams, who had both been GSO3s at Gallipoli. But the corps became involved in the internecine squabbles that frequently emerge when supposedly friendly intelligence organisations operate on the same territory. When the Allies sanitised the front of civilians up to a depth of 60 miles from the front line, a network of area intelligence officers, often supported by a band of brigands, provided counter-intelligence and rear area security and infiltrated behind Bulgarian lines.

7
The Western Front, 1916

After being criticised for his handling of the Battle of Loos in late 1915 during a British and French attempt to break through the German defences in Artois and Champagne, on 18 December, ill health led to Field-Marshal French handing command of the BEF to Haig, now promoted to field-marshal.

When General Sir William Robertson was appointed CIGS in December 1915, one of his first actions was to advise Lord Kitchener that the General Staff would control operations and that he was not to interfere. He also appointed Brigadier-General Macdonogh to be the DMI. Brilliant, and a survivor of Robertson's purge of French's staff in early 1915 when he was the BEF chief of staff, his Roman Catholicism, reticence and realistic briefings in a year of gloom had led to him collecting enemies, in particular Haig. One of his first instructions was to order that every theatre of operations should be supported by an intelligence department. Major Dunnington-Jefferson was posted in mid-February 1916 and replaced by the previous assistant from the Intelligence Corps, Major Arthur Fenn DSO (Royal Fusiliers); however, he was something of a martinet and was unpopular.

While forced to accept the weak-willed General Lancelot Kiggell as his chief of staff, Haig appointed John Charteris as his brigadier-general on the General Staff (Intelligence) BGGS(I). His briefings were concise and well presented and were generally slanted to support Haig's prognosis that attrition was the only strategy to defeat Germany. Charteris was a large, social and articulate man and a foil to the dour and at times insecure Haig to the extent that he was labelled as Haig's 'evil counsellor', on the one hand, and his 'principal boy' on the other. When he commanded the First Army, Haig had relied on the optimistic views of Charteris more than those provided by Macdonogh. General Monro, fresh from commanding the MEF in Gallipoli, assumed command of the First Army.

GHQ was now located on the hilltop town of Montreuil-sur-Mer overlooking the River Canche and flatlands criss-crossed by narrow canals winding their way through market gardens 20 miles from Bolougne and its port. The railway station was on the line to Paris. Dispatch riders on motorcycles could reach all the corps and divisional headquarters between Arras and Amiens within the hour. Networks of telephone lines laid by Royal Engineer signallers connected GHQ to London, Paris and the front line. Virtually every building in the town had been commandeered. Exercise for most was a twenty-minute walk around the ramparts and a tennis court squeezed into the moat. Heavy punts used to take vegetables and fruit to market were often hired by officers and soldiers to meander through the countryside to one of the island cafes selling hot red wine, bread and fried potatoes. The town was liberally sprinkled with places to eat. While the director of operations was in the Hotel Dieu, the Intelligence Branch was located in the Military School.

On 23 December 1915 General Robertson split the Directorate of Military Operations into the Directorate of Military Operations and the Directorate of Military Intelligence, in order to improve the control operations at the Western Front, in the Middle East, Greece and the Balkans, and East Africa, as well as those places where there was no direct military or security threat to British interests. The MO branches 2, 3, 4, 5, 7, 8 and 9 were now prefixed by Military Intelligence (MI). MO6 became the Secretariat as MI1. MO5 (g) (Secret Service Bureau) split into MI5 (Secret Service) and MI6 (Secret Intelligence Service). The GHQ BEF Intelligence Department establishment consisted of the BGGS (Intelligence) and about eight to ten GSOs and the same number of Intelligence Corps officers. Broken down into six departments, its organisation was replicated at the DMI:

I(a) Operational Intelligence	Five sub-sections responsible for the German order of battle; organisation, recruiting and conscription; documentary intelligence, artillery intelligence; drafting daily and weekly intelligence summaries and intelligence reports and maps, studying and analysing information from covert sources behind the enemy lines, assessments of enemy tactics, information about lines of communication and the dissemination of intelligence reports to consumers.
I(b) The Secret Service	Four sub-sections responsible for running sources and agents behind enemy lines; co-ordinating liaison with the War Office and French and Belgian agencies; producing and disseminating intelligence; managing counter-espionage and control of the civil population; censorship as it affected counter-espionage operations; debriefing of repatriated soldiers, escapers and civilians; and issue of passes and permits.
I(c) Topography and Mapping	Single sub-section responsible for the supply of maps, terrain charts; supervision of field survey units; printing, lithography and photography.

The one field survey unit attached to each Army HQ was responsible for sound-ranging and location of enemy artillery.

Special Intelligence I(d) Press; plus four sub-sections.

I(e) Control of ciphers and codes.

I(f) Visitors; plus four sub-sections.

I(g) War Trade. This was an offshoot of the War Trade Intelligence Department of the War Office (WTID), the task of which was to examine any commercial transaction which might have had a bearing on the economic situation in Germany.

I(h) Postal and Telegraphic Censorship. Responsible for press censorship and liaison with correspondents, the control and escorting of visitors, propaganda, collection of economic information from within Germany, photography and cinematography, censorship regulations and breaches of censorship, liaison with Allied censors and the issue of censorship stamps.

I(x) Intelligence Corps. The administration of Intelligence Corps officers and Intelligence Police.

While the purpose of the General Staff intelligence officers at army, corps and division level was evolving, the role of the Intelligence Corps had changed from a spare pair of hands running headquarters messes and acting as orderly staff officers with little incentive and reward to one of taking over some intelligence duties from staff officers. For the infantry officer armed with his revolver leading his men 'over the top' and across the shambles of no-man's-land, leadership, gallantry and regimental loyalty were fundamental. But increasingly important was the older-than-average lieutenant interrogating low- and high-value prisoners of war and extracting intelligence from grubby postcards and documents smudged with mud and blood.

The corps still attracted worldly-wise individuals with linguistic and analytical skills that the average army officer did not possess. Most were products of the public school ethos of restraint, honour, self-sacrifice and loyalty; however, their non-conformity, untidiness, eccentricity and lateral thinking were regarded with suspicion by conformists. Dr Beach comments:

They were untidy, the unmilitary, the unusual, the eccentric and the lateral thinkers. The BEF needed these talents to conduct effective intelligence work, but on the other hand, they constructed a framework around these officers to ensure they did not step beyond their clearly defined remits. These 'auxiliary intelligence officers' are therefore an unusual and illuminating example of the challenge of harnessing the talents of citizen soldiers.

Such was the framework of the historical rejection of intelligence embedded in the British army that the Intelligence Corps at Montreuil shared E Mess with logistic staff officers, not with General Staff officers, and it was thus inevitable that fractious relationships and scant disregard for senior officers would emerge. Unfortunately, the prejudice would remain well into the latter half of the twentieth century, except during the Second World War when the Intelligence Corps, as a whole, again demonstrated it had skills beneficial to the country.

Weaknesses within the General Staff meant that in 1916 Intelligence Corps personnel were maintaining operational maps and drafting daily and weekly intelligence summaries that were disseminated upwards, downwards and sideways to those who needed to know. Information sources included those from agents operating behind enemy lines. GHQ Intelligence regularly updated *The Index to German Forces in the Field*, which was better known as the *Brown Book*. It was delivered to every intelligence unit and listed the locations of most German divisions and their parent formations upwards. Improvements in air photographic interpretation promoted by Captain Romer led to each RFC reconnaissance squadron being supported by an intelligence section of air photographic interpretation officers managing the processing and examination and distribution of the product and telephoning or taking important information to the relevant corps headquarters. By 1916 Laws, now a major, was commanding the RFC School of Photography at Farnborough and was being recognised as the most experienced aerial photographic interpreter in England, if not the world. During the year, he invented the Model L (Laws) automatic and manual camera that could be mounted alongside the cockpit or pointed through a porthole inside the cockpit. Charteris insisted that intelligence officers requesting air reconnaissance should personally brief and debrief the pilot and observer.

The number of Intelligence Corps officers had increased significantly since August 1914. The selection process remained talent-spotting officers in Home Forces and the BEF with good language skills and an aptitude for intelligence. Front-line experience was desirable but not essential. Lieutenant Noel Dyson Williams, a Cambridge University graduate employed by Ealing County Council School, enlisted in a Public School Battalion in 1914 and was commissioned into the 3rd South Lancashires (The Prince of Wales's Volunteers) in 1915, the high casualty rate among front-line officers having led to suitable other ranks being encouraged to apply for commissions. His knowledge of German saw him transferring to the Intelligence Corps and being attached to HQ III Corps, in the Second Army, in

February 1916. On 27 March in heavy snow and using his motorcycle, Williams checked the state of about twenty roads for a corps move planned to avoid 'Hellfire Corner'. German gunners possessed an excellent view of the Ypres/Meni/Rouler junction and railway crossing 2 miles east of Ypres and shelled anything that moved through it; indeed it was reputed to be the most dangerous corner on the Western Front. Canvas screens were erected to shield activity and men and equipment moved at night. To study the German defences, some as close as 20 yards from the British trenches, Williams visited an artillery observation post on 2 April. In a letter to his mother he described the countryside as beautiful and outlined his role: 'Most important is to know exactly what parts of the country behind the enemy are visible from parts of our front. Then one can get an idea of how he will bring forward reinforcements up along avenues of approach trenches for our men.'

When he was appointed as an interrogator he welcomed the return to front-line comradeship and selected two dugouts in a communication trench to question prisoners. When an unexploded trench mortar bomb was brought to him, he used his experience to deduce the likely firing position by matching its fuse setting with a set of range tables. The problem was resolved by 8-in guns. Several British soldiers captured during a German raid on 4 May were rescued in a quick counter-attack in which a German was taken prisoner. Williams learned from him that his regiment was in good spirits, well led and in a year's time, there would be a German victory.

An interesting development was the acceptance that other ranks were capable of intelligence and counter-intelligence duties. Sergeant Harry Plant, of the 11th 'Accrington Pals' East Lancashires, was involved in prisoner interrogations at HQ Fourth Army. His recollections have been collated in *Somme Intelligence 1916* (2013). Private Howard Spring (Army Service Corps), a journalist, who later became an author, worked in I(a) (Intelligence) as a shorthand typist:

> I was employed by the Department of Intelligence, which was then commanded by Brigadier-General John Charteris, a robust and bustling, loud-shouting, very human person. Our work was clerical and mechanical, tedious and deadly boring: typing and filing all day long. Never was the King's uniform worn by less heroic persons. Then back to our typewriters to the everlasting 'Summary of Intelligence' and the filing of that vast conglomeration of reports that poured in daily: from spies, from newspapers, from air observation, from prisoners' stories. All through this time, I was doing what I had been doing as a newspaper reporter: I was a detached observer of a life in which I had no essential participation.

By 1916, the Security Duties Section had been re-formed as the Intelligence Police. Reporting to I(b) (Secret Service), its role was fivefold. Firstly, it had to prevent the collection and transmission to the enemy of information about Allied military operations; secondly, it needed to detect the presence of enemy agents and the control of the movements of suspects, possible suspects and undesirables; thirdly, it was a link in a chain of counter-intelligence control in the BEF sector by monitoring those hostile to the Allies. It also had to ensure that even if a suspect was not caught in the act, hostile acts were expensive in terms of effort, risk and finance. And finally, it had to investigate every security incident and extract the intelligence from it.

As the front stabilised to positional warfare, a need emerged for counter-intelligence and protective security measures to protect depots, supply dumps and the lines of communications to the Channel ports. The British, French and Belgian counter-intelligence authorities had agreed in early January 1915 that any Briton entering France required a pass and that the British and French would co-operate in the defence of coastal areas. A year later, GHQI(b) (Secret Service) developed plans to implement counter-intelligence in four operational Zones A, B, C and D in the British sector, each largely corresponding to the tactical area of operations of the four armies. Each consisted of three sectors enforced by military police manning check points. The Forward Zone was the operational front-line sector. The Middle Zone housed second-line billets, supply dumps and casualty clearing stations. The zones often contained civilians living in cellars of shattered houses, who had to be watched in case they were engaged in espionage. The village of Armentières was not only well known from the marching ditty sung by British soldiers, 'Mademoiselle from Armentières', but for the comely Tina who sold crumpets to soldiers and was said to have collected every cap badge of the BEF. Other characters included Gaby, of the '5 o' Clock' in Rue des Trois Cailloux, Amiens, and Madamoiselle 'Jamais', who was reputed never to have refused a kiss across the counter. The Rear Zone included the Channel ports and the large base at Etaples, about 15 miles south of Boulogne, which contained supply depots, sixteen general hospitals and a convalescent depot, military prisons and several divisional infantry base depots near the railway and the notorious Bull Ring battle camp on sand flats and dunes. Its courses lasted a fortnight and were designed to prepare all troops for the front line, including those returning after being wounded. The camp achieved considerable notoriety for its hard regime where everything was done at the double.

In charge of the security duties detachment at Boulogne was Sergeant Edwin Woodhouse, a former Special Branch officer, who had met Lenin at a nihilist gathering in Jubilee Street in London and had been part of the protective surveillance team as guardian detective for King Edward VII, King George V and several European crowned heads, statesmen and diplomats. In mid-November 1914, Lieutenant His Royal Highness the Prince of Wales (Grenadier Guards) had joined Field-Marshal French's staff as an aide-de-camp and had spent a short time as an intelligence officer. Woodhouse had been involved in the arrest of Private Percy Topliss, who regularly masqueraded as a British army officer and wore a monocle.

When he was tracked to a bar in a village, Woodhouse disguised himself as a priest and, riding into the village on a horse, entered the bar and arrested Topliss. Two French policemen then arrived and were confronted by a priest holding up a monocled British captain at gunpoint. Immediately arrangements were made for his court martial, but Topliss escaped.

Inside each zone, each corps usually had an intelligence police company of two Intelligence Corps officers and forty NCOs, the latter divided into fifteen intelligence police detachments of a sergeant and corporal or private based in police stations covering an area of about 50 square miles and about ten French 'communes'. They were not restricted by regimental discipline, had greater freedom of action and usually wore plain clothes, for which they received an allowance but they were expected to adhere to the standard operating procedures issued by each army. Good conduct, discretion and self-discipline were essential. Those who breached discipline risked being returned to unit. The company was supported by about ten signallers and five runners using bicycles. Two batmen, a cook and drivers for a lorry and staff car were located at company headquarters.

From his memoirs lodged in the Military Intelligence Museum, Sergeant James Camp was serving with the Corps of Military Police at Woolwich Barracks, London, when he responded to a memorandum seeking anyone who spoke French. Reporting to Room 226 at the War Office, he and several others were inducted into the Intelligence Police and instructed to report to HQ Intelligence Corps in St Omer. By now the intelligence police included the former Security Duties Section, police officers from the Metropolitan Police and regional constabularies, the Indian Police, the Corps of Military Police and non-police organisations. It grew from a force that numbered about eighty officers and 460 other ranks in 1916 to 800 all ranks in 1918. A small detachment from Indian Political Intelligence monitored radicals in the Indian army.

As part of their probation, intelligence police spent several days with town assistant provost marshals and dock police in order to understand their duties and become familiar with passes, permits and cachets. For some, the conversion from investigating crime and ill-discipline and immorality in the British army to counter-intelligence was interesting, particularly when it meant exploiting character weaknesses to unearth espionage and subversion. Good relations with the military police were essential because intelligence work often commences where their investigation finishes.

After several days at St Omer and as part of his probation, Camp was instructed by Major Malcolm Lamb, Intelligence Corps since 1914 and a stickler for protocol, to report to Captain Joseph Priestley (Intelligence Corps), a former professor of botany at Leeds University, then involved in port control and the central railway station passenger control at Le Havre. Camp accompanied a French Sûreté officer checking ship manifest lists and helped arrest several individuals suspicious enough to warrant further interrogation. In one incident, MI5 knew that a diplomat arriving from South America had a valuable document in his diplomatic bag and when he boarded a train, two Special Branch officers diverted his attention while a third threw the bag out of the railway carriage window to another officer. During the Second World War, Intelligence Corps Field Security Sections could be found at all the United Kingdom maritime and air points of entry.

Camp later moved to Calais where he worked with Captain the Honourable Hugo Baring (Intelligence Corps), brother of the RFC intelligence officer Maurice. After a German aircraft had attacked an ammunition dump, he reviewed control of access and investigated to see if someone had left a target marker. Moving to Paris-Plage, Le Touquet, he warned young officers not to share information with an attractive Frenchwoman whose husband was a French army deserter living in Spain. Based at Le Touquet was No.1 British (Duchess of Westminster's) Base Hospital. Camp recalls the town was full of 'aliens', many probably from 35,000 French deported from Germany to Switzerland because the country was unable to feed them. The Swiss sent them to France where they proved valuable economic and political intelligence sources of the situation in Germany.

The intelligence police also had a tactical role in offensives of accompanying leading infantry brigade HQs in a detachment that consisted of the GSO3, an Intelligence Corps officer, assistant provost marshal and town major, if relevant, although it was accepted that the intelligence police might arrive in a captured village before any of them, in which he was to report to the senior officer. Their roles were to search enemy dead and wounded for documentary intelligence, to search captured HQs' dugouts and communication trenches for code books and maps, and to search for and retain technical intelligence, such as wirelesses and listening sets. They also conducted the preliminary tactical questioning of prisoners, and helped to search prisoners, in particular officers and NCOs liable to ditch documents. Junior ranks were generally not searched until they reached a divisional cage. The intelligence police were issued with an updated brief translation guide of military terminology.

By its very nature, documentary intelligence tends to be scooped up and sent back quickly, in case of counter-attack, which sometimes led to intelligence offices, at all levels, being swamped by sandbags full of muddy documents, some blood-stained, some ripped, some crumpled. Examples are a document captured on 18 June 1915 listing lessons learned by German pioneers, infantry and gunners, and the tactic of leaving grenade-throwing detachments in special shelters and the sealing of trenches for counter-attack and, a year later, a month-old captured instruction detailing the battalion in the attack and new tactical deployments of machine guns. While official documents provided operational intelligence, letters and postcards projected hints about morale and the home front and helped to link field post office numbers to units. It was documents left in a box that proved German interception of British front-line field telephone networks. A GHQ intelligence summary in September 1916 described that the New Zealand Division had found a 'bit of crumpled paper' that listed German reserve divisions. Interestingly the Germans failed to impose any sort of field censorship until 1917.

Private Norman Shaw recalled that his equipment included iron rations, water bottle and canteen, first field dressing and iodine ampoule, respirator and smoke helmet, steel helmet, waterproof cape, second pair of boots, blanket and pack, road map of the forward areas, assistant provost marshal's pass with photograph, notebook with carbon sheets and pencil, twelve field service envelopes, revolver and ammunition, compass, electric torch, chain and padlock for his bicycle and goggles, overalls and gaiters for motorcyclists.

In February, the newly formed Fourth Army commanded by General Sir Henry Rawlinson assumed responsibility from the River Somme to Fonquevillers from the French. To its north was the Third Army. Although the French had applied a 'live-and-let-live' approach since 1914, their intelligence picture assessed that the Germans had built two belts of wire entanglements, a third one was under construction and that the thirty-four German battalions were good quality. In March, General Joffre proposed a major offensive astride the River Somme aimed at shattering the will of Germany to fight. In line with French military doctrine, enemy entanglements and trenches would be destroyed by shelling and then the infantry would prise open the German line sufficiently wide for the cavalry to attack the rear areas. In early April, Rawlinson advised Haig that since the Fourth Army was relatively small, he could not achieve the frontage of 20,000 yards and advance 5,000 yards per day and asked his frontage be shortened to between Maricourt and Serre and that he be permitted to advance in two bounds of 2,000 yards each, which would give him time to feed in fresh troops and maintain the momentum. Haig insisted that the first bound must be beyond the first enemy trench, a decision that he took from his experience in the Battle of Loos when the assault demoralised the German front line. When Haig also insisted on a 20,000-yard frontage and a shorter bombardment, Rawlinson reluctantly selected the Pozières–Grandcourt–Serre ridges as his objectives for day one and the German second line on day two. While British morale was high, the cynicism of the British Tommy was also clear:

We beat them on the Marne.
We beat them on the Aisne,
We gave them hell at Neuve Chapelle
And here we are again!

During Easter, an Irish republican demand for independence was crushed. On 31 May, the Royal Navy clashed with the German fleet at Jutland and then a week later Lord Kitchener was lost at sea when the cruiser HMS *Hampshire* taking him to Russia hit a mine off the Orkneys. Killed with him was Detective Sergeant Matthew McLoughlin of of the intelligence police.

By February 1916 the Royal Engineers had consolidated its BEF survey resources forming a field survey depot and attaching a field survey company to each army consisting of a HQ and topographical, maps, sound-ranging and printing sections. By 1917, each corps had a survey company and by 1918 they were enlarged into field survey battalions.

Artillery had become a battlefield-winning weapon, indeed about half of Allied casualties were from the shelling of the front line or during offensives. While enemy batteries could be identified from air photographs and pilots could act as airborne forward air controllers, a serious obstacle to counter-battery fire was locating artillery positions in depth. While the British were not the first to experiment with sound ranging to pinpoint the location of guns, Lieutenant William Bragg (Royal Horse Artillery), an Australian scientist and Nobel laureate, discovered from French experiments that the sonic boom of the shell could be separated from the sound when the gunner pulled the lanyard. Corporal William Tucker, formerly of the physics department, London University, then invented a low-frequency microphone capable of separating the components of the sonic boom and the gun firing. Promoted to second-lieutenant, he formed an experimental sound-ranging section in the UK and found the optimum layout to pick up the sounds to be an array of listening posts arranged in a shallow curve equipped with microphones and oscillographs to record the strength and direction of sound waves. Calculating the effects of meterological conditions, locating enemy artillery to within about 30 yards was regularly achieved. Another method of artillery acquisition was flash spotting, a system developed by Captain Harold Hemming, a Canadian artillery officer serving with the Third Army, of using triangulation from guns as they fired to pinpoint gun positions. Aircraft were often used to triangulate long-range guns.

Security vetting involving checks with MI5 and Special Branch had been introduced throughout the armed forces in early 1916 in which the loyalty of servicemen with enemy surnames, heritage and connections were challenged; and this in a country in which the monarchy was closely related to the Kaiser. One of those trapped was Second-Lieutenant W.A.M. Doll (Intelligence Corps), who was married to a German. Arriving in France in November 1914, he had been attached to 1/9 Gurkha Rifles; however, in June 1915 he was instructed to resign his commission after the commanding officer declared 'his sentiments that his sympathies were undesirable'. Most others returned to the colours, as did Doll as an Intelligence Corps officer with the 1919 Archangel expedition. The Intelligence Corps has always welcomed anyone with a skill set needed to match its operational requirement. Corporal Vincent Shirley, formerly Fritz Schurhoff, was of German extraction. Since his family lived in the midlands, he joined the Royal Warwickshire Regiment but when his fluency in German was noted, he joined the VI Corps

Intelligence Police, south of Arras. By late 1917, no one with enemy connections was permitted to join the Intelligence Corps.

In April, Brigadier-General Charteris took four weeks' sick leave in England with pneumonia and Brigadier-General Macdonogh sent the thoroughly capable Major Cornwall to act as BEF head of intelligence at a time when much of the intelligence effort was directed towards the 'Big Push' along the River Somme. As he was giving the daily intelligence briefings to General Haig:

> I soon discovered that the views held by Charteris and reported by him to Sir Douglas Haig regarding Germany's manpower reserves, morale and economic resources differed widely from the estimates made by the Director of Military Intelligence at the War Office, Colonel Cox, head of MI3, and the combined best intelligence brains at the disposal of the country.

Charteris appeared to be committing the cardinal sin of briefing the intelligence that the commander wanted and giving his largely untested views, as opposed to providing proven intelligence backed up with collateral. But there was little Cornwall could do except monitor the passage of information to Haig and report his views to Macdonogh. To add to the dilemma, Haig was about to commit the BEF to battle based on Charteris's optimism using Kitchener's six army groups of volunteers to an infantry charge on a broad front in the vicinity of the River Somme to 'fight and hold' and invite the Germans to retake lost ground, followed by cavalry exploitation. Major-General Kiggell was concerned that the divisions were insufficiently trained, but he lacked the self-confidence to pursue his concerns.

From analysis of British correspondence of senior intelligence officers, it is clear that the Germans predicted the time and place of the first offensive of the Battle of the Somme: poor censorship highlighting the 'big push' and accumulation of war stores, increased raiding and artillery registration providing clues. Deception was not attempted. Intelligence collection was largely limited to raids and air reconnaissance. The VIII Corps Intelligence Summary dated 26 June stated that 'raids attempted all along the Corps front were unsuccessful, in some sectors owing to the failure to cut the wire, and in others to intense machine-gun and rifle fire'.

According to research conducted for the television programme *The Somme: Secret Tunnel Wars*, in spite of the warnings the night before the troops went over the top, German listeners in a tunnel heard a British officer using a field telephone to wish a colleague 'good luck tomorrow morning' and possibly alerted the Germans to a time for the expected offensive. The day before the battle, Brigadier-General Charteris, commenting on the development of intelligence wrote to his wife: 'Even more remarkable is the progress on the scientific side of the war. Observation balloons, aeroplanes, air photographs, Sound Ranging etc.'

The opening day of the Battle of the Somme was a disaster. Although the troops had been assured that the pre-assault bombardment would be destructive, guns were defective, fuses faulty and there was insufficient high-explosive and consequently the artillery failed to destroy the defences. The Germans sat out the bombardment in deep trenches and once the shelling lifted would take up their positions arranged in depth. While the 34th and 19th Divisions were preparing to attack the fortified villages of Ovillers and La Boiselle, a brigade major ignored protests from his subordinates and issued the operational orders over a field telephone. Although two large mines were detonated near La Boiselle, the attack cost 11,000 casualties. A written transcript of the orders were found in a German headquarters dugout. A Signals historian later wrote: 'Hundreds of brave men perished, hundreds more were maimed for life as the result of this one act of incredible foolishness.'

Pigeons flying through the shelling and noise brought messages, some released at a time during the day when they were normally roosting and made for a comfortable roost until daylight. Some messages were tied to the pigeon's leg with string instead of using the container and, in one case, one bird arrived with the message tied around its neck with a shoelace.

In an attempt to prevent the Germans from moving troops from the quiet sectors near Fromelles, on 19 July the 61st (British) and 5th (Australian) Divisions attacked after a seven-hour bombardment but intelligence failed to register that the Germans had withdrawn 200 yards and the attack was shredded by counter-bombardment. While the British withdrew with 50 per cent casualties, the Australians reached the German trenches to find them flooded and indefensible, but at the expense of 90 per cent casualties. A British officer was captured with, against operational security principles, a copy of an operations order.

By 1916, the Germans were making extensive use of wireless at army level and were beginning to feed trench wirelesses into the front line. These developments and the capture of trench listening sets galvanised GHQ BEF into taking greater interest in wireless intelligence. MI1(e) (Wireless Intelligence) had been formed in July with specific responsibility for the intercept of wireless telegraphy, direction finding and the issue of codes and ciphers. It was the smallest of the military intelligence desks at DMI, but as wireless intelligence became increasingly valuable, Macdonogh directed that it should be integrated into the intelligence resources and thus prevented the culture in the Royal Navy of Room 40 not contributing to the intelligence picture. Macdonogh insisted, whenever appropriate, that intercept information was included in intelligence summaries.

The capture of a German Moritz trench listening device in mid-1915 led to Captain Ronald Nesbitt-Hawes, a former private in the Royal Engineers Signals Service, developing the 'Intelligence Telephone'. Nicknamed the 'I-Toc', it consisted of three ground aerials arrayed in a U-shape placed as close as possible to the enemy in order that the pulses from field telephone conversations could be intercepted by an amplifier of three electromagnetic valves and headphones. The listening post was usually located in reinforced dugouts in the front line or robust buildings several hundred yards from the front. Access was controlled. The Germans responded to the threat by devising voice procedures and codes. Eventually, three Intelligence Telephone detachments supported each corps.

To meet the demand for more signallers, the Signals Service began selecting suitable soldiers. John Revie, for instance, was a science teacher and amateur radio enthusiast living in Coatbridge, Scotland, who had enlisted in November 1914 under the short-lived Derby Scheme in which men in reserved occupations could be conscripted. Although his preference was the Royal Army Medical Corps, when he was called up in early 1916, he was sent to the Wireless Training Centre at Diglis, near Worcester. The need for interpreters led to the army trawling for those with good German, particularly among other ranks. Corporal Shirely was transferred to one of the first intelligence telephone detachments (I-Toc) at Achicourt-le-Grand, in June, working from cellars and barns. On 10 July, Sergeant R.A.B. Young (6th King's Own Scottish Borderers) responded to a call from the Intelligence Corps for German speakers. Within the day, he arrived at Hant's Farm near Ploegsteert, just 500 yards from the front line, where his expectations of a 'cushy number' disappeared when he and another Intelligence Corps returned to the front line, this time to a reinforced concrete bunker into which access was controlled by a special pass issued by the division. Inside was the I-Toc amplifier. Their first job was to set up the equipment in no-man's-land. Young:

> I quickly realised, however, the now enhanced value of my life to my country and also the impossibility of getting 'Jerry' to allow me to run the wire over his parapet, and was therefore reduced to crawling parallel with his trenches, finally pegging in, with, I must confess, an odd coil or two to spare. I then returned slowly and horizontally to 'safety' and all was set.

While many of the intercepted messages were mundane, Young collected information that such substantial stores were being delivered to part of a German trench that a mine was suspected. The gunners responded, much to the 'grateful awe of troops in the front-line'. I-Toc detachments also monitored British communications for breaches of security. On 3 July, an I-Toc intercepted operational orders being given in clear from HQ 12th Division during the Battle of Albert. Young's detachment listened one evening to a wiring party being tasked to dismantle barbed wire entanglements in preparation for a trench raid for the following night. His report prevented the raid from going ahead and disciplinary action was taken against those who had committed the breach.

As the importance of the I-Tocs grew, the competency of Intelligence Corps operators in interpreting German and their knowledge of German military terminology was tested. About 30 per cent were returned to their units, including several soldiers who were sons of German-born, naturalised British parents but were considered to be a security risk. Sergeant Young later transferred to the intelligence police, one of his tasks being to collect homing pigeons from outlying lofts and take them to coops in their billet at Boulevard de Faid'herbe in Armentières. He was involved in investigations, including one in which several Frenchwomen had been watching movements of troops and even, in some instances, noting the positions of guns.

As a counter-measure to the Moritz, Captain A.C. Fuller (Royal Engineers) had developed the Fuller Trench Phone. Superseding the D3 handset, intercept was reduced by the signallers at both ends synchronising the 'buzzers' and thus forming a simple scrambling mechanism. The Fuller Phone was sufficiently flexible to transmit Morse, including over damaged lines lying on the ground, and could be operated by signallers wearing gas masks. As 1916 drew to a close and the security of British battlefield communications improved with formal voice procedures, such as using codes to identify users (known as call signs), information leaked to the Germans began to dry up. Meanwhile, Captain Hugh Lefroy (Royal Engineers), who was commanding an RFC signals unit, was examining the feasibility of extracting intelligence from communications between intercepted German airborne artillery controllers. This later became known as traffic analysis, for instance, patterns of communications may indicate an event, such as shelling, raid or an offensive. In Great Britain, wireless intelligence was playing a vital role against the Zeppelins.

The expansion of wireless intelligence led, in 1917, to the formation of several wireless operating groups to support the expeditionary forces. On the Western Front, each army was supported by a wireless company that consisted of an army HQ section and corps and divisional subsections and typically consisted of twenty-seven all ranks, rising to thirty-four in 1918. When Private Review joined the BEF in early 1917 he was posted to the GHQI(e) (Wireless Intelligence) and plotted the movements of key enemy wireless stations and tracked enemy bombers in preparation for the forthcoming offensives against Messines and Vimy Ridge.

Being taken prisoner is a risk that everyone in the armed forces accepts and thus interrogation on being captured is, for some, a probability. To that extent interrogation is an extension of the battlefield.

The British captured about 400,000 Germans, of whom about 330,000 were taken in 1918, the majority in the summer and autumn as the German army collapsed. The Battle of Flers-Courcelette between 15 and 22 September introduced tanks to the Western Front. A rolling barrage protected the 2,500-yard infantry advance to the villages of Courcelette, Martinpuich and Flers. Among the prisoners was Lieutenant Richard Schade of the 181st (Württemberg) Infantry Regiment, which was part of 40th (Saxon) Division. Interrogated by Captain

W. W. Torr (West Yorkshire Regiment) an Intelligence Corps officer with III Corps and and commanding Lieutenant Dyson, Schade discussed German intentions, relief practices, support lines, orders of battle, morale, locations of supply dumps of food and ammunition, the merits of the new German machine-gun detachments and their developments in the German army.

In August, German machine-gun units were standardised to three companies of six machine guns per regiment. Independent machine-gun sections were formed as divisional and corps reserve assets. Schade said that morale was very good, the men were getting hot meals in the front line brought up by carriers, the losses were heavy and that reinforcements arrived promptly. He considered British artillery to be accurate but that some shells, especially those of the larger guns, in particular the 9.2in howitzer, were nearly all duds. Schade believed that the British attack had only just begun and commented that south of Martinpuich, there were strong redoubts and assembly trenches into which German troops could retire. The positions at Flers were stronger than the old front line. Other interrogations and air photography provided collateral to Schade's claims and when Haig insisted that Martinpuich must be seized, by the afternoon of 15 September, the 15th Scottish Division overran a village flattened by shelling and stoutly defended by Bavarian troops.

Human intelligence through interrogations of prisoners and deserters has always been a prime intelligence resource, but they are a nuisance because they need to be guarded and administered and prevented from gathering intelligence. During the First World War, the British term for interrogation was 'examination'. The objectives of prisoner intelligence were and remain to obtain information on the enemy, to deny information to the enemy through resistance to interrogation, and to discover what the enemy knows about friendly forces.

Signatories of the 1899 Laws and Customs of War on Land, Article 9, Chapter 2 (On Prisoners of War) stated that: 'Every prisoner of war, if questioned, is bound to declare his true name and rank, and if he disregards this rule, he is liable to a curtailment of the advantages accorded to the prisoners of war of his class.'

The Intelligence Corps learned during the Battle of Neuve Chapelle that prisoners were reliable sources of strategic and tactical intelligence and that the quicker they reached prisoners, the better, in order to exploit the psychological condition of the shock of capture. But natural battlefield empathy means that the condition can be degraded by capturing units using prisoners as porters and stretcher-bearers and supplying them with cigarettes and food. From this emerged the concept of tactical questioning of interrogators reaching prisoners very soon after capture and before transfer to 'cages'. Other ranks generally could be relied upon to express their opinions, for instance Prussians despising Saxons, Bavarians and others in the new state of Germany and vice versa. NCOs usually possessed low-level tactical information. Officers liked to be treated according to their social class. Reasonable conversation, as always, proved most successful; however, exploiting the principle of knowing or pretending to know more than the prisoner and then inviting prisoners to fill in the gaps proved particularly efficacious, as one would expect.

Initially, prisoners were held in an infantry barracks near St Omer before being transferred to prison camps in France and Great Britain. By 1916, the British had developed an effective system that combined the collection of intelligence, prisoner security and transfer to prison camps. One method was for Intelligence Corps interrogators to accompany columns of prisoners and chat. Prisoners were assembled in divisional 'cages', a term still evident today, usually located near casualty clearing stations in order to take advantage of roads. Interrogators were supported by intelligence staff from the reserve divisions. Reserve divisions also supplied guard forces.

Typically, a cage consisted of several compounds erected around existing buildings, for instance a farmyard. In 'arrivals', officers and other ranks were separated. Where possible, prisoners were kept in their units in order to provide continuity of information. In 'screening', German-speaking intelligence police and listening set linguists helped select prisoners worthy of interrogation. In order to maintain the shock of capture, one ploy was to exploit the German culture of militarism by setting up a phoney orderly room to create a familiar environment in a period of their lives when the future was uncertain and they did not understand the language of their captors. Junior officers and other ranks were marched in and formally asked for their personnel details, their unit and activities. The method usually resulted in a decent quantity of information over a short period. When a specialist, for example a gunner, was captured, an artillery officer might assist with technical issues. During the Battle of the Somme, Charteris took Haig to see a prisoner-of-war cage and arranged that fit soldiers were taken out of sight, so that Haig only saw demoralised prisoners in poor physical condition, in order for Haig to be convinced that the German army was near to collapse.

A valuable source was deserters. Some were conscripts from countries with little loyalty to Germany or Turkey, for instance Poles and Syrians; others had political reasons for taking the dangerous path across no-man's-land. But in an era of patriotism, honour and service, deserters were considered to be cowardly. Interrogators learned to put their views aside and found most were valuable sources of information on morale, manpower levels and home fronts. Lieutenant Blennerhasset tempered his lack of military protocols with a reputation for reckless courage that included, in 1916, crossing no-man's-land and persuading several German soldiers to desert. With his knowledge of Germany and fluent in German, he proved particularly adept as the disarmingly friendly interrogator.

Prisoners selected for further examination, such as officers, signallers and engineers, were sent to corps cages where interrogators usually worked to a list of intelligence requirements, such as identifications of neighbouring units, personalities and locations, descriptions of strongpoints and fallback positions and future intentions. 'Pigeons' of linguists dressed in captured uniforms exploited the desire of prisoners to bond with fellow prisoners. Wounded prisoners were considered to be fair game. A wounded German officer captured near Ypres in 1915 was transferred to a field hospital near Poperinghe, but his refusal to answer questions led to the belief that he had something to hide. A 'wounded pigeon' was installed in a bed next to him and they began to chat. The following morning the ward sister, who knew about the ploy, was dressing the wounds of the 'pigeon' when she burst into giggles from his fake moans and groans. The Germans also used 'pigeons', the Eton and Oxford-educated Air Force officer the Grand Duke of Mecklenburg Streliz VI mingling with captured aircrew as a captured RFC pilot. Those likely to be retained for further interrogation, such as senior commanders, engineers, signals and artillery, were sent to army cages. The 'evacuation' compound was for those ready to be sent to prison camps or ferried to detailed interrogation centres, most of which were joint services, also dealing with captured U-boat survivors and aircrew. Among the interrogators was Captain Bernard Trench (Royal Marines Light Infantry), who was one of the enthusiastic young officers who had been arrested while spying in Germany before the war. He had been released at the same time as Captain Bertram Stewart.

During September, the German high command assessed that the casualty rates during the fighting on the Somme and at Verdun were unsustainable and, since withdrawal was inevitable, proposed to withdraw to fortifications protecting the border. Ordered by General Paul von Hindenburg, over the next six months German military engineers, contractors and Russian prisoners of war constructed the *Siegfriedstellung* (Hindenburg Line), of nine redoubts stretching from the Belgian coast to Metz using the basic strategy that defence should be flexible and counter-attack swift and in strength. The basic defence consisted of the forward zone of wide anti-tank ditches and several layers of wire entanglements designed to blunt attacks; the middle zone usually of concrete pillboxes and redoubts about 1,100 yards in depth; and the rear zone of intricate networks of zigzag trenches.

Two lines of artillery on reverse slopes, whenever possible, were later moved into trench weapon pits and tunnels. In front of the defence was a scorched-earth policy to deny the enemy the cover of buildings and woods. The pulverisation of the countryside further removed navigational features and waymarkers. Since the fortifications were in a generally straight line, as opposed to salients and kinks, the length of the German front line was reduced by about 25 miles, which released about thirteen divisions to join the reserve army.

While the fighting on the Western Front was hitting the headlines, an unseen war was being fought behind both front lines as the opposing intelligence services competed. But resistance, as always, was risky, as several First World War memorials in Brussels bear witness.

Gabrielle Petit, aged 21 years and employed as a saleswoman in Brussels when Germany invaded Belgium, joined the Belgian Red Cross. After helping her wounded fiancé to rejoin his regiment in Holland, she collected information on German troop movements and technical intelligence, distributed the clandestine newspaper *La Libre Belgique* and helped several Belgians to cross into Holland until she was exposed by a German counter-intelligence officer masquerading as a Dutchman in February 1916. Convicted of espionage, she was shot on 1 April. Like Edith Cavell, Petit became a martyr and was given a state funeral with military honours in 1919 and is commemorated by a statue in Brussels. In the 'Garden of Aurora' in Bruges, a memorial records those executed by the Germans, including the Pagnien Group, which collected intelligence on airfields, military installations and troop movements in northern France and Flanders, lost its leader and had six members executed in Ghent. Thirteen people from Waregem were executed for supplying the British with information about German troop movements in mid-1917. M. Reseau Algoet, formerly in the Belgian army, was one of six executed in Ghent for observing railway traffic in south-west Flanders.

In December 1915, Captain Stanley Woolrych had been posted from 7th Division to GHQ Intelligence. He had been transferred from the division laundry to intelligence duties in December 1914 and had scoured no-man's-land for items of intelligence interest among enemy dead and wounded, for which he was mentioned in dispatches. On Boxing Day he wrote to his father that the previous afternoon he had been in the divisional rear sector near Fromelles when he met some soldiers, who told him other soldiers were 'talking to the Germans half-way between the trenches'. They directed Woolrych to a major who suggested that he use his linguistic skills to talk to the Germans but by the time he reached the front line, both sides had returned to their trenches. Notwithstanding the possibility of being shot, Woolrych, waving his arms, crossed no-man's-land and met three Germans, who had climbed from their trenches, one of them a corporal from Hamburg. After introductions, the corporal fetched a captain, who said that he hoped the unofficial Christmas truce would last until the New Year. Woolrych believed the truce was expunged from the divisional war diary because it was regarded as 'unsoldierly' by politicians and senior officers.

In January 1916 Major Kirke sent Woolrych to the GHQI(b) (Secret Service) office in Folkestone where he joined Lieutenant Payne-Best screening passengers arriving on the ferries from Holland. Needing more staff, Kirke selected him to replace Captain Campbell in Geneva after the GHQ1(b) section at the nearby Annemasse border and quarantine crossing point had been closed in November 1915 when the Swiss police began to suspect Campbell. Kirke then decided to open a permit office in Paris and sent Woolrych and the enthusiastic Belgian Lieutenant Monthaye, an interpreter and former lawyer who had served in the French army, to look for an office. Finding suitable premises at 41 Rue St Roch, they separated the legitimacy of the permit office from its clandestine intelligence activities by securing a large room in Rue Soufflot, on the Left Bank, as an agent training school. Woolrych later equipped it with tailors' dummies wearing German uniforms complete with insignia and drawings pinned to the walls with types of troop trains and maps. They also talent-spotted several Belgian refugees stranded in France willing to return to occupied Belgium as agents. Noting that intelligence operations managed by the War Office DMI complemented each other and risked duplication to the extent of running the same sources and therefore providing unreliable collateral, Kirke persuaded Smith-Cumming to concentrate on political intelligence and to focus on Switzerland, unoccupied Belgium and Germany while GHQ focused on Holland, France and occupied Belgium.

Major Kirke recognised that prisoners were a valuable intelligence resource able to supply information on the German rear areas and the home front, and when he heard that the French had devised a 'parcel fund' to communicate with their prisoners of war in the summer of 1915, he wondered if British communications between prisoners and correspondents could be used to pass information. Some families had developed codes to transfer information in letters and were sending welfare parcels in which maps, compasses and survival rations were secreted. Kirke had little regard for the British Red Cross, because he thought it an aimless organisation unwilling to conduct its patriotic duty by collecting intelligence from prisoners, and thus it was no surprise that his request that it follow the French example of a formal parcels fund was rejected by the Red Cross parcels on the grounds that if contraband were found, the Germans would refuse to accept welfare parcels. Indeed, in October 1914, Colonel William Gordon VC (Gordon Highlanders), the senior British officer at Torgau prison camp, had written to the *Times* in October 1914 asking that in letters and parcels, 'above all, no information about the war should be either openly or by some secret means included in any communications'. He emphasised that unless the conditions were fulfilled, the privilege of receiving mail might be withdrawn. Nevertheless, Miss Dorothy Done, an Englishwoman, was employed in the French Ministry of War managing the French parcel fund to transfer her work to British prisoners with a specific role to aid escapes and receive intelligence.

Three other women who used the Paris office were Charlotte and Sylvia Bosworth, both sisters to two Intelligence Corps officers, who had responded to a personal appeal from Brigadier-General Charteris, and Miss L. Brooking, who had worked in a department of GHQ counter-intelligence attached to the Paris *Deuxième Bureaux*, to collate information from captured pay books. They worked closely with Captain Alexander Scotland (Inns of Court Training Corps), who had spent several years in southern Africa, including serving four years in the German South-West Africa *Schutztruppe*. During the Second World War, he commanded Camp 020, the 'London Cage'.

The well-travelled South African Captain Henry Landau (Royal Field Artillery) was posted to Rotterdam in 1916 to run the military intelligence section in Richard Tinsley's MI6 group. He scored a crucial success by convincing a gunsmith named Dieudonne Lambrecht, who had crossed the border intending to join the Belgian army, to form a train-watching network at Liège. Lambrecht recruited a network of observers and couriers, but German counter-intelligence trapped a courier carrying some instructions and Lambrecht was arrested and then shot on 4 March. Walter Dewe, a cousin, and Herman Chauvin, both telephone and telegraph engineers, reinvigorated the network and named it *La Dame Blanche* (White Lady) after the legend of the white ghost whose appearance would induce the downfall of the Hohenzollern dynasty. Financed by a Liège banker, they built the *Corps d'Observation Anglais* of about 1,300 agents, who styled themselves as 'soldiers without uniforms', and organised them into battalions, companies and platoons manning fifty-one train-watching observation posts spread across occupied Belgium, Luxembourg and France that supplied GHQ with about 75 per cent of the 'train watch' intelligence collected in Belgium. The corps was evenly split between men and women, many of the latter middle-aged and single. Laure Tadel, who commanded 3rd Battalion in Brussels, which included eighty priests and nuns, managed a school with her sister and was in her 40s. Cut-outs and dead letter boxes reduced the risk of penetration. Broom handles were hollowed out so that dried beans could be inserted to denote numbers of soldiers, horses and guns on trains. The family home of Edward Aimiable, a friend of Lambrecht, at Fournies overlooked the important railway junction at Mezieres. The group re-emerged during the Second World War as *Corps d'Observation Belge*.

During the summer Major Kirke recruited his most successful agent, smuggler and former soldier Victor Marie, whose house near the German-Belgian border overlooked the railway from Cologne to Namur. He signalled when conditions were right for a pigeon parachute drop by hanging out his laundry. By the end of the war, forty-three members had been arrested, two of whom were shot.

By 18 November the autumn rains soaking the countryside, long casualty lists, a dip in morale and political and social concerns on the home front led to the Battle of the Somme stuttering to a halt.

S.S/103.

ORDERS
regarding the sending of Messages within 1,500 yards of the firing line.

O.B./630.

1. Messages sent by buzzer on any circuit which has an " earth " within 1,500 yards of our front trenches, are liable to be overheard by the enemy.

2. As a circuit, even if metallic, may be earthed, either through damage to the conductors by shell fire or other causes, it is necessary to ensure that as far as possible messages transmitted shall not give information of value to the enemy.

3. No written message is to be sent by buzzer from or to any office in the zone 1,500 yards from the front line trenches without the sanction of an officer who must sign the message as being authorized for transmission within the dangerous zone.

4. Every station working buzzer in the dangerous zone is to be given a station call which will *not* be the recognised signal call of the unit. These calls will be allotted by Divisions.

5. Names of units are not to be " buzzed " in any messages. Only the code names of units as laid down and published by Corps and Divisions should be used.

1 Order issued by GHQ BEF front line in 1915 designed to minimise the effectiveness of German intercept of front-line field telephone networks.

2 Brigadier-General David Henderson. His progressive thoughts led him to being regarded as the 'father' of the Intelligence Corps. He was also a founder of the Royal Flying Corps.

3 Second-Lieutenant Rolleston West and a family group prior to him joining the BEF Intelligence Corps in France in August 1914. Note the goggles on his cap. He was awarded the DSO for helping to blow up a bridge. (Military Intelligence Museum)

4 The cavalry, in this instance 9th Lancers, initially provided valuable scouts but were then restricted by trench warfare until 1918 when they pursued retreating Germans. (Courtesy of Queen's Royal Lancers & Nottinghamshire Yeomanry Museum)

5 Battle of the Marne, 8 September 1914. Troops of the 1st Middlesex under artillery fire on the Signy–Signets road. The figure holding his head is one of the 'Original 55' of the Intelligence Corps. He later died from his wounds. (Imperial War Museum)

6 With a maximum speed of 72mph, the BE-2 had a limited 'dogfight' capability; however, its stability proved ideal for air reconnaissance. (Courtesy of the Medmenham Collection)

7 An RFC corporal checking a Type-C Camera fitted to a BE-2. (Courtesy of the Medmenham Collection)

8 The Western Front. An annotated photo of German positions. The zigzags denote three positions marked 1, 2, and 3 of 'Any trench apparently organised for defence'. The triangle denotes a supply dump. (Courtesy of the Medmenham Collection)

9 Palestine. An air photographic interpretation unit in a tent. Note developed photos drying on a line.

10 Macedonia, 1917. A British intelligence officer uses a stereoscope to interpret aerial reconnaissance photographs. (Imperial War Museum)

11 The Bosworth sisters used their linguistic skills to translate and interpret captured German paybooks. Their brother was in the Intelligence Corps. (Courtesy of the Military Intelligence Museum)

12 Wirelesses were used to transmit messages and intercept enemy communications; however, they were large, heavy and took time to assemble.

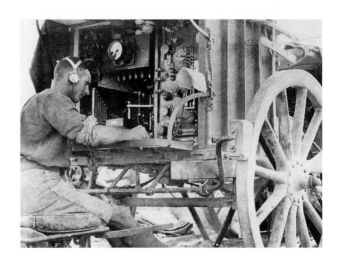

13 Pigeons being transported to and from the front line. In the background is a mobile coop. Pigeons were a generally reliable form of communication, if unable to differentiate between friend and foe. (Great War Archive)

14 The Western Front, September 1917. German prisoners being escorted through Ypres after the Battle of the Menin Road. (Great War Archive)

15 The Western Front. An intelligence officer, identifiable by his armlet, questions German prisoners of war in a trench for tactical information.

16 The first Special Security Section provided by the Metropolitan Police Special Branch. Standing: PC Cuthbert Park; PS Pat Barratt; Insp. Charles Frost; Insp. Jock Bannon; PS Albert Canning. Seated: PS Leo Gough; PC William Palmer; PS Lionel Kirchner; PS Bob Brown; PC Durkin. (Courtesy of Metropolitan Police Crime Museum)

17 The Western Front, 1916. Sgt Rowe and, on the motorcycle, Cpl Cousins, of No. 9 Intelligence Police Station at Bailleul. (Courtesy of the Military Intelligence Museum)

18 The Western Front, August 1918. An Intelligence police sergeant questions a suspect civilian in Bethune after a bombardment.

19 Brig.-Gen. John Charteris CMG DSO was the senior Intelligence officer to Douglas Haig for several years. While generally regarded as an effective, he was discredited when it emerged that he had fitted intelligence to match Haig's beliefs.

20 East Africa, July 1915. The German cruiser *Königsberg* lying damaged deep in Rufiji Delta after being trapped and bombarded by the Royal Navy. (Great War Archive)

21 The ensign of the *Königsberg* being displayed in the Intelligence Corps Museum, Ashford before it was handed to the National Maritime Museum. (*Kentish Express*)

22 German East Africa, November 1917. Capt. the Hon James Crichton, a GSO3 in the Nigerian Brigade, Capt. Eric Stobart, the Brigade Intelligence Officer and Capt. Austin Gardner at Makania. (Imperial War Museum)

23 North Russian Intervention, 1919. In Murmansk, Bolshevik prisoners employed as servants to Capt. William Blennerhassett (Intelligence Corps). (Imperial War Museum)

24 Gallipoli. Intelligence dugout at Anzac Cove. (Imperial War Museum)

25 Gallipoli. 42nd (East Lancashire) Division interrogators questioning Turkish prisoners captured during the Third Battle of Krithria on 4 June 1915.

26 Mesopotamia. Lt-Col Gerard
Leachman DSO (Royal Sussex Regiment),
masquerading as a desert Bedouin, ran
intelligence operations before and during
the war. He was murdered in 1920 during a
factional dispute.

27 Akaba, 1916. Capt. Thomas Lawrence
(Lawrence of Arabia) after the capture
of the town. He regularly dressed as
Bedouin noble. (Imperial War Museum)

28 Palestine. Motorised patrols complementing mounted troops proved ideal in the desert.

29 Members of HMY *Managem* crew. Sitting left to right are Maj. Ian Smith MC, Lt-Cdr Alan Cain DSC and Capt. Weldon MC. Smith controlled clandestine operations in the eastern Mediterranean.

30 The eastern Mediterranean. Her Majesty's Yacht *Managem* used by Capt. Weldon for clandestine operations. Weldon spent almost the entire war landing in the occupied eastern Mediterranean area meeting agents and delivering arms and ammunition.

31 Palestine. The Aaronsohn family formed the NILI network, which supplied intelligence crucial to General Allenby's advance. From left to right: Rifka (sister to Aaron); Alexander; Samuel (brother); Chaim Abraham (husband of Sarah) and Ephraim (father). Sitting at the foot of Samuel is Sarah and behind him is Aaron. (All rights are reserved to Beit Aaronsohn, Zichron Ya'akov, Israel)

32 Lt Alexander Aaronsohn DSO (Intelligence Corps). (All rights are reserved to Beit Aaronsohn, Zichron Ya'akov, Israel)

33 Maj. Robert Bruce ran GHQ BEF Secret Service operations from Paris. He wears an intelligence brassard. With him is Father Cambron, who collected information. (Courtesy of Lord Balfour of Burleigh)

34 Madame Lise Rischard CBE was recruited by Maj. Bruce to form a train-watching circuit in Luxembourg that provided crucial by supplying intelligence during the final German offensive in 1918. (Courtesy of Lord Balfour of Burleigh)

35 In June 1918, the Belgian Lt Albert Baschwitz Meau DSO crossed German lines at night in a balloon and linked up with Mme Rischard. He was the first agent to be delivered by air into enemy territory. (Courtesy of Lord Balfour of Burleigh)

36 The Italian Front, 1917. A British intelligence officer, probably from 7th Division, interrogating an Austro–Hungarian prisoner. (Imperial War Musuem)

37 Gallipoli, 1915. Lt-Col Charles Doughty-Wylie, the GHQ GSO1 (Intelligence), was awarded the VC for rallying troops at V Beach landed from the River Clyde. Exchanging his walking stick for a rifle, he was killed in Sedd al Bahr on 26 April 1915. (Courtesy of the Royal Welch Fusiliers Museum)

38 Aden, 1919. Turkish prisoners are brought by the narrow gauge military railway from Lahej prior to repatriation.

8

The Western Front, 1917

In early February 1917 the German army began withdrawing to the Hindenburg Line. On 9 April, amid snow showers and behind a rolling barrage, the British Third Army and I Canadian Corps, commanded by General Allenby, attacked Arras and Vimy Ridge and breached two defence zones within two hours but were held up by the third. The attacking troops were struck by the scorched-earth policy and were wary of booby traps and mines.

Although his promotion had been meteoric and there were doubts about his intelligence conclusions, Brigadier-General Charteris had converted the BEF intelligence infrastructure from the muddled organisation of August 1914 to a function that exploited intelligence and security resources and enabled the dissemination of daily intelligence summaries from every division, corps and army. A Second Army Intelligence Christmas card in 1916 described intelligence as:

To describe the indescribable,
To discern the indiscernible,
To define the indefinable,
And to unscrew the inscrutable.

Developments in air photography for artillery and intelligence purposes during the Battle of the Somme led the RFC to taking vertical, high-angle and wide-angled photographs that could be developed into a control map into which low-level photographs could be inserted. But air reconnaissance of the Hindenburg Line met stiff opposition from the German air force. Artillery intelligence had improved significantly with maps showing unoccupied and occupied gun positions, but in the struggle for air reconnaissance and artillery spotting before the advance, seventy-five British aircraft were shot down at a cost of nineteen pilots killed. Nevertheless, the French insisted that Field-Marshal Haig maintain the pressure at Arras in the spring, largely because mutinies were beginning to affect the soldiers. The Canadian Corps had an extremely well-developed intelligence function and developed rigorous communications security measures to prevent leakages of operational information; indeed, the counter-measures caught the Germans off guard.

Charteris tended to employ Intelligence Corps officers in GHQ Intelligence for long periods. He also selected a cohort of officers he could dispatch on a mission at short notice, for instance liaising with the French, interrogating captured staff officers and briefing war correspondents. As the demand for intelligence increased, it fell not on the shoulders of the General Staff intelligence officers, but, according to Dr Beach, on to a 'loosely controlled and rather egalitarian pool of around 100 inexperienced amateur-soldiers' of Intelligence Corps officers fusing information from a variety of sources into intelligence for exploitation by the General Staff.

John Freeman, of the University of Birmingham, researched *A Planned Massacre? British Intelligence Analysis and the German Army at the Battle of Broodseinde, 4 October 1917*:

> As the divisional staffs were so busy during operations, it was felt impossible to dedicate a GSO solely for intelligence purposes. It was clear, however, that these officers were too busy doing 'all the bottle-washing of operations'. Officially the GSO was still in charge though, in practice, the trained Intelligence Corps officer became the de facto focus within the staffs.

Charteris and Macdonogh had followed British military protocols that Intelligence Corps would not fill General Staff intelligence appointments because they should be filled only by officers with command experience. It was a protocol that lasted well into the twentieth century. The Intelligence Corps, as the experts on the enemy threat, dispositions and likely intentions, drafted intelligence summaries and prepared briefings; however, as the workload increased, the Intelligence Corps took on more intelligence matters. Generally, intelligence summaries were divided into Part One, a general overview, and Part Two, detail from interrogations, neighbouring units and documentary intelligence. Wireless intelligence was also maturing with GHQI(e) producing daily intelligence summaries identifying unit locations and moves. On an average day in 1917, traffic analysis was listing the locations of about one third of the German divisions, which was far more than gained from prisoners of war, battlefield detritus and observation. Intelligence Corps officers also ensured that during troop rotations at every level, maps and air photographic mosaics were handed over to incoming units.

Intelligence Corps officers began wearing cypress green collar tabs and hat band and a green and grey brassard in 1916. GSOs continued to wear the distrusted red tabs and the red hat band of the General Staff:

> The green-tabbed official of the Intelligence Corps was at first regarded with the utmost suspicion. His reserve was very marked and he had an instatiable curiosity, a combination of characteristics which the average Britisher resents, and this rather led the soldier to imagine that his efforts were not so much

directed towards gleaning information about the enemy as the state of the unit that he visited, and he was consequently looked upon first as suspect. Gradually the feeling wore off when it was found that the visitor often supplied interesting tit-bits of news and that the information given to him became reflected in Intelligence Summaries which reached the troops and, again, in subsequent field operations.

Officers joining the corps did so as a posting from regiments and corps and were inducted 4th Class agents if involved in counter-intelligence, or interpreters, when involved with operational intelligence. The highest grade of 1st Class led to automatic promotion to captain, but since there were only twelve such posts in the BEF, career aspirations were limited until a career path was developed taking them from divisional headquarters through corps and army to GHQ. An example was Captain (1st Class Agent) Frederic Bell who was appointed GSO3 (Intelligence) at HQ First Army in March 1918, having joined the Intelligence Corps in September 1914. In 1917, the corps formed a unit of volunteers, nicknamed the 'Suicide Club', at Bruay. Their role was to accompany the cavalry in breakthroughs and infiltrate into German rear lines and report enemy activity. Recruited and trained by Captain William Hazeldine, it was unfortunate that formation HQs were wary of the secretive nature of the 'Club' and consequently it suffered from shortages of supplies and equipment. Experiments were conducted with wirelesses, but since their weight of about 57lb precluded their use, trials were held in using pigeons as couriers. Cheekily, Captain M.G. Pearson claimed that since he had crossed the pigeons with parrots, the latter could give verbal reports.

GHQ Intelligence had established Central Collecting Centres to fuse information, co-ordinate collection and disseminate intelligence summaries and intelligence reports and was producing results. Below is an intelligence order dated 16 May 1917 before the attack on Messines-Wytschaete Ridge:

1. Intelligence Collection Methods

    The transport of PoW to Advanced Collecting Stations where they will be searched and subjected to initial tactical questioning before being sent to a PoW Collecting Station where intelligence officers will conduct a more thorough examination.

    The study of captured maps and documents by intelligence officers at Corps PoW cages and tactical information to be transmitted immediately to front line units.

    Intelligence collected as a result of penetration of the enemy's lines by reconnaissance patrols.

    Intelligence gathered by observation posts.

Reports by observers with the Royal Flying Corps which will be dropped at advanced positions near divisional HQs. After landing the observer will report directly to the intelligence officer in his Squadron HQ.

Air photography should take place several times a day and oblique photos should be used in conjunction with panorama photos from the ground.

Flash spotting and sound ranging systems to be confirmed by air photography.

Signal and wireless interception of the enemy's ground wireless stations, enemy aircraft transmissions operating with his artillery. The use of Compass Stations to locate enemy wireless sets and artillery positions and listening sets at the front line to listen to the enemy's trench conversations.

Intelligence emanating from the enemy's rear areas consisting of reports from agents, refugees, repatriated prisoners and documents retrieved from prisoners.

2. Dissemination of Intelligence

Messages are considered the most positive and rapid means of transmitting information to higher and lower formations.

Daily Intelligence Summaries are to be issued by Division, Corps and Army Intelligence Staffs at noon and during the evening.

Intelligence Staffs are to participate twice daily in conferences to discuss intelligence and artillery intelligence.

Use Standard Trench Maps at the scale of 1:10,000 and 1:20,000 and Special Attack Maps at a scale of 1:5,000 for Platoon Commanders and Royal Artillery and Royal Flying Corps Observers.

3. Counter Espionage

Reports from the Intelligence Police and the Provost Marshal on the actions of the inhabitants both military and civil in their respective areas.

The development of the Hindenburg Line quickly attracted the attention of air photographic interpreters. New cameras, including one with a 20in focal length, gave greater detail, for example types of shells in ammunition dumps and purpose of strongpoints by the number of footpaths around and between positions and studying the adjacent topography. In October 1916 Major-General Trenchard had proposed that each corps reconnaissance squadron should be supported by a resident RFC intelligence officer to brief and debrief aircrew and interpret photographs. Two months later, Macdonogh decided the posts should be filled by Intelligence Corps officers supported by two Royal Engineer draughtsmen and a clerk with typing skills. Trenchard defined their role at the end of March 1917 to be to debrief observers immediately after landing to gain as much 'hot' information as possible; to disseminate information quickly, especially to army and corps headquarters; and to examine, annotate and issue photographs obtained and to create photo-maps, if required.

By the end of 1917 there were a total of nine Intelligence Corps officers and six intelligence clerks attached to RFC squadrons. Trenchard later commented:

> My Intelligence Department provided me with the most thorough information on all targets such as gas factories, aeroplane factories, engine factories, poison gas factories etc. Each target having a detailed and illustrated plan. Maps were prepared of every large target that was within each. These were supplemented in a large way by the aerial photographs made by reconnaissance machines.

In addition to the standard photographic interpretation equipment of stereoscopes, magnifying glass, rulers and pens and pencils, sections were equipped with self-contained portable Ellam flatbed duplicators for the dissemination of reports. Lieutenant-Colonel M.N. MacLeod (Royal Engineers), then commanding 4 Field Survey Company supporting the Second Army, had devised a system that rectified nuances in aerial photographs transferred to mosaics. As more air photographic interpreters began arriving in January, their postings were administered by Captain Maurice Baring at HQ RFC. Meanwhile Major Brabazon-Moore, now in charge of air photography at HQ RFC, had published on 2 January 1917 the first handbook on photographic interpretation entitled *Photographs Taken by the Royal Flying Corps*. It detailed types of photography, conventional symbols to standardise the annotation of photographs, and guides to the identification of defence works and fortifications, trench systems, interpretation of communications equipment and other battlefield features, such as types of artillery bunkers.

The handbook appeared shortly before the General Staff in France published its *Notes on the Interpretation of Aeroplane Photographs*, which consisted of Part One, instructions on the interpretation of air photography with detailed description of artillery, machine gun and mortar emplacements; trench works; defence systems; communication system and military installions, such as headquarters; and Part Two, an album showing types of vertical and oblique photographs to illustrate the techniques used in Part One.

With Bolshevik revolution ripping Russian imperialism apart, U-boats sailing from Belgium attacking shipping in the North Sea and the combination of the grim fighting at Verdun and defeat of the Nivelle offensive culminating in French mutinies, the Allies planned an offensive before mutual solidarity splintered. Although morale in the British army was largely intact, there was a major mutiny in September at Etaples after a military policeman shot dead a corporal. Resentment against the military police and the General Staff, poor camp administration and lack of respect towards those who had served in the front line by officers and instructors at the Bull Ring and, above all, war weariness were the principal causes. An intelligence police detachment under command of Captain Frank Joy (King's Own Scottish Borderers), a Somerset county cricketer, investigated the causes of the mutiny, looking in particular for political subversion. None of note were found. Public morale in Great Britain was wavering.

Three weeks after the raid against the Zeppelin sheds at Cuxhaven, on 19 January 1915, Germany conducted the first of many air raids against Great Britain over the next thirty years when L-3 bombed Great Yarmouth. In early June there was a welcome breakthrough when Sub-Lieutenant Reginald Warneford, of No.1 Squadron RNAS, on his way to bomb the sheds at Evere and Berchem-Ste-Agathe in a Morane-Saulnier Type-1L monoplane, saw LZ-37 returning to base. Machine-gunners defeated his first attack, but he followed and hand-dropped six 20lb fragmentation bombs, the last one hitting the Zeppelin as it landed. Bursting into flames, the Zeppelin crashed near Ghent. Warneford was awarded the VC.

The potential air threat had been considered by the progressive Committee of Imperial Defence in 1909; however, based on the available information, air attack was considered unlikely because North Sea weather conditions would hinder navigation. It was accepted that bombing would cause significant damage. And thus when the Zeppelin air raids began in 1915 there was no co-ordinated air and civil defence. The Royal Navy was responsible for defence of the mainland. Visual observations were telephoned from police stations, military installations, railway stations, and lightships with callers asked to be precise when giving location and direction of travel. However, in some parts of the country telephones were uncommon and it was not unknown for reports to be forwarded by post. Room 40 intercepted Zeppelin transmissions usually giving departure time and directions, sighting of ships and checking positions with German direction-finding stations, but the strict need-to-know basis meant that the intelligence was not always shared with the operations staff.

July 1916 saw responsibility for air defence transferred to the army and a reorganisation. A searchlight belt stretched from Sussex to Northumberland. A sound locator system and the Metropolitan Observation Service of observation posts were connected to seven control posts commanded by anti-aircraft controllers able to predict air raid warnings. MI1(e) (Wireless Intelligence), in War Office Room 417, shared information and thus controllers had the options of using either guns or RFC aircraft. Attacks by aircraft usually forced Zeppelins to climb to about 19,000ft; however, long missions in unpressurised and freezing cabins and exposed persistent aircraft made life intolerable and by September 1917 the Zeppelin menace had largely been replaced by Gotha and Giant bombers. The public quickly learned to live with air raid warnings, blackouts and night bombing. Air defences were strengthened with anti-aircraft artillery fire sectors, aircraft patrol sectors and a barrage balloon apron wrapped around London. To speed up the passage of intelligence formation, the Metropolitan Observation Service expanded outward from London and its observer posts were equipped with equipment that enabled the height and flightpath of bombers to be plotted onto a gridded map on an operations table manned by plotters and overseen by the senior controller on a dais.

While the French preferred to wait for the arrival of American armies, Haig planned to attack through Flanders to destroy the U-boat bases and defeat the German army, which Brigadier-General Charteris was briefing to be near collapse. In preparation for the offensive, the Canadian Corps deployed twice the usual number of listening sets and acquired a substantial intelligence picture. As part of a deception, the Germans were fed wireless traffic suggesting that there was no increase in the number of divisions in the front line and preparatory deployments took place at night. It was still difficult to shield air reconnaissance, the building of railways and roads to move men and material and an increase in tented camps, supply centres and casualty clearing stations. Efforts were made to divert German attention with a feint, but even this was largely limited to an artillery bombardment. The greatest danger to the compromising of an offensive was a captured soldier telling his German interrogators about preparations, orders and training associated with an attack.

The launching of the attack against Messines Ridge by the Second Army, commanded by General Sir Herbert Plummer, was the detonation of nineteen mines underneath German mines on 7 June. His tactics favoured 'bite and hold'. The remains of Messines-Wytschaete Ridge was captured, but Plummer was prevented from advancing toward the village of Passchendaele by Haig. Code books and ciphers captured during the fighting gave GHQI(e) (Wireless Ridge) valuable clues to German code structures. The village overlooked the railway junction at Roeselare, which had become an important logistic centre for the German Fourth Army. German counter-attacks continued until 14 June, by which time the Messines salient was in Allied hands.

Plummer captured the Menin Road Bridge on 20 September and 'Polygon Wood' six days later; meanwhile, the German Fourth Army had retreated to Broodseinde Ridge. During the fighting, Temporary Captain Frederick Hotblack (Norfolks/Intelligence Corps) was awarded the Military Cross for 'conspicuous gallantry, initiative and devotion to duty' as the Tank Corps intelligence officer. At the beginning of the summer, Private Revie was posted to Third Army Wireless Company and found himself in the front line with an I-Toc detachment. During his time with the company, it lost Privates James Marrian and Frank Jago killed on 14 May and John Fenton dying at home on 23 June from wounds received a week earlier. At the end of June, Revie was transferred to the Second Army Wireless Company near Messines for the next six months. The Germans learnt from intercepts that the British were planning an offensive in July. GHQ commented:

> There is evidence indicating that our telephone messages between Brigade and Division are now being intercepted by the enemy. Prisoners state that a new and

improved apparatus is now in use. The following details are given regarding the
new instrument:

a.   The amplifier comprises four valves of a new type.

b.   The whole amplifier is contained in one box.

It is of vital importance to obtain further details and, if possible, a sample of the
new apparatus.

Studies of intelligence on the Western Front and its use are generally rare, so
the study by John Freeman, of the University of Birmingham, of the Battle of
Broodseinde on 4 October gives a rare insight in the days before battle. The Second
Army GSO1, Lieutenant-Colonel Charles Mitchell (Royal Canadian Engineers),
had a firm grip of intelligence. Previously the Canadian Corps GSO1, he had
welcomed innovation, one of the most important being to promote the use of
maps at intelligence briefings. HQ II ANZAC, which was part of the Second
Army, reported on 28 September that the 'enemy front-line ran from Zonnebeke
to Staden and was a single line of trenches, yet to be completed. Communication
trenches had not been dug. West of the trenches were defensive positions in shell
holes supported by several concrete dugouts.'

Photographic interpretation the previous day showed four posts connected
by trenches north of Zonnebeke Church. There was no enemy activity around
Dochy Farm. British observation posts monitored both features and Israel House
where a new trench was thought to lead to 'an advanced post'. The Australians also
learnt that the 4th (Bavarian) Division and 44th Reserve Division were fortifying
mutually-supporting shell holes. A captured German instruction read:

> When, as in the case of Company A, no small pieces of trench are already dug,
> the foremost shell craters are to be joined together in such a manner as to provide
> positions for groups [i.e. one NCO and six men]. The crater-field in between
> the 'group' positions is to be filled in with barbed wire, to hinder the enemy
> establishing posts.

A captured map showed the line to be heavily wired but with incomplete trenches.
From prisoners and documents captured in trench raids, HQ I ANZAC identified
four divisions on Broodseinde Ridge. Nine prisoners from 73rd and 92nd Reserve
Infantry Regiments, of 19th Division, claimed that soldiers sheltered in craters close
to British trenches to escape harassing artillery fire. They also said that the division
had spent six weeks training for the Russian Front and had been on the Western
Front for a week. The Second Army believed the recently arrived 4th (Bavarian)
Division was a counter-attack division. During the fighting at Verdun, the German
infantry had developed three-man assault detachments (*Sturmtruppe*) tasked to lead
attacks. These had evolved into assault battalions (*Sturmbataillon*) of four pioneer

companies supported by light artillery and trench mortars, machine guns and flamethrower detachments. Counter-attack divisions had also been formed to lead attacks and to be withdrawn as the follow-up fought through enemy positions. Their presence was regarded as an intelligence indicator of enemy intentions. The Australians knew 4th (Bavarian) Division from heavy fighting at Mouquet Farm in the Battle of the Somme. HQ II ANZAC Intelligence commented:

> It has been at Armentieres since the beginning of July but does not appear to have had many casualties on that front. However when it relieved 23rd Division, incoming units suffered very heavily under our intense artillery fire, in particular the 2nd Battalion, 5th Bavarian Reserve Infantry Regiment. The company trench strength may now be said to average out at about 80. The morale of the division appears to be indifferent and had probably suffered through a prolonged stay on a quiet front.

A 77th Infantry Regiment prisoner captured by II ANZAC then supplied the German regimental tactical order of battle as two battalions up front and one in reserve; each battalion had three companies in the front line and one in reserve, and each company had two platoons in the front line and one in support.

The change from the usual one battalion in the front line, the second in direct support and the third in reserve about 5,000 yards from the trenches meant that the enemy front line was being held more strongly than previously calculated and that a counter-attack was a distinct probability. The Second Army confirmed this with documentary intelligence indicating the Langemarck-Gheluvelt and Hanneback trenches were objectives. However, a general intelligence assessment suggested that the German army had lost the initiative and, in order to maintain morale and combat effectiveness, the high command was having to rotate divisions quicker than normal. Brigadier-General Charteris wrote to his wife that 'things are going very well in the battle and the Germans are far nearer to giving in than ever before'.

It was quiet on 29 September with the Australians reporting artillery-harassing fire screening the German reorganisation of their defences. When a New Zealand intelligence summary suggested that resting German battalions deployed in depth were for defence and that only the front line was held in force, II ANZAC treated the assessment with caution and rated it 'subject to confirmation'. Although the New Zealanders were wary of the quality of the source, since its claim suggested a shift in the German defensive strategy, at least they had the confidence to pass their views to Corps HQ. Confirming intelligence from multiple sources is the sign of a well-organised intelligence structure. 4th Field Survey Company plotted seven enemy batteries pinpointed by sound ranging and by the RFC from gun flashes. From interrogations, the Australians learnt that the 15th Reserve and 3rd Reserve

Divisions were using old and damaged trenches and fortifications. A 3rd Reserve Division NCO admitted his company had recently arrived from Russia and that its trench mortars were using shell craters while machine guns were in old emplacements. Morale was high and the food good. Conversely, a prisoner from the 75th Infantry Regiment, 17th Division said that his company should have rotated and that morale was poor. A I ANZAC intelligence assessment confirmed that the Germans were not repairing the badly damaged Zonnebeke-Staden line and were alert to the threat against Broodseinde Ridge:

> At present he [the enemy] still retains the advantage of being able to concentrate troops under cover of this ridge, and in his efforts to retain it, further severe fighting and strong resistance can certainly be expected. That the enemy fully appreciates the situation was clearly indicated by the disposal of his counter-attack regiments, and the promptness with which they came into action in the fighting of 26 September.

The following day, as X Corps relieved V Corps, the two ANZAC divisions adjusted their frontage until they were opposite the 4th (Bavarian) and 19th Reserve Divisions. The intelligence summaries make interesting reading:

> At 1.30am it was reported that the Germans were massing at J.16b. Patrols were sent out and this was found to be correct. A barrage was therefore arranged at 4.45am and was put down to good effect. About 5.15am the enemy were seen to be advancing to the attack with their left on the Ypres-Menin Road. Visibility was poor despite the moon by reason of a ground mist; while it was further impaired by the German use of smoke bombs and flammenwerfer [flame-thrower]. Despite these advantages, the front-line garrison overwhelmed the attack […] before it could reach our trenches. About 6am the attack was renewed […] but again the enemy was driven off leaving two prisoners and one MG machine gun in our hands, while the ground in front of our lines was strewn with his dead. The counter-attack was pressed until 8 a.m. when it was finally dispersed by 'the very heavy artillery fire that was turned onto him'.

After three prisoners were captured from 92nd and 78th Reserve Infantry Regiments, 19th Reserve Divisions, the 92nd Regiment prisoners confirmed that their division had replaced 17th Division the previous day because of its heavy losses. The fighting had undermined the Second Army view that the German army was collapsing; indeed, I ANZAC reported increased mortar fire and sniping while X Corps experienced shelling from Keiberg, Broodseinde and Droogenbroodhoek, followed by two infantry attacks on its right flank aimed at straightening the German trenches. II ANZAC reported:

The study of aeroplane photographs taken during the last few days reveals no trace whatever of any trench work being done by the enemy West of the Zonnebeke-Staden Line. This line itself has been very badly damaged and appears in poor condition. Those pieces of trench which exist appear shallow. The only area where they observed any maintenance of these defences was an intersection between the main line and the Bellevue Spur. By correlating this information with their existing intelligence, II Anzac Corps found this lack of maintenance surprising. […] In view of the fact that captured German maps show that a considerable amount of new defence work had been projected in this area – including a great deal of wiring – this lack of work on the part of the enemy is somewhat remarkable. It seems probable that the enemy is at present determined to hold the whole area west of the Zonnebeke-Staden line merely as a crater position in spite of the fact that he must have at least three battalions west of this line. On the other hand he may be tempted by the present lull in operations to construct a line along the Gravelstaffel ridge. The erection of new wire should in particular be looked for.

The Second Army believed that the Germans were concentrating on defending the most tactically important areas, such as Broodseinde Ridge, at the expense of less important features such the Zonnebeke-Staden line. By assessing front-line rotations, studying enemy air reconnaissance routines and a report of the enemy consolidating its artillery into four groups, the Second Army predicted an attack on 1 or 2 October, but the objective had yet to be identified. Lieutenant-Colonel Mitchell noted that:

> Local counter-attacks will of course continue […] but should these fail it is unlikely that he will use up all his intact counter-attack units and reserves by flinging them too hastily into battle. It seems more probable that he will rely more on his artillery to keep our attack within bounds … In fact his future defensive policy may probably be in the nature of a carefully prepared counter-offensive which would take place one or several days after our attack and when the position in the forward areas had resumed a more or less normal aspect.

During the morning of 1 October, the New Zealand Division reported a working party digging a trench near Oeylker and that snipers had shot five of thirty enemy working on shell holes and that about twenty Germans seen near 'Dear House' were adapting shell holes and ruined buildings. The New Zealand front line and several battery positions had been heavily shelled during the night. Three attacks between 'Cameron Covert' and 'Joist Farm' allowed HQ Second Army to report that evening, 'Situation unchanged'. Reports from X Corps that some prisoners had been at Verdun until the end of August led to the conclusion that the Germans were transferring units from one active front to another active front because the Third Battle of Ypres was draining their divisions. On the same day, General Robertson assessed the probability of a German counter-attack:

> The enemy appreciation of the present situation doubtless turns largely on his experiences and the result of his tactics during the September fighting; two main considerations are probably prominent in it:
> 1. His tactics for counter-attack have failed.
> 2. He confidently expects our offensive will continue at (a) Menin Road, and (b) Broodseinde Ridge.
>
> The former needs no comment except that he doubtless now sees the necessity for a change in his defensive tactics. The latter will enable him to make plans for counter measures well in advance of our resumption of the advance.

Lieutenant-Colonel Mitchell wrote:

> That the enemy is changing his tactics is now evident. He has already engaged in a counter offensive independent of our last advance after we have become established on our new line. This has taken the form of deliberate well organized attacks on our new line about Menin Road Ridge [...] and Polygon Wood. These have followed our last advance after an interval of three days in which he has perfected his preparations after the confusion of his former failures. He will doubtless make another similar attempt in the same place or somewhere on the battle line within the next two days. This analysis clearly predicted the German counter attack at Broodseinde. The information collected over the last few days enabled even further prediction of the German Army intentions. The likelihood is therefore that he will wait until our advance with limited objectives ... has become established and consolidated and that he will [...] launch a large well organized attack or series of attacks at a time long enough after zero to ascertain our new positions. To do this would require at least 10-12 hours [...] It is more likely that he would defer the attack until daybreak employing the night in getting up and assembling his assault troops and putting on the heavy preparatory bombardment of our line.

There was little enemy activity on 2 October. The New Zealanders reported that during the night a new trench connecting the network of fortified shell holes in front of Boettler was being deepened and two new positions had been sighted near 'Dear House'. Two men carrying a long object had entered 'Deuce House'. From prisoners captured at Dochy Farm, 77th Infantry Regiment, 20th Division was identified; it had arrived from Russia a fortnight earlier. Soldiers from 79th Infantry Regiment and probably 92nd Infantry Regiment, both belonging to the 20th Division, previously located in Roulers, had been seen. The 79th Regiment was on the left flank of 77th Regiment, whose 3rd Battalion was in the front line while 1st and 2nd Battalions were believed to be in reserve billets east of Moorslede. The location of the 4th (Bavarian) Division was now uncertain. Thought to have relieved 23rd Reserve Division in the front line, prisoners were indicating its use as a counter-attack division, not as a relief. If correct, it meant that II ANZAC was opposed by the 20th and the 45th Reserve Divisions holding the line from the Ypres–Roulers Railway southwards. While there was confusion about the identity of the counter-attack division, the 4th (Bavarian) had been marked on a captured map in a concentration area about 1 mile north-east of Passchendaele, ready to counter-attack in a south-easterly direction.

Ten Corps confirmed the enemy opposite were the 19th and 45th Reserve Divisions. Because of the attacks over the previous two days, Mitchell had so much information that he was producing daily intelligence summaries in the morning and the evening; his overriding intelligence picture was of an offensive. When prisoners from the 77th Division told II ANZAC interrogators that German 'artillery aircraft have been unusually active throughout the day', this was reflected by the shelling of the front line of a fire mission to register a defensive barrage line and the Second Army confirming enemy aircraft directing divisional artillery fire onto British gun positions.

The Second Army saw a marked increase in enemy activity next day with II ANZAC and X Corps suffering from increased artillery registration. A prisoner captured during a raid confirmed the order of battle assessment on 28 September of two battalions per regiment in the front line. It was suggested by II ANZAC that the differing information given on 28 September and 2 October needed to be resolved because, if the latter was correct, it indicated a massing of troops. Captured maps and documents still indicated that the Langemarck-Gheluvelt and Hanneback sectors as objectives but since this information was dated 25 September, it was conceivably out of date.

With an attack seemingly imminent, Mitchell produced a supplementary intelligence report describing no-man's-land to be passable to waterlogged. Unlike the ground behind the Germans, the British struggled across networks of ditches, streams and canals usually providing natural drainage, but now churned up by rain and wrecked drainage into a thick muddy swamp littered with shell holes. A decrease in enemy air activity allowed RFC air reconnaissance from which 2nd Field Survey Company photographic interpreters located enemy batteries between the Ypres–Roulers Railway and the Menin Road, thus confirming X and II ANZAC reports that German artillery was being consolidated rearwards. Second Army interpretation of interrogation reports suggested that 25th and 19th Reserve Divisions were in the front line and that 20th Division had relieved the 4th (Bavarian) Division in the Passchendaele sector during the night of 28–29 September. The rotation of the Bavarians was significant because it had been assumed that 4th Division was the counter-attack division, but that it had been in the line for one day suggested the Germans were their rotating divisions in the front line daily, thus making calculating orders of battle difficult. While it was unclear if the 45th Reserve Division had taken over the sector south of the Ypres–Roulers, it was thought that 236th Division had been relieved on 27 September by the Bavarians. To add to the problem, prisoners were now indicating that a regiment from the 45th Reserve Division had been assigned a counter-attack role.

During the evening, Secret Service information from train-watching agents in Lille, dated several days earlier, reported that troops travelling from the south might be relieving or supporting the division between Zonnebeke and Gheluvelt and might be the 19th Reserve Division. However, Mitchell believed they might the 4th (Bavarian) Division or the two missing regiments of the 45th Reserve Division. BEF Intelligence had noted a rise in troop, aerial and artillery activity throughout the day and that probing counter-attacks at 'Cameron Covert' and 'Joist Farm' had been defeated. In spite of the confusion over the counter-attack divisions which was making prediction difficult, 3 or 4 October was now predicted to be the most likely date for an assault. Meanwhile, the Second Army had been planning a spoiling attack on 6 October to disrupt the Germans massing on Broodseinde Ridge. This was brought forward to 4 October. The German Fourth Army had intended to attack on the 3rd but their lack of success over the previous two days meant that the attack, codenamed Operation *Hohensturm*, was planned to start a day later at 6 a.m., also on 4 October.

With the 4th Bavarian and 19th Reserve Divisions waiting in their trenches, as the 45th Reserve Division, the counter-attack division, advanced across no-man's-land, the Second Army artillery opened fire at 5.25 a.m. with a rolling barrage intending to cover the advance of the leading British divisions and catch the Germans in the open. Within a few minutes, 45th Division lost eighty-three officers and 2,800 other ranks killed and wounded, while the 4th (Bavarian) Division lost eighty-six officers and 2,700 other ranks. A German officer later wrote: 'What actually happened in that swampy area in the dark and the fog, no pen of a living author can ever write.'

The crushing of the Fourth Army generated a severe loss of morale and a command crisis among the Germans but as it prepared to withdraw toward the Belgian coast, the curse of the Western Front, heavy rain, fell later in the day. The rainfall that autumn was the heaviest for many years and the British advance slowed to a cold, sodden crawl across flooded plains. Nine days later, Haig was forced by the conditions to cancel further offensives. Although the Fourth Army gained more ground with fewer casualties than on the Somme a year earlier, he was heavily criticised for persisting with an offensive that became increasingly unlikely to succeed. He had rejected Plummer's suggestion of using Messines Ridge as a launch pad and stuck with his philosophy of attrition in the belief that Germany could ill afford major losses of men and material, particularly with the US entering the war. Passchendaele was captured by British and Canadian forces a month later.

This review of the Battle of Broodseinde Ridge shows how fluid intelligence can be to identify enemy intentions and calculate orders of battle. Nevertheless, it is clear from research conducted by John Freeman just how far intelligence on the Western Front had developed since late 1916. The combination of tactical intelligence and reports from train-watchers had allowed the British to predict a major German counter-attack, although it appears to have been more by luck than judgement that British and Dominion gunners decimated the German Fourth Army. It later emerged in a train-watching report dated 3 October that the 4th Guards Division had been earmarked to deploy to the north but was diverted at Lille. Freeman concludes:

> The specialist training and expertise of the Intelligence Corps officers combined with good analytical discipline helped piece together the jigsaw of the German Army. It was thanks to the rise of the Intelligence Corps as a professional body that allowed this organisation to play an important part in the battle.

In November, Macdonogh was promoted to brigadier-general and appointed to the post of brigadier-general, intelligence, at the War Office.

For several weeks, the new Tank Corps had been pressing for 'tank raid' as a mobile alternative to the slow attrition of the Third Battle of Ypres. Haig badly needed a victory to deflect the criticism and selected the Third Army to attack Cambrai, a town that the Germans had captured in 1914 and which was a junction on a lateral railway route behind their lines. It was also on the St Quentin Canal that connected with the River Scheldt and Antwerp. To the east of the town were formidable German defences about 6 miles wide. Tank Corps commanders had selected Cambrai because they were convinced the ground was to their advantage.

The sector was regarded as generally quiet and defended by three divisions graded by GHQ as 'very good', two divisions graded as 'average' and a *Landwehr* division of men aged between 17 and 45 years unfit for active service, but not exempted for military service, graded as 'poor'. Documentary intelligence suggested that three more divisions were in transit from the Eastern Front, an assessment supported by train-watchers in occupied Belgium reporting increased rail traffic from the east on 18 November. Interrogations were also identifying units transferring from the Eastern Front. But since these reports would upset Haig's attrition strategy, Brigadier-General Charteris directed that the fresh divisions should not be marked on the GHQ railway map or mentioned in intelligence reports.

In a case of misplaced deception, General Sir Julian Byng, who commanded the Third Army, ordered that operations in the Cambrai area were to be reduced, which led to the Germans becoming suspicious. During the night of 17–18 November a raid near Havrincourt Wood captured several British soldiers and some documents; the Germans concluded that an offensive was imminent in the Cambrai area. Two days later, the Battle of Cambrai opened with the first demonstration of a modern all arms battle when 1,000 guns, 300 aircraft on air reconnaissance and artillery spotting, 250,000 infantry and 324 tanks stormed the Hindenberg Line on a 6-mile frontage. The cavalry divisions anticipated a canter through the mud and blood to a gallop across the green fields beyond. Captain Hotblack was still a Tank Corps intelligence officer and since one of his duties was to ensure that the tanks stayed on firm ground, he decided the best way to achieve this was to walk in front of them, marking the route with white tape. He guided one tank to its objective by walking ahead, under fire, to a strongpoint at Quennemont Farm. For this gallantry, he was awarded the DSO and earned a bar several days later when he took control of infantry who had lost their officers and organised an attack with tanks. Not surprisingly, Hotblack became a highly decorated Intelligence Corps officer earning two DSOs, two MCs and four mentions in dispatches. Thirty-nine tanks were destroyed by a German battery near Flesquieres that had not been identified by air reconnaissance, and seven by a lone German artillery corporal who was the only German soldier to be mentioned in dispatches during the war.

The following day GHQ Intelligence learned, probably from train-watching or wireless intercept, that the experienced 107th Infantry Division was en route from Russia and would be inserted into the line in the same area where Byng planned to release his cavalry across the St Quentin Canal. Meanwhile, GHQ Intelligence concluded from train-watcher intelligence that three more divisions were scheduled to be inserted into the line on 22 and 23 November – as part of rotation, it was assumed. Above the fighting, Baron von Richthofen and the German air force had air superiority. Snow was falling as tanks entered the village of Fontaine, but their crews were unprepared for their vulnerability in fighting in built-up areas. Meanwhile, four more Germans divisions were fed into the line between 25 and 27 November, which GHQ again interpreted to be reliefs. The next day fourteen divisions under command of the German Second Army overran British gains. Four divisions had slipped through the GHQ intelligence assessments. A German dressed in a British officer's uniform ordering troops to attack the Germans was shot as a spy. On 4 December, Haig instructed Byng to withdraw into trenches.

The defeat was a political and military embarrassment and a scapegoat was needed. At a Cabinet meeting on 4 December, into the sights of Prime Minister Lloyd George stepped Brigadier-General Charteris. Lloyd George accused him of not providing accurate intelligence to General Haig:

> General Charteris, who was an embodiment of the Military Intelligence which he directed, glowed with victory. For him, the news was all good. If there were

any elements that might have caused doubt in more discriminating minds, General Charteris had not discerned them and if he had, he was proof against their maleficent influence.

He then instructed Secretary of State for War Lord Derby to tell Haig to dismiss his senior intelligence officer. Behind the scenes, Lieutenant-Colonel Philip Sassoon, Haig's private secretary, had been lobbying that Charteris was incompetent and a risk to Haig retaining his position. Within the week, Haig reluctantly convinced him that he should leave his appointment as BEF director of intelligence early in the New Year; nevertheless, he insisted that his performance during the Battle of Cambrai should be formally investigated. Lloyd George intervened by persuading the editor of the *Times*, Geoffrey Dawson, to press for an inquiry into Cambrai. After Dawson had accused him as being 'Haig's worst enemy', Charteris bowed to the inevitable.

The Haig–Charteris relationship is regularly discussed at the School of Military Intelligence in terms of 'should the intelligence officer provide intelligence to suit the motives of a commander or should the intelligence officer provide a balanced view of the enemy situation, irrespective of the commander's beliefs?' Charteris was intelligent, popular, was an accomplished staff officer and valued the opinions of Macdonogh; however, his motives had become suspect after Major Cornwall had acted as head of BEF intelligence.

On 7 December 1917, GHQ BEF and the director of military intelligence agreed a BEF Intelligence Corps establishment of 3,000:

Army HQ Intelligence Company	9 officers
	36 other ranks
	3 cars, 10 motorcycles and 8 bicycles
Corps Intelligence section	5 officers
	17 other ranks
	7 motorcycles and 10 bicycles
Divisional Intelligence section	1 officer
	1 batman
	1 NCO
	1 motorcycle
Lines of Communication Company	26 officers
(Intelligence Police)	222 other ranks
	5 Metropolitan Police officers ranked inspector and above
	9 Metropolitan Police ranked sergeant and below
	1 car, 17 motorcycles and 110 bicycles

Intelligence Corps	Commandant
	Adjutant
	16 other ranks
	10 cars, 15 motorcycles and 2 horses
Headquarters Company (consisting of GHQ, War Trade, Cavalry Corps, Tank Corps and RFC intelligence sections, a Wireless Section and a Special Duties Section)	98 officers
	124 other ranks
	12 Women's Auxiliary Army Corps
	2 cars and 16 motorcycles

The presence of Women's Auxiliary Army Corps is the first mention of the long association the Intelligence Corps has had with women in uniform.

Italy had joined the Allies in 1915, which prompted a war fought in the Italian Alps against Austria. The Italians made little headway and after being defeated at the Battle of Caporetto between 24 October and 19 November 1917 they were driven from their positions until the pursuing Germans and Austrians outstripped their supply capability 20 miles north of Venice. In November, the Second Army contributed XI and XIV Corps as part of an Anglo-French expeditionary force of ten divisions rushed to reinforce the Italians.

Included in the force was its intelligence company of ninety-eight officers, three warrant officers, 109 NCOs and twelve clerks commanded by a commandant. The corps was spread between the corps, divisional and RFC headquarters and wireless intelligence. Lieutenant-Colonel Mitchell was the GSO1. One intelligence officer was Lieutenant Julian Huxley, later the influential evolutionary biologist. Lieutenant Louis Gluckstein (Suffolks), (later Colonel Lord Gluckstein MP) was at Victoria Station waiting to leave for Italy when he was handed a package and instructed to deliver it to GHQ. It contained the new cipher books. Intelligence officers maintained close links with the Italian army and censored news sheets issued to the troops and to supervised correspondents. An immediate intelligence problem was the multi-ethnicity among the prisoners of Czechs, Slovaks and Poles wanting to please, voluble Romanians overloaded with useless detail and disinterested Slavs. To ease the linguistic problem, prisoners and deserters helped interrogations through interpreters. Air reconnaissance proved a critical asset to cover the alpine terrain. The intelligence police, working with the Italian *Carabinieri*, confined their operations to the British zone.

9

The Western Front, 1918

Although Brigadier-General Charteris transferred to be the GHQ deputy director of transportation on 5 January 1918, General Haig continued to seek his advice. Appointed chief of intelligence was Major-General Sir Herbert Lawrence, a curious choice considering that he had resigned from the army in 1903 when Haig was promoted over his head to command the 17th Lancers. Recalled to active service in August 1914 as a major, he fought in Egypt, Gallipoli and on the Western Front. But within a fortnight Lawrence was appointed BEF chief of staff and was replaced by Brigadier-General Edgar Cox, who began the war as a captain.

Nine months after the Paris permit office opened, Lieutenant-Colonel Kirke moved Captain Woolrych to Switzerland and replaced him with Captain George Bruce, of the Argyll and Sutherland Highlanders. Bruce had been badly wounded at the Battle of Neuve Chappelle. His brother, also in the Argylls, had been killed at Le Cateau in 1914. After the War Office refused his application to return to active service, his fluency in French and German and ability to ride a horse and motorcycle saw him directed to the DMI and then transferred to the Intelligence Corps in mid-1915. Within the year, he was masquerading as an assistant provost marshal in Amiens, in reality on counter-intelligence duties. However, he contracted jaundice and returned to Scotland to recuperate. Still determined to return to active service, in January 1917 he applied to join the newly formed Welsh Guards, whose Scottish commanding officer was seeking Scottish officers. Kirke, on notice to rejoin his regiment, and Charteris failed to persuade him to replace Woolrych in Paris, a situation that was resolved by Field-Marshal Haig personally ordering him to do so for four months, with a commission in the Guards. By now, the Belgian Monthaye held an honorary British army commission as a lieutenant.

In June 1916 two German motor torpedo boats had intercepted the ferry *Brussels* and four months later the Flushing to Folkestone ferry. British intelligence reports were seized and details of espionage networks captured. Although a replacement ferry service was provided between Harwich and the Hook of Holland, it only operated when a warship was available. By 1918, Kirke believed that the English Channel had become a barrier and realigned the BEF GHQ covert operations by separating Folkestone from Paris and instructing Paris to take over Zurich and

Geneva. A member of the Geneva section was Captain Somerset Maugham. The decision infuriated Major Cameron because he regarded Paris as a subsidiary to Folkestone and sent a lieutenant to be his liaison officer. Kirke then handed GHQ Secret Service operations to Lieutenant-Colonel Reginald Drake and departed to be deputy director of operations at the War Office. However, Drake found that competition between Cameron and Commander Tinsley was unhealthy and leading to duplication. Matters were not helped by French and Belgian networks producing parallel intelligence.

After the 1871 Franco-Prussian War, Germany took over the management of the railways in Luxembourg and during the war, Luxembourg station and its marshalling yards had become a focal point for troops and material destined to the Western Front. After her father's release from prison in 1916, Margriet Ballegeer resumed her activities and, by 1917, was part of the train-watching network formed by Henri van Bergen, a former diplomat, whom she planned to marry. But the network was betrayed by Inspector Woulters of the Antwerp police and Margriet was condemned to death along with twenty-four others. Although she was reprieved on the eve of execution, van Bergen and Father Moons were shot on 16 March 1918 in Fort Edegem in Antwerp. Margriet eventually settled in Eastbourne.

One freezing February morning in 1917, Lieutenant Julian Fuller, MI(b)'s (Secret Service) main agent at Evian, and the Paris office interpreter, Jean Chocqueel, were at Annemasse waiting to meet a Jesuit priest who had the potential to report on German railway activity in Luxembourg. Bruce had someone else in mind, someone with first-class connections and desperate to return home.

Madame Lise Rischard had travelled from Luxembourg to France in January 1916 to visit her son, who had been conscripted into the French army. Her value was that her husband, Dr Camille Rischard, was the senior doctor for Luxembourg State Railways. A French citizen by virtue of her first marriage, several applications for a permit to return home through Switzerland had been rejected and then, in mid-March, she was introduced to Captain Bruce and Captain Campbell, both wearing uniforms, in Paris. They invited her to take a message to Luxembourg in return for a permit. She refused because respectable people did not engage in subterfuge and even though she became increasingly despondent each time her application was rejected, she continued to reject approaches from Bruce until a priest at confession suggested it was her duty to serve her country. At her next meeting with Bruce, Madame Rischard agreed with his proposal and while training in Paris was accommodated with Dorothy Done.

After several complications that tested her resilience and ingenuity, she returned to Luxembourg in early February 1918 and invited her astonished husband into her embryonic network. Having recruited several stationmasters and Edouard Bram, who worked in the marshalling yards and knew the railwaymen, Madame Rischard sent coded reports of German railway traffic to Captain Bruce in letters until she accepted an offer to write for the country newspaper, the *Landwirt*, and then convinced the editors to allow her to insert coded messages in her articles. In order to outwit German censors, the editors agreed to insert very minor adjustments to the Gothic text as a signal that the edition included a coded message. The British Embassy then bought copies and sent them by diplomatic courier to BEF GHQ via the Paris office. At the GHQ Cipher Office, Captain A.W. Speyers decoded the content and sent the results to the GHQ Intelligence Section for collation and, when relevant, information marked on the 'railway map'. Nil reports could be equally significant as a detailed report.

Such was the value of Madame Rischard that Drake and Bruce decided to send a Belgian officer named Lieutenant Albert-Ernest Baschwitz Meau to help her and to improve communications. He had lived in the Belgian Congo for several years and, in August 1914, had joined the *Corps de Volontaires Conglais* but was captured three weeks after war broke out. He escaped several times, twice with British officers, before making a successful home run. However, he was prevented from returning to the front line and his name was passed to Captain Bruce by Captain Sidney Buckley, an RFC observer shot down in April and now teaching escape and evasion in Paris, having taken over this aspect from Woolrych. He knew Baschwitz Meau from his escapes. On 30 January Baschwitz Meau transferred to the British army and began training in Paris, which included an exercise in the Fifth Army area of operations near Hazebrouck. The next problem was to infiltrate him into occupied Belgium.

Early on 13 September 1915 Captain Thomas Mulcahy-Morgan (Royal Irish Rifles), of No.6 Squadron RFC, took off in his BE-2c with a Belgian agent named van der Leene as a passenger; he landed near Oygem in Belgium shortly before dawn but the aircraft hit a tree in a wood and his passenger broke both legs. Van der Leene was cushioned from further injury by a basket of homing pigeons he was carrying. Both men changed into civilian clothes but were captured about an hour later. Mulcahy-Morgan was sent to a prison camp. Van der Leene was never seen again. Mulcahy-Morgan later escaped and reached England in April 1917. The experimental flight led to the RFC forming Special Operations flights in direct support to GHQ Intelligence. This included agents with baskets of homing pigeons strapped on their backs being parachuted from Handley-Page bombers. Kirke tried to convince the RFC to deliver pigeons, but the pilots were distinctly unenthusiastic about having anything to do with them, let alone being involved in a dogfight while carrying a basket.

Successful experiments by the pigeon-fancier Sergeant Lynon to drop a basket by parachute led to GHQ directing the RFC to deliver baskets into occupied Belgium. Another experiment was for an alarm clockwork to release a basket carried by balloon. Attached to the leg of the birds were sheets headed

'*Pour La Patrie!*' '*Vivent Les Allies!*' '*Demand de Renseignements*' and instructions for finders asked to fill in a form detailing German locations and units, insert it in the aluminium capsules and release the birds. Although the punishment in occupied Europe for being found with a pigeon was usually execution, the Germans never solved the problem. Pigeons released at 11 p.m. could be back in the GHQ loft within ten hours. The expected homing success rate was set at 5 per cent, although it actually achieved 40 per cent. When air losses meant that the RFC were unable to deliver Baschwitz Meau, Major Bruce investigated the option of using a balloon, suggested by Captain Payne Best.

Having analysed the German defence in depth during the grim fighting of 1917, the British were in the process of changing the front line to an 'outpost zone', later renamed the 'forward zone', to blunt an attack, supported by strongpoints in the 'battle zone' designed to mount stiff resistance. When the Fifth Army took over French positions the defences were incomplete and there were too few troops to organise defence in depth. The battle zone consisted of battalion redoubts but not all were mutually supporting and were therefore vulnerable. By the middle of February, the GHQ Intelligence Section was predicting a German offensive against the Third and Fifth Armies, but Haig concentrated on the former defending the ports and coalfields, leaving the Fifth Army on its right thinly spread.

The wintry weather of January improved in February and March and allowed air reconnaissance. During one week, air photographic interpreters analysing several thousand photographs noted clear evidence of a steady build-up of troop concentrations and small supply dumps nicknamed 'lice'. The political turmoil after the Bolshevik Revolution led to Russia and Germany signing the Treaty of Brest-Litovsk on 3 March, bringing the fighting on the Eastern Front to an end. Overnight, the Germans were able to transfer large reserves to the Western Front. As the Germans redeployed, the French believed that main weight of an offensive would be against them in the Champagne region with Paris as the objective; however, with its intelligence picture BEF GHQ Intelligence believed a German attack near Royce to be most likely. Brigadier-General Charteris noted on 3 March:

> The Third Army is rather concerned about some new marks on air photographs in the fields by the road of the German back area. The track leading to them may mean some form of German tank. I think there are too many in one place to be tanks. The Fifth Army has something of the same sort from its photographs of areas near St Quentin, and thinks it is ammunition brought up on artillery tractors. Whatever they are, it points pretty conclusively to a very early offensive.

German diplomats were spreading information that Calais was the objective. Brigadier-General Cox used the railway map in his briefings to Field-Marshal

Haig to show German divisions transferring from the Eastern Front. Train-watcher intelligence suggested 100 artillery batteries moving to Cambrai. By mid-March, strong intelligence indicating that the Third Army near Arras was likely to be attacked was being strengthened by deserter information and air reconnaissance. Signals and documentary intelligence identified that the experienced General Oskar von Hutier had arrived from Riga with his battle-hardened Eighteenth Army. Lieutenant-Colonel Stephen Butler, the Fifth Army GSO1 (Intelligence), was not convinced by the intelligence and he believed the ground in front of the Fifth Army was unsuitable for a major assault. In spite of the increasing threat, in early February Cox appointed Lieutenant-Colonel Stephen Butler as his deputy chief of intelligence, from his appointment as the Fifth Army GSO1 (Intelligence) and replaced him with Lieutenant-Colonel Francis Piggott (Royal Engineers) from the army's Operations staff in mid-March. When two Alsatian deserters crossed the lines in the Fifth Army sector and claimed they had overheard two officers discussing a major offensive planned for 21 March, the information was sent to GHQ, but the two Intelligence Corps officers sent to conduct a detailed interrogation crashed their car.

During the foggy early morning of 21 March, after nearly five hours of bombardment spread across 150 square miles, in Operation Michael three German armies attacked the Fifth Army and the right wing of the Third Army. Covered by gunners, who had lowered their sights to hit the front line, stormtroopers spearheading the offensive bypassed strongpoints and infiltrated the British front line to a depth of about 4 miles and attacked HQs, logistic centres and gun positions. Corporal Shirley had been interrogating prisoners and translating captured documents at the Arras prisoner-of-war cage and at HQ VI Corps until he returned to the front line with an I-Toc detachment in September 1917. His detachment remained in position for as long as possible and, in close-quarter fighting, he then he joined a platoon as a rifleman and would be awarded the Military Medal for gallantry. As the British front line creaked badly, the intelligence police in the Forward Zones evacuated their offices, taking as many documents as possible, helped town mayors move civilians, disconnected telephone lines and destroyed homing pigeons. The following day Paris was shelled by very long-range guns.

Although the BEF fought hard it lost 20,000 killed, 21,000 captured and 35,000 wounded as it was driven back toward the Somme. On 24 March, as the Germans drove a wedge between the British and French near Bapaume, the French reverted to defending Paris and appealed to the US army for help. Although the RFC had lost thirty aircraft and the air staffs believed that bombing railways was counter-productive because trains could be quickly rerouted, attacking junctions, depots and marshalling yards were seen as effective. Luxembourg station and its yards were bombed. But the offensive lacked a coherent strategy and while the Germans relied on pushing troops into gaps, by 27 March the troops were exhausted and also demoralised by the lack of food and supplies in villages, fields and captured dumps. The Allies used the weakening impetus to counter-attack with fresh British and Australian divisions protecting the railhead at Amiens. Within the week, the German offensive finally stalled with a long and irreplaceable casualty list. On the other hand, the Americans had increased the confidence of the Allies.

Throughout the fighting, Madame Rischard had sent vital intelligence of German divisions arriving from the east, as well as the 200th Division from Italy, but having not heard from Major Bruce, she was not sure that the *Landwirt* was being received, although she did know from correspondence that 41 Rue St Roch was still operational. By 19 April her group had identified 206 divisions, a further nineteen in reserve and the locations of rear supply and ammunition dumps. GHQ felt that the Germans would attack Arras and that a subsidiary attack to the River Lys was a diversion to draw reserves from the town; however, HQ Fifth Army remained unconvinced that the ground was suitable for military operations. The sighting of German reconnaissance patrols between the Lys and the La Bassee Canal was assumed to be a deception, a view strengthened by prisoners claiming they had been instructed to divulge that Calais was the objective. When the First Army took over the River Lys sector, a badly organised rotation led to the Portuguese 2nd Division defending 7 miles of trenches. Fourteen German divisions then used gas to overrun the British and Portuguese. GHQ underestimated the weight of the assault to be six divisions. Arras appeared to be the objective. By next day, eleven enemy divisions had been identified but since they were not included on the known German order of battle, their presence was still assumed to be a diversion with the railhead at Hazebrouck the objective and the ports of Calais, Boulogne and Dunkirk then exposed. Amid increasing uncertainty about German intentions, on 11 April Haig issued his famous 'with our backs to the wall and believing in the justice of our cause, each one of us must fight on to the end' order.

In order to restrict U-boat operations, on St George's Day, the Royal Navy landed Royal Marines to blockade their base at Zeebrugge and although the attempt largely failed, the raid boosted home morale at a time when the sacrifices of the Western Front seemed pointless. Prior to the operation, Ulysse Knappen, a Belgian Lancer officer, his wife and two sons were arrested on 1 February 1918 for supplying information on Ostend and Zeebrugge harbours.

The following morning Brigadier-General Cox strayed into operational matters by suggesting that the British line should be shortened and that several divisions should be transferred from Italy and the Middle East as reinforcements. Intelligence reports suggesting that the offensive had stalled allowed GHQ Intelligence to insist on its assessment that the German advance toward Hazebrouck was indeed a diversion. In fact, the German logistic chain was near to collapse with railheads some 50 miles from the front and road convoys unable to lift sufficient ammunition and food and evacuate casualties.

Over the next month intelligence flowing into GHQ indicated that the German emphasis was shifting towards the French to the south. On 26 May, agents reported German units moving from Belgium and then documentary intelligence from a captured letter suggested an attack on the River Aisne. The Germans then drove the French from Chemin des Dames and headed toward the Aisne with the aim of splitting the exhausted British and French line before US forces could intervene. Wireless intelligence again convinced Cox that the attack was designed to draw the British from Arras, but Haig felt that the Germans would exploit their success by advancing toward the River Marne, which proved to be correct. Long-range artillery shelling again caused panic. The British rejected a French appeal for assistance because train-watching information was suggesting forty German divisions had not yet been committed.

The combat effectiveness of the German army was a point of disagreement between the British and the French in the early summer. While air photography and wireless intelligence provided information, it was the human intelligence gained from prisoners that became crucial. In mid-June, Second Army interrogations indicated that an attack against Ypres had been postponed, probably because the Spanish influenza that would devastate the world after the war was already affecting a demoralised German army weakened by poor food, lack of medicine and four years of fighting. An 11th Reserve Division prisoner said in mid-May that morale in his regiment was low from poor food and rags as uniforms, but as trenches and supply depots were captured and as it passed through thriving French villages, morale had risen; indeed, an incentive to advance was food. The abundance of supplies also had a demoralising effect because press reports in Germany were suggesting that U-boat attacks had driven Great Britain to near starvation. By now, severe restrictions of fuel were depriving the Germans of the ability to fly air reconnaissance sorties. Further indications of low morale were several instances of insubordination. Knowledge of enemy morale has always been an indicator of combat effectiveness. While suggestions that German proposals for prisoner exchange and preliminary peace talks indicated to Haig that the Germans were anxious, Brigadier-General Cox generally excluded political intelligence assessments from his intelligence summaries.

Meanwhile, Captain Bruce and Lieutenant Baschwitz Meau, in Paris, investigating the use of a balloon to infiltrate him across the front line, had calculated a flight path to a suitable landing place. Selecting the optimum meteorological and wind conditions, he launched at 2.20 a.m. on 19 June from about 5 miles behind the British lines. Rising into the night sky, Baschwitz Meau drifted over the front lines and landed 25 miles north of Luxembourg. Baschwitz Meau, now using the *nom de guerre* Conrad Bartels, released the balloon to disappear into the dawn and walked to Luxembourg where he introduced himself to a decidedly suspicious Mme Rischard.

On 4 July reports from prisoner and train-watching networks of an imminent attack on the French in the Champagne region did not convince the British to change from predicting an attack in the Lys salient. On the same day, the capture of about 1,470 prisoners during an attack by the Australians and Americans at Hamel was significant because the rationale for the attack was based on the German low morale. Australian patrols then revealed the suitability of the open and firm terrain south of the Somme for a larger offensive. After the battle, British aircraft dropped 100,000 rounds of ammunition. When three German armies attacked the French in the Rheims area on 15 July, Haig transferred four divisions but remained convinced the main attack would be against Ypres in order that the Germans could improve their tactical position for the winter, as opposed to the previous view of a drive to the Channel ports. But within three days, the offensive stalled.

In spite of several successes, after three months of manoeuvre warfare, the Germans were demoralised and exhausted. Train-watching intelligence of the arrival of Austrian divisions led to GHQ Intelligence concluding they were a powerful reserve; nevertheless, it was an assessment based on order of battle, as opposed to combat effectiveness and motivation. Cox still believed the Channel ports were the objectives. In the first week of August, he returned to Britain on sick leave, having succumbed to influenza. One of the privileges of the intelligence police was to provide King George V with close protection when he visited the Western Front in August 1918.

In spite of the American Expeditionary Force itching to become involved in an independent role, the Allies drove the Germans from the River Marne. After the BEF had been reinforced with divisions rushed from Palestine and Italy and replacements held in Britain, French and British commanders decided to force the Germans from the vital Amiens–Paris Railway. They selected the River Somme as the inter-army boundary and aimed to make best use of the tank country of the Picardy countryside, as opposed to the poor going in Flanders. The defending German Second Army was weak in a sector regarded as quiet and was regularly raided by the Australians. As part of a deception, two Canadian infantry battalions, a wireless unit and a casualty clearing station were sent to near Ypres. Troops allocated for the offensive moved only at night, artillery acquisition was conducted by sound ranging and air reconnaissance. When the Germans learned after a trench raid that an offensive was imminent on 10 August, Haig attacked early on 8 August with Australian, British and Canadian infantry and 500 tanks of the Fourth Army. They broke through German lines near Amiens, capturing 17,000 prisoners, and cavalry and armoured cars poured through a 15-mile gap south of the River Somme. Field-Marshal Erich Ludendorff, the German commander, called the defeat 'the Black Day of the German Army'. Armed with results from interrogations and documentary intelligence captured at a German Corps HQ near Wancourt, the BEF advanced towards the Hindenburg Line.

In November 1931 a former No.35 Squadron technician was sorting personal papers when he found his 1918 diary and noted that the entry on 28 September referred to a briefing for the attack on the Hindenburg Line and that squadron commander Major D.P. Stevenson had said there had been a change of plan because 'a subaltern took some papers from a German Staff Officer and they contained a complete plan of the defences of the Hindenburg Line'. When the technician asked the newspapers to investigate, this resulted in Lieutenant-Colonel Valentine Vivian, the Fourth Army GSO1 and a former Indian Colonial Police officer, confirming that information from the captured maps and documents had enabled the Fourth Army to change its plans, but that he did not know who had found the maps. Indeed, the finder probably did not know of their significance. Vivian's view was that 'Intelligence men do not go across No-Man's-Land and see exactly what the enemy system is. Intelligence must obtain their whole information from this side of No-Man's-Land', and that 'when you take good prisoners, do not kill them, for a dead Hun is no good to the Intelligence'.

Vivian said that during the fighting a German Corps HQ had been identified in a farmhouse at Wancourt near Frameville, not far from Amiens, and he had instructed that it be raided by a combined cavalry-armoured car force with instructions to kill or capture enemy in the complex and to search for documents. Every officer was given a detailed map of the German HQ. The force probably included Intelligence Corps interpreters. The raid infiltrated the shattered defences near Brettoneux and 9 miles later, overran the HQ and scooped documents, maps and publications into sandbags. Three hours later, the force reached British lines along with 200 prisoners and the sandbags delivered to Vivian. The newspaper then discovered that the 'subaltern' was Lieutenant Ernest Rollings MC, then serving with the 17 (Armoured Car) Tank Battalion, then attached to the ANZAC Corps. Born in Hereford, when his parents moved to Knighton, Radnorshire, he joined the Glamorgan Constabulary and on the outbreak of war was permitted to enlist in the cavalry. Bored with its inactivity, he transferred to the infantry and, after being wounded in 1915, was commissioned into the Machine Gun Corps in January 1917. He had then transferred into the Heavy Branch and became one of the first 'tankies'. During the Third Battle of Ypres, while commanding a Pioneer tank of C Battalion, he had crossed the River Steenbeck and been awarded an MC for rescuing a wounded officer and his men pinned down by enemy fire. Soon after the raid, Rollings was again wounded, in the head, and took no further part in the fighting. Awarded a bar to his MC, on being demobbed in 1920 he rejoined the Glamorgan Constabulary as a constable and remained in obscurity until his role as the finder of the map brought him fame. Lady Lucy Houston, the benefactor and philanthropist, presented him with a cheque for £5,000 and a scroll in a silver casket that was treasured by his family. In January 1932 he was made a Freeman of Neath and five years later was promoted to inspector. He left the police in 1943 as acting chief constable and worked in the Investigative Department of the Board of Trade until retirement. Rollings died, aged 73, in February 1966, his exploit largely forgotten.

General Haig then lost his third chief of intelligence when Brigadier-General Cox drowned while swimming at Berck Plage near GHQ at Etaples. During the German offensive, he had focused on providing intelligence at the expense of eating and sleeping and had become a heavy smoker. Lieutenant-Colonel Butler took over his role. On 2 September, the Second Army outflanked the Hindenburg Line and forced the German army to withdraw. During a visit to the First Army, Haig learnt from Lieutenant H.L. Watts (Intelligence Corps) that German discipline and morale had collapsed and the German army would retreat into Belgium. Aware that fresh divisions were occupying the Hindenburg Line, GHQ Intelligence remained cautious even though air reconnaissance had shown that the Germans had few strong positions in depth. In mid-September Brigadier-General Sidney Clive, head of the British military in the French GHQ since 1915, took over from Butler, who had never really gained Haig's confidence and whose strategic vision did not match Clive's.

As the Allied advance beat an army weakened by demoralisation, anarchy and mutiny and entered a starving Germany, the intelligence police were formed into sections of about eleven NCOs per corps. They were controlled by a GHQI(b) (Secret Service) officer split between two corps. During the advance they searched enemy HQs for documents and courier pigeons, checked for booby traps and mines, searched for concealed telephone lines and interrogated military stragglers and deserters. According to a Second Army report, most collaborators had left with the Germans, but a large number of people classed as 'undesirables' were rounded up for further investigation. In Germany, the detachments joined the occupation authorities formed usually of an Intelligence Corps officer, a GSO3 and assistant provost marshal or a town major, and liaised with mayors and local authorities. They also debriefed civilians repatriated from enemy-held territory. They also helped the military police post proclamations, enforced regulations restricting the movement of civilians, detained those unable to provide proper documentation, and kept a constant watching brief on individuals notified by GHQI(b). In conducting an accurate census, the intelligence police arranged for communities to receive food, notified the medical authorities of those with infectious diseases, attended to the old and infirm and arranged the billeting of troops. And, as always, collected information.

10

Arabia

During the war the economy of Arabia dived as the Royal Navy blockaded ports and prevented the delivery of grain and other food. When the number of pilgrims had dwindled to almost none in 1915, thereby restricting intelligence collection opportunities, British ships began to deliver pilgrims to Jeddah, from where they were guided to Mecca.

Judging by documentary intelligence captured in 1918 the Turks had considered landing in Cyprus in December 1914 after a deputy governor of Alexandretta had supplied HQ Fourth Army in Syria and Palestine with details of British forces and Greek-Cypriot attitudes. The governor also revealed that his son, an army officer and a man familiar with Cyprus, had spent two hours with a Turkish-Cypriot customs official in Larnaca, during which they learned that the coast was practically defenceless.

Great Britain had annexed the island from Turkey on 5 November 1914 and found that ethnic tensions between Christian Greek Cypriots and Muslim Turkish Cypriots were rife, as was factional rivalry between pro- and anti-Young Turks and royalist and nationalist Greek Cypriots. An added complexity was that some Turkish Cypriots held grievance because they had contributed funds to the two Turkish navy battleships seized by Great Britain.

When Sir John Clauson, a civil servant with a reserve commission in the Royal Engineers but no active service experience, arrived as the second high commissioner, he found that the equivalent of the Defence of the Realm Act had not been applied. Establishing a defence committee, he introduced post and newspaper censorship, detained German and Austro-Hungarian ships and their crews and appointed courts at which enemy aliens were required to sign to say they would not leave the island without permission and would not engage in activities hostile to British interests. Crucially, no Turkish Cypriots had been deported.

On New Year's Eve 1915, as a slaughterman in Larnaca opened his premises, he was confronted by three uniformed Germans, but his report was disbelieved by Clauson and the police as a hallucination. As Turkey gained the upper hand at Gallipoli in the summer, Turkish Cypriots contacted prisoners of war held in the large camp at Karaolis, north of Famagusta, and used 'dead letter boxes' to pass information, such as distances to the coast and methods to reach Syria.

When, in March 1916, Great Britain and France agreed that Cyprus should be included in the French sphere of operations, Major Samson, who was running clandestine operations in the Eastern Mediterranean, sent Captain Woolley to establish an intelligence base on Cyprus, in addition to the one he used in Port Said, and to work with the French. Leonard Woolley, who had been part of the 1913–14 Wilderness of Zin project, was the Port Said I(b) (Secret Service) representative and was using a variety of vessels to deliver and collect agents and information into Palestine, Syria and Anatolia. One vessel he was using was the smart 150ft x 23ft Royal Yacht Squadron steam yacht *Zaida*, formerly owned by Lord Rosebery. While Commander S.B. Crabtree was brought out of retirement to command it, Woolley was in overall command of operations. Whenever Woolley was on deployment, Captain Weldon managed the Port Said office, if he was available. While in Cyprus, Woolley conducted disinformation to keep alive the notion that the Allies planned to land in Alexandretta Bay and thus force the Turks to defend its lines of communications. Shortly after landing two agents on Provencal Island (Dana Adasi), west of Mersin Bay on 17 August 1916, Woolley decided to reconnoitre the bay for agent rendezvous beaches and its coastal defences, but the *Zaida* struck a sea mine that killed a dozen men. The survivors, including Woolley, were captured. Not only was the Admiralty annoyed that an army officer had been in command of a vessel, but the French were furious that a minefield had been compromised.

Meanwhile, Major Holt-Wilson had reviewed intelligence operations in the Middle and Near East and recommended to Vernon Kell and Mansfield Smith-Cumming that R Organisation should be reformed as the East Mediterranean Special Intelligence Branch (EMSIB) with the role of supporting both Egypt and Sudan GHQs with A (Positive Intelligence) Branch and B (Counter-Intelligence) Branch. R Organisation had failed to recruit a single officer in the Turkish army as a source. Captain Richard Hadkinson (Intelligence Corps), sent to Cyprus, persuaded the French to release five tugboats to patrol the Cyprus coast. Captain Ian Smith (Somerset Light Infantry) in Port Said controlled clandestine operations in Palestine and southern Syria. He had been a vice-consul in Anatolia in 1914 and had witnessed the first stirrings of the brutal Armenian genocide.

Captain Weldon also returned to Egypt on board the *Aenne Rickmers*, which had been repaired at Mudros and was manned by the crew of the *River Clyde*. When it had been fully repaired in dry dock, he recommended floatplane and clandestine human intelligence operations along the coasts of Syria and Asia Minor. One issue was the increasing number of U-boats in the Mediterranean and the ship provided air support for a French cruiser searching for their lairs. In August, the ship raised the White Ensign and was renamed HMS *Anne*. Following a brief bombardment of Haifa by two French warships, the ship opened fire on a Turkish schooner close to the shore en route from Cyprus to Tripoli and watched the shell explode among a troop of Turkish cavalry. Welford provided more air support for French warships loitering in the Alexandretta Bay and then off Beirut. One aircraft reconnoitered the railway to Damascus. On arriving back in Port Said, Welford checked the GHQ map store to see if any of captured maps had anything of a confidential nature of Sinai and then remembered a draughtsman in the Surveyors' Department had been German.

At the end of August, Welford was on his way to repatriate twenty-nine prisoners when he used the guards, from the Glasgow Yeomanry, to reinforce a French landing force about to seize Ruad Island, a few miles south-west of Tartus. During the evening he landed two agents in a captured sailing boat with instructions to return to the island, but they never arrived. The following day, as part of a GHQ propaganda operation, a floatplane he sent to Nazareth dropped letters from prisoners of war praising their treatment. The observer saw nothing of interest. In early September, the ship helped evacuate several thousand Armenian refugees from the Bay of Antioch.

In October, the prevailing winds in the Eastern Mediterranean veering to an easterly proved hazardous for the underpowered aircraft. One failed to return from a reconnaissance of Beersheba. In November, Welford received a censored letter from the pilot, then a prisoner in Constantinople, in which he described the aircraft suffering engine failure; the two aircrew were rescued from hostile Arabs by Turkish officers and had been taken to Beersheba. The writer, Captain Sir Robert Paul, mentioned they had been escorted by an 'aviation officer', a snippet of intelligence indicating air activity at Beersheba. In the meantime, GHQI(b) (Secret Services) had made contact with a group of young Jews living in the village of Zichon Ya'aqov, about 20 miles south of Haifa.

The spread of railways during the late nineteenth century had seen European Jews migrate to Palestine, many agitating for a homeland. Among them was the Aaronsohn family from Romania. Aaron Aaronsohn, the eldest son of the patriarch and an internationally recognised agronomist, had established the Jewish Agricultural Experimental Station Centre at Athlit, near a crusader castle above a cove and about 2 miles from the village, to help the new arrivals learn about farming. The combination of the expulsion of 6,000 Russian Jews from Jaffa in December 1914, the genocide of the Armenians, a severe plague of locusts, and Djemal Pasha, the governor of Syria and commander-in-chief of the Fourth Army, threatening to send the Jews to 'another place', induced the Jews to fear for their lives.

Aaronsohn was conscious that apart from the Zion Mule Corps at Gallipoli, the Jews, as a nation, had not markedly contributed to the Allied war effort and believing that the British would attack Palestine, he realised he could help by supplying military, economic and political information, and by informing the world of the danger in which Jews in Palestine found themselves. Realising that his investigation into the locust plague would provide him with cover to form a network of contacts in positions throughout Syria and Palestine, he persuaded Djemal to appoint him as his scientific adviser.

During the mid-summer, Aaron's younger brother Alexander completed four months' conscription in a labour battalion in southern Palestine and when he infuriated Djemal by accusing an officer of corruption, Aaron persuaded him to escape to Cairo and offer the services of the family as a British intelligence source. Armed with the address of a naval interpreter, Alexander embarked on a US warship and presented himself at GHQ in Cairo, as a 'walk-in' source, something about which the department had very little, if any, knowledge. A month later, in an interview with Lieutenant-Colonel Stewart Newcombe (Royal Engineers), then commanding the GHQI(a) (Intelligence) at DMI Cairo, he explained that his family was well placed to organise an espionage network throughout Palestine and that his brother was a 'special adviser' to Djemal. But when he denied that gratuity was their motive, Newcombe appears to have concluded that the offer was too good to be true, especially in the Middle East where everything had a price tag, and he ordered Alexander to leave Egypt. Alexander then left for the US to seek financial and moral support.

Hearing nothing from his brother, in late August 1915 Aaron sent Avshalom Feinberg, a Russian poet, to Egypt, also using the US warship. When he met Captain Woolley, Woolley realised that Feinberg had something to offer and they agreed a plan that, provided it was safe, an intelligence ship would call at Athlit to pick up information. Woolley introduced Feinberg to Captain Weldon, but it was not until the moonless night of 8 November that HMS *Anne* was hovering about 3 miles out to sea. Weldon took Feinberg ashore in one of the ship's boats to the cove, in the expectation that he would return a month later. Assuming that a link had been established with the British, Aaronsohn then conducted a detailed reconnaissance by horse of north Palestine, during which he had conversation with German officers and filled three notebooks with information. Although ships were twice seen offshore, none approached the cove; Aaron was unaware that winter storms were preventing landings and HMS *Anne* badly needed repairs. The ship had also lost a second aircraft on a reconnaissance to Beersheba with the pilot captured and the observer, Lieutenant Horace Ledger (Indian army), shot by Bedouin while trying to burn the aircraft. Realising the plan had failed, Feinberg volunteered to take the intelligence to Cairo. Masquerading as a Turkish officer, he was crossing the Sinai Desert by camel when he was intercepted by a Turkish patrol within sight of the British forward positions and was taken to Beersheba prison where he was interrogated. While imprisoned, he wrote a poem in honour of Lieutenant Ledger. Aaron persuaded Djemal to release Feinberg and was making arrangements for him to go to London via neutral Romania when, in mid-March, a swimmer left a note from Woolley at the research station, but no more ships appeared.

Frustrated and unaware that Woolley had been captured, but still determined to contact the British, Aaron persuaded Djemal to allow him to go to Europe to meet other scientists. Taking the Baghdad–Berlin Railway, he then made his way to Denmark where he boarded a US ship bound for the USA and disembarked in the Orkney Islands. Arriving in London in October, Aaron was vetted at Scotland Yard and was immediately sent to the War Office where he met with Major Walter Gribbon (King's Own Royal Regiment) at the DMI. Gribbon, an expert on Turkey, was concerned that GHQ Cairo had failed to exploit the contact made by Woolley.

In September 1914, Lord Kitchener had tasked Ronald Storrs, the chief oriental secretary, to dangle the prospect of a caliphate in front of Sharif Hussein bin Ali al-Hashim, the powerful amir of Mecca, provided that he rebelled against the Turks. Hussein's powerbase was in the Red Sea province of Hejaz through which the Turks had built a railway between 1900 and 1908 connecting the holy city of Mecca and the important junction at Deraa in Syria. The British also needed a figurehead from one of the five principal Arab chieftains in modern Saudi Arabia to protect the left flank of the IEF D advance to Basra. After the government of India assessed that one was pro-Turkish, one was loyalist and three were uncertain, in October 1914, Captain William Shakespear (17th Bengal Cavalry), the political agent in Kuwait and a noted desert explorer who had mapped the An Nafad Desert, successfully negotiated support from the charismatic Emir Ibn Saud, the future king of Saudi Arabia. Saud had recaptured almost half of the remote Najd Desert in 1902 from the rival Rashidis but, after being defeated by a Rashidi–Turkish coalition two years later, he then waged a guerrilla war that saw him conquer the Najd and the eastern coast of Arabia by 1912. He then assembled the nomadic Bedouin into agrarian communities owing allegiance to a military-religious brotherhood. When, in January 1915, Hussein mentioned to Saud of the value of *jihad* against the Turks, Shakespear assured him it was British policy to protect Islamic holy places. Saud duly signed a treaty with the government of India in December; however, the death of Shakespear in an engagement with the Rashidis proved untimely.

Meanwhile, the British were becoming aware from defectors, desertions and prisoner interrogations at Gallipoli that subversive *Al-Fatah* societies existed within the Turkish army. Their principal motivation was that the nationalism promoted by the Young Turks was causing proud Arabs to be second-class citizens to the Anatolians. One proposal was that in exchange for an independent Arab state stretching from Aleppo to Aden, a British landing in the Gulf of Alexandretta would be supported by five Arab divisions in the area changing sides. But the failure of R Organisation to recruit any Turkish army officers to lead such a coup d'état was proving a hindrance. Newcombe could have resolved the problem if he had recognised the credibility of Aaronsohn's links with the Fourth Army.

When *Al-Fatah* offered Sharif Hussein bin Ali al-Hashim, the powerful amir of Mecca, leadership of the societies in January 1916, he appointed his third son, Feisal, to be his intermediary. It was perhaps inevitable that when Turkish counter-intelligence discovered that the plotters had links with the French diplomat Francois Picot, several were executed. But Hussein was not aware that under the March 1916 Sykes–Picot Agreement, once Turkey was defeated, the British would govern Mesopotamia, Transjordan (Jordan), and Palestine, while the French would govern Lebanon and Syria and the Russians would receive Kurdistan and Armenia. An international body would govern Jerusalem. The 'Sykes' was Lieutenant-Colonel Mark Sykes (Green Howards), assistant secretary to the War Cabinet and an expert on the Middle East. In 1915, he was convinced that the promotion of *jihad* by German intelligence officers was undermining British interests, but Egypt and India were reluctant to address the issue collectively because their priorities were defending the Suez Canal and Aden, Gallipoli, addressing German influence in East Africa and protecting oil interests in Mesopotamia. Lord Kitchener, the Foreign Office, the India Office (London) and the War Office and Admiralty directors of intelligence then jointly agreed that an organisation should be formed in Cairo, under the auspices of the Foreign Office, to co-ordinate military and political intelligence. Although the government of India objected to interference in their theatre of operations, compromise was agreed and in January 1916 the Arab Bureau was formed as part of Sudan Intelligence under the authority of the high commissioner of Egypt and the head of military intelligence, Colonel Gilbert Clayton.

After the evacuation from Gallipoli, the MEF reformed under command of General Sir Archibald Murray, who had been relieved as CIGS in January by General Robertson. Its intelligence function was divided between a section dealing with Egyptian and Sudanese affairs under the control of Clayton in Cairo and Khartoum and the MEF Intelligence Branch under the command of Lieutenant-Colonel Gerald Tyrell, who had fought at Gallipoli, at Ismailia. Each had a Department of Military Intelligence dealing with intelligence, counter-intelligence and censorship. The MEF also had Intelligence, Suez District and 5th Wing and the RNAS in support. After GHQ MEF moved to Ismailia, Clayton remained in the Savoy Hotel in Cairo with the Arab Bureau and began to assemble a group of Middle East experts. Commander David Hogarth RNVR, from Naval Intelligence and an archaeologist with great experience of Cyprus, Syria and Asia Minor, managed the function. Others included Major George Lloyd, an expert on regional politics and commerce, who had fought at Gallipoli.

On 6 June Lieutenant Lawrence edited the first of the 114 editions of the *Arab Bulletin*, a 'secret magazine of Middle East politics for officials and military commanders', of articles and comment on strategic and tactical intelligence of the Turkish armed forces, regional politics and tribal dispositions. It was essentially an intelligence summary. Hogarth summarised its editorial policy:

Since it was as easy to write it in decent English as in bad, and much more agreeable, the *Arab Bulletin* had from the first a literary tinge not always present in Intelligence Summaries. Firstly, it aims at giving reasoned, and as far as possible definitive summaries of intelligence, primarily about the Hejaz and the area of the Arab Revolt. Secondly, the *Arab Bulletin* aims at giving authoritative appreciations of political situations and questions in the area with which it deals at first hand. Thirdly, it aims at recording and so preserving all fresh historical data concerning Arabs and Arabic-speaking lands, and incidentally rescuing from oblivion any older facts which might help to explain the actual situation: likewise, any data of geographical or other scientific interest, which may be brought to light by our penetration of the Arab Countries during the present war. It is part of the Editor's purpose that a complete file on the *Bulletin* since its beginning should be indispensable to anyone who hereafter may have to compile for official use a history of the Arabs during the last three years, an Intelligence Handbook of any Arab district or even a map of Arabia.

The *Bulletin* quickly achieved the important military intelligence aim of immediacy of information, quality and credibility Sources of information, some open, some highly classified, included:

- Documentary intelligence from open (published) and closed (unpublished) enemy statements, newspaper and communiqués and letters.
- Human intelligence from the interrogation of prisoners, debriefing of informers and neutral travellers and agents in a network spread throughout Syria before the war through consular officials and agents. One station-master kept a record of every man and parcel transported into Damascus by the Hejaz Railway. Nomadic Bedouins in Sinai proved particularly valuable.
- Topographical and imagery intelligence.
- Wireless intelligence and intercept.
- Human intelligence, including from informants and 'walks-in'.

On the outbreak of war, censorship was enforced at telephone and telegram bureaux in overseas post offices under British control; information was collected from regional newspapers and intercepted mail and telegrams, and was collated in the Military Intelligence Branch in Cairo. When Lloyds at Port Said intercepted encrypted messages from US warships delivering financial aid to Jewish communities in Palestine in late 1914, this was brought to the attention of Brigadier-General Clayton, but Cairo lacked the ability to decode them and the raw material had to be sent to either England or India. Contributor identity added content credibility: for example, Gertrude Bell had travelled extensively in Iraq, Syria and Transjordan. It was assumed that recipients had good knowledge of events and individuals in the Middle East. Specific subjects were included in the equivalent of supplementary intelligence reports. The Foreign Office later described the *Arab Bulletin* as 'a remarkable intelligence journal so strictly secret in its matter that only some thirty copies of each issue were struck off [...] Nor might the journal be quoted from, even in secret communications.' That wireless intelligence and imagery intelligence played key roles in the Arab Revolt remained unrecognised until Dr Polly Mohs published her *Military Intelligence and the Arab Revolt: The First Modern Intelligence War*.

British wireless intelligence operations in the Middle East presented significant opportunities because the Turks had undeveloped communications security and very little crypto-analysis capability: it was largely dependent on civilian telephone networks which tended to be in the major cities. Shortly before the declaration of war between Britain and Turkey, a cipher used by Turkish diplomats was handed to an agent sufficiently long enough for it to be photographed. After its failure to bounce the Suez Canal, the Fourth Army laid 1,800 miles of landline for military communications from Damascus to Beersheba and Awja. Although two of the five mobile stations were carried by camels, the stations in Syria were largely inactive. In November 1916 a Turkish officer intercepted in the Red Sea was found in possession of cipher used by VII (Yemen) Corps. The communications of the German Asia Corps were managed by 105 Wireless Detachment with detachments at HQ VIII Corps in Sinai, the regional HQ in Beersheba and 300 Air Force Squadron and a fourth detachment deployable when required. Generally, the Turks were apprehensive of intercept, while the Germans accepted it as fact. In one instance in mid-1917 they sent a false message about a crashed British aircraft and ambushed a flight sent to destroy it.

In early 1916, GHQI(e) (Wireless Intelligence) began interception and soon unearthed important military wireless stations at army HQ in Damascus and corps HQs at Beersheba and Medina and modern Lebanon. In March, Captain Walter Gill (Royal Engineers) established an intercept station in Cairo targeting Palestine and found the perfect site for its aerials on top of the Great Pyramid at Giza; he was able to cover Anatolia and Northern Syria, intercepting Turkish and Asia Korps mobile traffic up to a distance of 1,000 miles and fixed stations 3,000 miles distant. His section was enlarged from fifteen to sixty all ranks. An Oxford physicist specialising in electromagnetic phenomena, Gill, too old to be commissioned in 1914, had enlisted as a private digging trenches on the Isle of Wight. When his expertise was recognised he was commissioned into the heavy artillery where his knowledge of trigonometry helped to locate enemy artillery. As the army developed wireless intelligence, he was transferred into the Royal Engineers Signals Section.

The Fourth Army was a critical target. Intercepts tracked the transfer of the 3rd Cavalry Division from Gaza to Jaffa and the arrival of the 16th Division commander in Damascus pinpointed his formation. By mid-1916, the British were reading virtually every message sent in Mesopotamia and Palestine including one sent by Enver Pasha compromising his use of his strategic reserve. Turkish orders of battle emerged, but analysts faced the same problems as interrogators of illiterate prisoners identifying their units by the names of commanding officers, which meant that unit nomenclatures could change quickly when commanders were changed, killed or captured. It was also difficult to identify the type of unit – division, brigade or regiment? Traffic analysis became important.

Initially, few of the operators were Turkish or German linguists and so encoded reports were sent to the War Office by wire, but it took about four weeks for translations to be returned, which meant intelligence did not always reach those who needed it in time to be of value. Oliver Strachey, a civil servant in India, transferred his considerable cipher skills to Egypt and within four months he and his small team were decoding an average of sixteen telegrams a day which strengthened intercept, crypto-analysis and dissemination. If there was a weakness, it was an inability to predict enemy intentions but this was resolved once intelligence staff realised how wireless intelligence slotted into the intelligence cycle.

Major Hugh Lefroy (Royal Engineers) arrived with a Special Wireless Section (SWS) of fifteen soldiers from Salonika, where he had evolved intercept and direction find, and was appointed to manage wireless intelligence operations throughout the Middle East and Eastern Europe. The SWS had also intercepted civilian communications, such as journalist dispatches. Two new stations at Larnaca on Cyprus covering Anatolia and northern Syria led to the SWS increasing its establishment to ninety-six all ranks. Further rationalisation took place when Lefroy took responsibility for co-ordinating intercept throughout Egypt, Mesopotamia and Salonika. Captain Gerard Clauson, then head of I(e) in Mesopotamia, took control of crypto-analysis in the same theatres, an arrangement that allowed an efficient exchange of findings and ideas. Decoding remained the responsibility of the DMI in London, which, to some extent, degraded the effort. Sometimes, wireless intelligence was deemed too precious for information to be disseminated, except as 'a usually reliable source' or, as Clauson preferred, 'as absolutely reliable'.

When Feisal and Ali learnt from *Al-Fatah* in Damascus that the Turks were planning another attack on the Suez Canal, on 5 June, they launched the Arab Revolt in Damascus. While Ali rallied 30,000 tribesmen and damaged 150 miles of the Hejaz Railway to delay Turkish reinforcements from the north, Feisal attacked Fortress Medina but encountered the gritty Fakhir Din Pasha, commander of XII Corps, whose troops repelled wild Arab charges. Five days later, after early morning prayers, Sharif Hussein symbolically fired his rifle at the barracks in Mecca from his home and within three days, the understrength garrison had surrendered. Ali's siege of the remainder in their summer station at Ta'if encountered a well-organised defence. The capture of Jeddah on 16 June opened an opportunity for support and supplies to be landed from Port Sudan.

Towards the end of January 1916, HMS *Anne*, HMS *Raven* (formerly *Rabensfels*), HMS *Empress* and HMS *Ben-my-Chree* (with British aircraft) had been formed into the East Indies and Egypt Seaplane Squadron. Weldon was appointed the military intelligence officer for *Anne* and *Raven*. The intelligence officer on *Ben-my-Chree* was Erskine Childers. In mid-April, *Anne* was rescuing the crew of one of its aircraft that had ditched off Wadi Gaza when it was bombed by two German aircraft. Since it was the first aircraft seen in the Eastern Mediterranean, Captain Weldon immediately wirelessed their presence to GHQ. In late April, the French floatplane squadron was disbanded. During its lifetime it flew 118 flights with no aircraft damaged during launches and recovery. An aircraft could be launched within five minutes and twenty seconds. Two aircraft had been captured and one airman killed. Commander Samson, now commanding the squadron, assured Captain Weldon that he was to continue his work from HMS *Anne*.

When Colonel Cyril Wilson, then governor of the Red Sea province of Sudan, was dispatched by Governor Wingate to assess the situation, he reported that the rebellion had been started 'without sufficient preparation and somewhat prematurely'; nevertheless, he remained in the port as a British resident in Hejaz province under the guise of 'pilgrimage officer' and not only established an Arab Bureau subsection, but also critically won the confidence of Sharif Hussein with his frankness. Major Kinahan Cornwallis and Colonel Alfred Parker, both from GHQ Intelligence, toured Hejaz in the month and concluded that a Arab victory at Medina was unlikely.

With their lines of communication to Medina threatened, the Turks rapidly repaired the railway and transferred supplies from the large garrison at Ma'an. When, in mid-July, Fakhri Din Pasha formed the Hejaz Expeditionary Force (HEF) at Medina and intelligence reports suggested that it included Germans, this presence had considerable negative psychological impact on the Arabs. An attempt by Cornwallis, Wilson and Major Pearson, an Egyptian army intelligence officer, in mid-June to transfer arms and ammunition, explosives, gold, two artillery batteries and mules from Port Sudan at Rabegh and Yenbo was met by successful Turkish subversion accusing Britain of intending to occupy Palestine and Syria. Cornwallis and Pearson eventually persuaded the sharif to allow one battery and its Egyptian protection to land. When HMS *Anne* delivered the second battery to Rabegh, such was the Muslim hostility that it was not permitted to land. In mid-July, the ship left the oppressive heat of the Red Sea and chaos of the ports and returned to its usual air reconnaissance and clandestine operations over Sinai, Gaza and Beersheba. Its aircraft spotted for the French bombardment of Mersina in Asia Minor and participated in a seaplane squadron raid on the railway junction at Afuleh and several raids on Turkish camps and a viaduct. On 31 August, HMS *Raven* was hit during a German air raid of the Port Said roads. In early August, Fakhri Pasha had sallied from Fortress Medina and drove Feisal 50 miles to a natural and formidable defensive barrier of hills 20 miles wide north of Mecca.

In a strategic review of an advance from Cairo through the Sinai Desert to Palestine, General Murray, believing that a diversionary landing at Aqaba would stretch the Turkish ability to protect their lines of communication, suggested to General Robertson in London that the revolt be controlled by GHQ Cairo. Robertson responded that for political reasons, it must remain under the political control of the high commissioner, and that he, Murray, must focus on advancing to Palestine. Murray withdrew the support of his Intelligence Branch. Meanwhile, intelligence was suggesting that the revolt had led to an increase in desertions, particularly by Arab officers resenting the Turkish–German alliance. Colonel Parker recommended distraction raids and naval bombardments of Syria and a landing to pin down Turkish troops, but his attempts to recruit Arab agents to sabotage the railway was largely unsuccessful. Meanwhile, the HEF had grown to 16,500 men, of whom 1,200 were confined to Fortress Medina and 8,000 formed the Railway Protection Group.

In late September, as Turkish forces advanced towards Feisal in Rabegh, Arab morale rose when his brother Abdullah, supported by Egyptian artillery, captured Ta'if. Ali then moved his forces from Medina to reinforce the defence of Rabegh. After the executions of several Syrian nationalists in Damascus in May, intelligence reports suggested that 15,000 deserters had formed two loose corps. Two officer deserters suggested that deserters could sabotage the railway near Ma'an. Meanwhile, Ali had formed a brigade of 5,000 Arab prisoners of war and deserters as a reliable component of his army.

Political disagreements in London and Cairo and Arab religious sensitivities led, early in the New Year, to the War Committee instructing the transfer of military and political assistance to the Arab Revolt to Governor Wingate. Clayton remained head of military intelligence. When Ronald Storrs met Abdullah at Jeddah to discuss military aid on the premise that Arab regional aspirations should not disrupt French interests in Syria, with him was Captain Lawrence, lying low after differences with senior officers in Cairo over the rationale of the revolt and Arab ambitions, and Colonel Wilson. Abdullah requested that a British brigade and a flight of aircraft help defend Rabegh, a suggestion that Sharif Hussein and Wilson had previously agreed was unwise, given that Christian intervention so close to Mecca might fragment the loose federation of Arab tribes. Admiral Sir Rosslyn Weymess, commander-in-chief, East Indies Fleet, and General Murray both acknowledged that although the Arabs were supported by warships, the Turks were not formidable and that wireless intelligence would give intelligence of Turkish intention. The War Committee rejected landing a brigade but did agree to aircraft. When discussions turned to the general conduct of the Arab Revolt, Lawrence impressed Abdullah with his linguistic skills, but he managed to be antagonistic, which led to Colonel Wilson writing to Clayton:

Lawrence wants kicking and kicking hard at that, then he would improve. At present, I look upon him as a bumptious young ass who spoils his undoubted knowledge of Syrian Arabs etc. by making himself out to be the only authority on war, engineering, running HM's ships and everything else. He put every single person's back up I've met, from the Admiral to the most junior fellow on the Red Sea.

Nevertheless, after Wilson agreed that he should conduct a five-day review of the Arab forces, Lawrence assessed Prince Feisal to be the most capable commander. He also returned with a shared vision of an independent Arab state. On returning to the Arab Bureau, he wrote an intelligence summary that overturned misconceptions in Cairo of the fighting in Hejaz. Examples of intelligence that he collected included that three Turkish regiments south of Medina had been reinforced by four battalions, each of 900 men; that cholera may have prevented a major advance to Mecca; and that the unpredictable nature of the Arab fighting methods and the long lines of communication were delaying an advance. He also confirmed earlier reports that the Turks at Medina had enough food were correct, but that they lacked forage.

He then proposed that:

- The Arab forces hold the barrier of hills between Rabegh and Mecca.
- The Arab practice of speed, raiding and loyalty suited guerrilla and irregular warfare.
- The headquarters of the three Arab armies be equipped with wirelesses to ease co-ordination.
- The Hejaz Railway should be attacked.
- The Arabs be equipped with artillery.
- While plunder should be payment for the Arab rank-and-file, the princes should be rewarded with money and that bribery and corruption should be ignored.
- A conventional army be raised from prisoners of war, deserters and nomadic Arabs to hold positions, fight formal battles and be a rallying point for flying columns, which essentially negated the suggestion of landing a brigade.

No sooner had Clayton instructed Lawrence to return to Hejaz as liaison officer to Feisal than a Turkish counter-offensive drove the Arabs back to Yenbo and the cover of the Red Sea Squadron. Hussein immediately requested six battalions – ideally Indian army Muslims, but he would accept Christians – but by the next morning he had changed his mind. With Murray still keen to draw Turkish troops from his planned advance to Palestine, Colonel Wilson offered support, seizing Aqaba as a base for attacking the Hejaz Railway. One prisoner reported that it was held only by a Turkish police company. In early September, HMS *Anne* returned to the Red Sea and provided naval gunfire support, bombing and conducting air reconnaissance of several Turkish-occupied towns. Wireless intelligence suggested the air raids were demoralising the Turks.

Although wary about Arab reactions to Christian pilots, in mid-November Sharif Hussein permitted C Flight, No.14 Squadron to land with four BE-2 fighters. It became known as the Rabegh Flight. In contrast to the Western Front features of inclement weather and the enemy, the pilots here flew in clear skies, rarely saw enemy aircraft and could penetrate deep into enemy territory to bomb and take photographs and sketch subjects of intelligence interest. However, midday heat affected engines and the best time to fly was early morning. Imagery intelligence of Aqaba and Wadi Rumm to the north reported that coastal artillery emplacements could be dealt with by naval gunfire.

After Colonel Wilson had persuaded Feisal in Yenbo on 27 December to outflank the Turks by seizing the port of Al-Weijh, 220 miles to the north, Lawrence joined as the liaison officer. Wilson undertook to provide imagery intelligence. Arab irregulars prevented the Turks counter-attacking from Medina and then on 4 January, Feisal advanced with 10,000 Arabs toward the port, his left flank protected by Red Sea Squadron, which was also carrying a landing force of 500 Arabs. By now, the Turks had learnt of the association of Lawrence and the Arabs and had posted a reward for him. Next day, Lawrence and a small patrol captured two Turkish engineers. One, a railway signals inspector from Fortress Medina, said he could only receive messages from Damascus and the lack of wireless operators had led to the risk of interception being ignored, a decision that had confined Turkish intelligence largely to low level human intelligence. The Turkish General Staff were also beginning to distrust their Arab soldiers. When the march was delayed by the failure of Feisal to send scouts to find wells and sources of forage, Lawrence cursed the lack of reliable topographical intelligence. On 23 January, the Red Sea Squadron landed 200 sailors and the 500 Arabs north of Al-Wejh and forced the surrounded garrison to capitulate thirty-six hours later. HMS *Anne* aircraft conducted air reconnaissance and 'spotted' for the warships, but lost an observer killed while he was transmitting messages. Documentary intelligence collected during the advance indicated that isolating garrisons, harassing lines of communication, the presence of Royal Navy in the Red Sea and the growing unavailability of gold to bribe sheikhs to stay on side was causing the Turks anxiety.

The victory marked a turning point in the Arab Revolt because, for the first time, Arabs had defeated the Turks. General Murray also welcomed that the siege of Fortress Medina and attacking the Hejaz Railway would divert significant Turkish resources from his offensive. British and French military missions arriving to strengthen the link between the Arab hierarchy and the Allies joined raids on the railway.

Colonel Wilson and Lieutenant-Colonel Newcombe, who commanded the British mission, both agreed with Lawrence that their arrival should be supportive, as opposed to executive as promoted by Wingate. Newcombe and his deputy, Major Phillip Vickery (Royal Artillery), who understood guerrilla warfare through his colonial experience as an Indian police officer, agreed the Arabs should be have a full role in the fighting. In mid-January 1917, wireless and imagery intelligence suggested that the HEF intended to tighten its perimeter by withdrawing from Rabegh and by reducing railway security by withdrawing small garrisons. The capture of a senior Turkish army officer carrying letters for Arab rulers in Yemen and a large amount of gold and war stores in a convoy heading east from Medina led to the Arab Bureau concluding that Turkish officials were reducing their links with sympathetic Arabs. Wireless and imagery intelligence targeted important Turkish units.

Meanwhile, General Robertson instructed General Murray to postpone any offensives and to send two divisions to the Western Front to replace losses suffered in the Battle of the Somme. After British forces in Egypt had crossed the Suez Canal and had defeated the Turks in a clash at Romani, Murray formed the Eastern Force and placed it under command of Major-General Sir Charles Dobell and in so doing, weakened his control of the advance across the Sinai Desert.

Meanwhile, Aaron Aaronsohn had arrived in Egypt in November and was being handled by Captain William Edmunds, a GHQ intelligence officer and former Levant consular service official. He was also interviewed by Major Norman Bentwich, a Zionist and officer in the Camel Transport Corps, to determine his trustworthiness and when this was recognised, Aaron learned that he would not be permitted to return to Palestine. However, he was a stranger in a strange land, the British army, and was impatient to prove his value and highlight the dangers to the Jews. On Christmas Eve 1916 he accompanied the trawler *Goeland* to Athlit. Also on board was Captain Ian Smith from EMSIB, who prevented Aaron from sending some food and gifts ashore. Indeed poor weather meant that two couriers were forced to swim from a ship's boat to the beach and worse, Smith refused to arrange shore-to-ship signals for future operations because they were less important and no influence on the military situation; more important was the delivery of military intelligence.

By early 1917, the EMSIB 'intelligence fleet' had been strengthened with the 160-ton yacht *Managem* hired from the Egypt Survey Department and the requisitioned Grimsby trawler HMS *Veresis* built at Selby in 1915. In December 1916, Captain Smith invited Captain Weldon to concentrate on the clandestine operations in Palestine and Syria using the *Managem* with Port Said and Famagusta as his bases. Lieutenant H.C. Salter (Intelligence Corps) controlled similar operations in Asia Minor in the *Veresis*.

In early January 1917 Aaronsohn moved to Cairo but still found himself sidelined by officers; nevertheless, he learnt of the Sykes–Picot Agreement. After a profitable meeting with Lieutenant-Colonel Wyndham Deedes, a senior intelligence officer, when Edmunds told him that someone who knew him in Palestine had arrived at Port Said, it turned out to be Josef Lishinsky, one of his researchers. After not hearing from her two brothers, Sarah Aaronsohn had sent Feinberg and Lishinsky overland to contact the British. Sarah had recently arrived from Constantinople and had witnessed the Armenian genocide. In her brothers' absence, she was controlling the network. As Feinberg and Lishinsky crossed the Sinai Desert, they had been ambushed by several Bedouin and Feinberg was killed. Badly wounded, Lishinsky pressed on and was found by an Australian patrol. As he was being debriefed, the quality of the information led to GHQ Intelligence transferring contact with Athlit to EMSIB. Two days later a swimmer landed at Athlit from a French motor torpedo boat that was lost in rough seas. After Israel overran Sinai during the 1967 Six Day War, an elderly Bedouin took an Israeli officer to a date tree known as the Jew's Grave, which turned to be that of Avshalom Feinberg. A seed in his pocket had sprouted. He was later buried in the Mount Herzl military cemetery in Jerusalem.

On a moonless night in mid-February at about 10 p.m., with Captain Weldon in command of his first operation with *Managem* and with Captain Smith and Aaron Aaronsohn on board, the yacht hovered about 3 miles offshore, while Weldon used a surf boat to land Lishinsky, who was to collect Liova Schneersohn and Reuven Schwartz with the intelligence from the Experimental Centre and meet the boat at midnight. To their delight, Aaron was on board. Schneerson returned to the *Managem*. During the voyage back to Egypt, Aaronsohn and Schneersohn agreed a password for the group: *Netzakh Yisrael Lo Yishaker* ('The eternity of Israel will not lie') from 1 Samuel in the Bible. Usually known as NILI, EMSIB knew NILI as A (Aaronsohn) Organisation. The network included a civil engineer providing information on roads, water, bridges and Turkish plans; a doctor who practised at Afule and Ramle who collected information from German and Turkish officers and British prisoner-of-war patients; a man running a fake store at Afule railway traffic and a Turkish army Jewish officer-cadet who reported on activity in Damascus and Aleppo and who used his friendship with a colleague to enter the main German wireless room. He also selected targets to be bombed. In Cairo, Aaronshon translated the information and suggested corrections to the intelligence map, but rather undermined his credibility by interfering with tactical decisions.

Over the next few months on moonless nights when the weather permitted, the *Managem* usually hovered about 3 miles offshore from rendezvous beaches. Generally dressed in a blue jersey, army tunic, dark flannel trousers and a pair of tennis shoes and armed with a rifle and a holstered revolver, Weldon would be rowed ashore by a couple of his trusted four Syrian boatmen – a father and his three sons – in a boat armed with a Lewes gun. On reaching the surf line, when calm, an anchor was dropped and the boat allowed to drift ashore, stern first, and Weldon and his group waded ashore. If it was rough, the boat skimmed through the surf on to the beach. When the sea conditions were too rough to approach the a beach, generally in the autumn and winter, a swimmer capable of swimming 500 yards in any condition to and from the boat was used. One was a Zion Mule Corps private who had fought at Gallipoli. Ashore, Weldon interviewed potential agents and sources and collected information. He also interviewed people in Cyprus likely to be of use in Asia Minor and Syria. Sometimes he collected documents and items from dead letter boxes buried in the sand. He usually navigated back the *Managem* by selecting a star. On the return voyage, he usually examined the information and enciphered it for transmission to EMSIB. Weldon fed the cover that the yacht was being used to hunt U-boats until the Cyprus chief of police mentioned it only left harbour on moonless nights.

One of his first deliveries was from an elderly Syrian near Tyre, who disguised himself as a beggar to mingle with Turkish soldiers, and was tasked to take messages to EMSIB agents and collect information. In mid-March, after several attempts, Smith was again on board when two NILI agents were landed at Athlit; one turned out to be unfit to land. Weldon was in the boat about 200 yards from the beach waiting to collect one of the agents when he noticed the *Managem* was drifting towards him from its position nearly 3 miles offshore. Unable to shout, he waited until the yacht was sufficiently close to hail the captain. The agent ashore was picked up the following night and then Weldon set course to Tyre to collect the elderly Syrian; however he was at the rendezvous and although the beach was searched and the dead letter box checked, there was no sign of the Syrian or his information. When he returned to Egypt, Weldon was able to acquire revolvers and ammunition for the EMSIB agents from a police armoury. He obliterated the serial numbers by filing.

Encouraged by the Anglo-French Congress opting on 26 February for a spring offensive, General Murray rejected the opinions of Aaron Aoronsohn. Historically known as *Azzah* ('the strong'), Gaza had been the gateway to the Levant from the desert for centuries. The town straddled an oblong hill and was surrounded by cactus and fruit orchards on the southern flanks and olive groves to the north and east. To the south was the 40-mile-long Wadi Ghazze and flat desert; to the south-east lay the hillock of Ali Muntar. The defence had been entrusted to Major Tiller, a German officer, commanding three battalions and two batteries of the Sinai Defence Force. On 10 March wireless intercept picked up a message ordering the wireless station in Gaza to transfer to Jerusalem. Although it actually referred to a routine deployment of wireless stations, GHQ Intelligence interpreted it as a Turkish intention to evacuate Gaza and encouraged opinion that the Fourth Army did not intend to defend the town. While the Turkish army had shown a weakness to exploit offensive operations – most recently at Aden and the attempt to cross the Suez Canal – they had shown at Gallipoli and Ctseshion a stubbornness in defence.

Ten days later, intelligence assessments suggested that the defence was 'steadily deteriorating' and there were 'heavy losses' of deserters. In fact, Tiller had been reinforced by seven battalions and three field batteries, one German and one Austrian; the 53rd Infantry Division at Jaffa had been warned to reinforce Gaza. When Colonel Friedrich Kress von Kressenstein, a member of the German military mission, moved his headquarters from Beersheba to Tel esh Sheria on 24 March, air reconnaissance showed more tents than usual and the building of a railway spur to the town. Wireless intelligence then indicated Austrian presence and the transfer of a wireless station from Beersheba. Interrogations suggested that far from withdrawing, the Turks intended to defend Gaza. Lieutenant-General Dobell issued orders that 'an early surprise attack was essential [...] otherwise it was widely believed the enemy would withdraw without a fight'. Significantly, his intelligence estimated the enemy order of battle to be 2,000 men; in fact it was 3,500.

The confidence that spread through Eastern Force was enhanced by the news that the Mesopotamia Expeditionary Force had recaptured Kut-al-Amara on 24 February. Maude had reformed II Corps into III (Indian) Corps. After the loss of Kut, Major Leachman disappeared into the desert with his faithful servant, a roguish Arab, and spent months rebuilding his intelligence networks, undermining German attempts to subvert the tribes and attacking Turkish supply lines using the River Euphrates. His activities gained him the accolade 'OC Desert'. A useful asset were children to whom he paid a small fee for information. He trained mounted Arabs to patrol the desert and help collect taxes. In return, he built an irrigation scheme at Ramadi. But he had his enemies among the Arabs, who tried to kill him.

During the advance, wireless intelligence had provided the line of retreat of every Turkish division. After being repulsed at the junction of the Diyala and Tigris rivers 35 miles south of Baghdad, Maude used wireless intelligence to block a surprise attack by shifting the majority of his army north, forcing Khalil Pasha to mirror the move. The remainder of his force Maude left in position to cross the Tigris and destroy the single regiment guarding the original crossing point. Khalil abandoned Baghdad, leaving Maude to enter the city on 11 March. Some 9,000 Turks were captured.

The Eastern Force had been strengthened by the desert column of the ANZAC Mounted Division and Imperial Camel Brigade commanded by Lieutenant-General Sir Philip Chetwode, an experienced cavalryman. In the opening phases of the battle for Gaza, on 25 March, ANZAC Mounted Division patrols found suitable places for the infantry and guns to cross Wadi Ghazze but the advance was delayed by early morning thick coastal fog that restricted the ability of No.1 Squadron RFC to take off. However, Turkish aircraft operating in clear blue skies machine-gunned the two leading infantry brigades. The Imperial Camel Brigade and ANZAC Mounted Division surrounded Gaza during the day, cut telegraph lines and captured the general commanding the Turkish 53rd Division and his headquarters, on their way to reinforce Gaza. But the jamming of wireless transmissions and weak staff procedures hindered the infantry attacking from the south. Dobell signalled Major-General A.G. Dallas, commanding 54th (East Anglian) Division, shortly before midday:

> I am directed to observe that (1) you have been out of touch with Desert Column and your own headquarters for over two hours; (2) no gun registration appears to have been carried out; (3) that time is passing, and that you are still far from your objective; (4) that the Army and Column Commanders are exercised at the loss of time, which is vital; (5) you must keep a general staff officer at your headquarters who can communicate with you immediately; (6) you must launch your attack forthwith.

Staff failures persisted in the afternoon and when 53rd (Welsh) Division became embroiled in the labyrinth of trenches networked into gardens of thick cactus during the early evening, Doball ordered a withdrawal, an order that puzzled those fighting in the town. He then learned from intercepts that Tiller had sent his wife a message bidding her farewell as he expected to be taken prisoner; Kress von Kressenstein instructed Tiller not to surrender and to attempt to renew the attack, but it was too late and Dobell ordered a general withdrawal to Wadi Ghazze.

The British press reported the battle as a success. The Turks responded with an aircraft dropping the message, 'you beat us at communiqués, but we beat you at Gaza'. The gates to the Levant remained closed. Activities were confined to patrolling, intelligence collection and the production of accurate maps from air photographs. Captain Joseph McPherson (Egyptian Camel Transport Corps Officer) accompanied two Royal Engineer officers on a reconnaissance during the afternoon of Good Friday, 6 April: 'We saw parties of Turks and mapped down new trenches they had made, got sniped at incidentally, and had to travel a good bit of the way on our bellies.'

In preparation for a renewed attack on Gaza, Murray ordered Dobell to attack with three infantry divisions, including the weakened 53rd (Welsh) and 54th (East Anglian) Divisions. Five Mark 1 tanks that had arrived in Palestine in January for trials and instructional purposes had proven ideal for desert warfare, and they joined Eastern Force. Providing twenty-five aircraft, 5th Wing RFC gained air superiority thus allowing reconnaissance to identify artillery batteries. By mid-April, Kress von Kressenstein had reinforced the defence of Gaza to 21,000 infantry, about sixty-five guns and 2,000 cavalry. The attack on 17 April soon ran into trouble. A reason offered by the official British historian was: 'It appears that the men of the 53rd Division still felt the effects of their losses, disappointments and fatigue in the battle fought three weeks earlier, for their advance, even up to Samson Ridge, had been much slower than that of the other two divisions.'

Although the desert column disrupted Turkish communications by cutting field telephone cables, after being advised by his divisional commanders that another assault would result in further losses, Dobell ordered the Eastern Force to withdraw to Wadi Ghazze.

The British mission in Heraz had rejected landing at Aqaba after wireless intelligence indicated that Djemel Pasha had instructed Fakhri Pasha to abandon Hejaz and withdraw to Palestine. The intelligence reached Captain Lawrence on 9 March and although he had been instructed by Clayton, now promoted to brigadier-general, not to share the content with Feisal, in case the Arabs eased up their operations, he did so because he felt including Arabs in the decision-making process was essential to their aspirations. Faisal responded by ordering his brothers to attack the Turks wherever and whenever they could. When human intelligence suggested that the stalwart Turkish supporter Ibn Rashid was receiving about 300 camels, arms and money, Wingate asked General Maude in Mesopotamia to disrupt any attacks he might be planning. Referring back to Medina, the Arab Bureau assessed that:

No reinforcements had reached the city, except two battalions of 163rd Regiment. However, they were part of 53rd Division based in southern Palestine and were likely to be recalled [...] Although a force had been formed to secure the railways, it was likely this had been formed from existing HEF units [...] While a Circassian cavalry unit and a new camel corps had been identified, it would be withdrawn as soon as the HEF had left [...] Medina was near to collapse with food scarce, increasing sick and wounded lists and passengers in trains being deposited 20 miles outside the city to continue their journey on foot.

The Arabs in Wejh were reluctant to attack the railway from Medina until a raid in early March led by British officers sparked an escalating enthusiasm to blow up trains, sabotage tracks, mine bridges, wreck water towers and stations, cut telephone lines and attack Turkish repair parties. Lawrence wrote: 'Ours should be a war of detachment. We were to contain the enemy by the silent threat of a vast unknown desert, not disclosing ourselves till we attacked [...] and develop a habit of never engaging the enemy.'

But the indiscriminate slaughter of passengers led to disgust among the officers, and Lawrence added: 'I'm not going to last out this game much longer, Nerves going and temper wearing thin [...] This killing and killing of Turks is horrible.'

Fortress Medina continued to resist. While the British mission believed that the Arab armies should drive the Turks from Hejaz and that Aqaba should be captured, Anglo-French politics were mitigating against advances to Damascus. Lawrence, who had helped interpret imagery intelligence of Aqaba, felt that an approach to Aqaba through the desert from the east was the best tactic. As the option developed, eleven Turkish prisoners captured in a Royal Navy operation on 20 April told Lawrence at Wejh that sea mines protected the port. He also learned that 'the garrison of gendarmes from Syria and Medina were located in three camps at Wadi Itm, about 10 miles north of the harbour [...] 2/161st Regiment provided a company on rotation [...] No other Turkish troops were in Western Arabia.'

The information added impetus to the landward option and, bypassing the British mission, Feisal appointed Nasir, the young sharif of Medina, as the expedition commander and invited Lawrence to join him, along with Auda abu Tayyi, the charismatic leader of the Howitat, a powerful tribe who lived in modern Saudi Arabia and Jordan.

On 9 May Nasir left Wejh and headed toward Aqaba on a 600-mile march through desert still patrolled by the enemy. The important telegraph station at Ghadi el Hal railway station was destroyed. A month later, Nasir reached their first camp at Wadi Sirhan and while he conducted a recruiting drive, Lawrence and a small Bedouin escort left on a 300-mile reconnaissance that took him north of Damascus to determine if Syria was ready for revolt, which it was not. He also discreetly met Ali Riza Pasha, the nationalist Arab governor of the city. By the time he returned on 18 May, Nasir had recruited 500 Bedouin with more promised near Aqaba. Lawrence accompanied an unsuccessful raid on the railway designed to distract Turkish attention and then cut the road from Aqaba to Ma'an. A battalion sent to recapture the outpost at Guwelia was surrounded at Abu el Lissal and massacred until Nasir and Lawrence spared the prisoners, which included the battalion commander. Interrogations revealed it had recently arrived from the Black Sea and was the only reinforcement that Fortress Ma'an could spare.

Meanwhile HMS *Slieve Foy*, penetrating into the Gulf of Aqaba, reported to naval headquarters in Egypt that the Arabs were friendly toward British intentions and that Aqaba was empty of troops. In fact, they had retired to shelters in the cliff to avoid bombardment. A prisoner helped write a letter to the Turkish garrison commanders of three outposts in Wadi Rum suggesting that they surrender. And then on 6 July, after Nasir had used the cover of a sandstorm to enter Aqaba, Lawrence and an escort crossed the 160 miles of the Sinai desert. He famously arrived at GHQ four days later dressed in his Arab clothes. The news that Aqaba had been captured was welcomed by General Sir Edmund Allenby, who had taken over from Murray, who been sacked by General Robertson. One reason cited his loss of control of Eastern Force from his headquarters in Cairo. Allenby, fresh from commanding the Third Army on the Western Front and a cavalryman familiar with manoeuvre warfare from the Boer War, assured Robertson that he intended to use the Arab armies. When he arrived in Cairo on 28 June, his top priority was to break into Palestine; however, he first needed to secure his left flank.

11

Palestine

While Allied intelligence co-operation in the Eastern Mediterranean had improved by 1916, with operations from Cyprus targeting Syria and Anatolia and Port Said concentrating on Palestine, Brigadier-General Macdonogh accused Cypriot agents of being 'useless'. High Commissioner Clauson was still giving concern at GHQ, but he was confident enough to summarise intelligence contribution being made by Cyprus:

- Local intelligence was working to prevent communication with the enemy.
- Cyprus was a base for obtaining intelligence from Asia Minor and Syria with intelligence staff stationed at Famagusta conveying agents by British vessels, French armed auxiliaries and requisitioned Cypriot motorised fishing boats. There were two wireless telegraphy stations:
  - Royal Navy detachment at Famagusta mainly used for military intelligence communication with Ruad and occasional communication with Egypt.
  - Army wireless intelligence section at Larnaca linked to other stations in the Levant intercepting enemy communications.
- French naval coaling base for their Syrian Patrol of eight armed auxiliaries at Famagusta.
- Troodos and Limassol housed convalescent hospitals with accommodation for 500 and 1,500 casualties respectively.
- Karaolis prison camp.

The French training base at Monarga was used for about 4,000 Armenians evacuated from Alexandretta after a forty-day rebellion against the Turks in 1915. Disembarked at Port Said, most were assembled into the *Légion d'Orient*, which had been officially established in Egypt on 15 November 1916 under command of Lieutenant-Colonel A.V. Romieu. The force was joined by about 2,000 Armenians from the USA in 1917.

Between late November 1916 and early 1917, 10,000 prisoners of war were sent from Egypt to a comfortable camp at Karalaos, Famagusta. Clauson believed that their presence would demonstrate to the Turkish-Cypriots that the enemy were not invincible. The floodlights were a sharp contrast to the dark city. There were public concerns that there was not enough food for the increasing population. Cyprus also accommodated several hundred Russian refugees evacuated from Crimea and Maltese and British Jewish refugees from Smyrna in Larnaca.

In January 1917 Captain Ian Smith warned that, because they were poorly paid and therefore open to bribery, Cypriot customs officers could become conduits for information from Egypt to Turkey. He highlighted the lack of control over visiting ships, in particular the weekly mail ship from Cairo that had yet to be threatened by a U-boat, which he found suspicious. He recommended improving the telephone network, that access to small harbours at night should be controlled and that troops should guard the five main harbours and prevent vessels from putting to sea at night. Clauson disagreed, but the senior customs officer introduced measures to prevent information flowing from harbours.

Captain M.C. Scott (Intelligence Corps), also of EMSIB, took over from Smith in March. When he discovered in May that four Turkish Cypriots and a delivery boy from Famagusta were passing letters to and from Karaolis prison camp, Clauson refused to detain them and suggested they should be tried at the Provost Marshal Court, a recommendation rejected by Scott, the police, military commanders and prosecutors because it would expose the investigation in open court. The five were therefore released. Scott also discovered from intercepted letters of prisoners that a Turkish officer had landed on Cyprus on several occasions to collect information and financial contributions for the Turkish army. Turkish Cypriots were discovered smuggling arms onto the island intending to arm the prisoners of war.

When in mid-June the lighter *Dolphin*, bound for Limassol from Famagusta, turned up in Turkey and then five days later an agent landing in Anatolia was shot, Scott believed there was a link between the incidents. Later in the month, Clauson rejected an appeal from Captain H.C. Salter, who had replaced Hadkinson, to instruct district commissioners to prevent boats skippered by Turkish Cypriots from leaving Cypriot coastal waters. He also reversed an order from the senior naval officer restricting Turkish Cypriot-crewed boats from fishing at night and from working on vessels. Captain Scott used these examples to complain to GHQ and the Colonial Office that internal security in Cyprus was hopeless because of the lack of co-operation from the high commissioner.

In a report of internal security, EMSIB concluded that while there was no evidence of organised hostile intelligence services, the potential for disruption from Greeks and Turks remained. The assistance to prisoners of war was limited to supplying advice and giving a little money. The EMSIB report concluded that Cypriots should not be included on the regional blacklist. Clauson rejected concerns that the Turks were collecting intelligence and denied suggestions that Germans and Austrians were living in Cyprus with few restrictions. But as criticism was heaped on Clauson, Allenby needed to secure his left flank and agreeing with his proposal that a General Staff officer be sent as an intermediary, appointed his GSO1 (Intelligence), Lieutenant-Colonel John Belgrave (Royal Artillery).

Giving a lecture to the Royal Military Academy, Woolwich in 1919, Major-General Macdonogh said:

> You will no doubt remember the great campaign of Lord Allenby in Palestine and perhaps you are surprised at the daring of his actions. Someone who is looking from the side lines, lacking knowledge about the situation, is likely to think that Allenby took unwarranted risks. That is not true. For Allenby knew with certainty from his intelligence of all the preparations and all the movements of his enemy. All the cards of his enemy were revealed to him, and so he could play his hand with complete confidence. Under these conditions, victory was certain before he began.

Intelligence would be critical in spreading disinformation and assessing whether the enemy had fallen for it. Wireless intelligence would be crucial with prisoners providing collateral and filling in gaps relating to unit cohesion and morale. Leaving Rear HQ in Ismailia, General Allenby established his Tactical HQ near Khan Yunis, near the coast several miles south of Gaza. Intelligence on the Palestine front was controlled by Brigadier-General Guy Dawney, EEF brigadier General Staff, while subsidiary fronts were controlled by Major-General Louis Bols, EEF chief of staff. The organisation of EEF Intelligence Section in the summer of 1917 was:

Military Intelligence: Lieutenant-Colonel Walter Nugent	I(a): Operational intelligence
	I(b): Advanced intelligence
	I(d): Topography
	I(e): Wireless intelligence
	7th Field Survey Company RE
	RFC
	RNAS
Political Intelligence: Colonel Wyndham Deedes	I(b): Espionage and counter-espionage
	I(d): Censorship, arrests
	I(g): Economic and political
	Arab army liaison
	EMSIB

Advanced Intelligence was commanded by Lieutenant-Colonel Meinertzhagen, who had recently arrived from France. Its purpose was to monitor Turkish forces in Palestine; however, Lieutenant-Colonel Nugent thought the concept to be surplus to requirements, particularly after Meinertzhagen contacted the Mounted Desert Corps for information on its intelligence procedures, instead of referring

to the HQ Eastern Force Intelligence Section. Meinertzhagen convinced
Brigadier-General Dawney to split it with him, taking control of the new Palestine
intelligence of I(a) (Intelligence), I(c) (Mapping) and the Indian Corps of Guides
and Interpreters. Major George Lloyd thought the split was unwise and was given
the forty officers and other ranks to form Advanced Intelligence, which he divided
into A (Espionage) and B (Field Security and prisoner interrogation) sections.

The Corps of Guides and Interpreters was closely linked to the Intelligence
Corps and initially consisted of about two locally recruited officers and two other
ranks employed as irregulars who supplied their own camels. The unit proved of
such value that by 1918 the officer establishment had grown to eighty-six officers
graded as 1st to 4th Class agents, mostly Egyptians, Palestinians, Sudanese and
Jews. By September it listed 106 officers and was commanded by Captain the
Honourable E.C.G. Cadogan (Suffolk Yeomanry).

As usual, the three corps and their divisions, brigades and regiments or
battalions each had intelligence representation. Cavalry and camel squadrons
had an intelligence NCO. A documentary intelligence analysis cell at GHQ had
subsidiary teams with divisional HQs tasked to search captured enemy positions
and headquarters, of any level, for documents, code books, sketches, letters, marked
maps and reports. An Arab military linguist was attached to the brigades. Field
security supported occupied enemy territory administration detachments and
protected lines of communication and rear areas from sabotage, espionage and
subversion; they were equipped with lists of agents, informers and potential agents
and a blacklist of Turkish collaborators and suspects.

Major Ian Smith was still controlling clandestine operations and with HQ EEF
needing detailed information, the Arab Bureau, EMSIB and several Arab officer
defectors developed a strategy in which couriers were landed and moved through
a network of cut-outs and safe houses to pass instructions and collect information
from agent networks in Mersin, Ladhiqiyah, Tripoli, Beirut and Tyre. An instruction
to increase train-watching intelligence led to contacts being established at Adana,
Aleppo, Muslamia, Homs, Rayaq, Damascus and Afula. Known double agents were
exploited as a channel for feeding disinformation.

The crews of the *Veresis* and *Managem* had become well practised in their
clandestine operations. Landings were hazardous because they took place on hostile
shores, with the ever-present risk of patrols and betrayal, and with the possibility
of landing parties becoming separated from the ship. Signal lights could not be
used and therefore navigation had to be precise. Captain Welford usually identified
a star before he left his ship. For some time, he used a Syrian father and his three
sons as his boatmen. Once the intelligence had been collected, Welford enciphered
the important items and dispatched by pigeon to GHQ Cairo. Information also
leaked from Cyprus of German air reconnaissance flights over Famagusta and
Limassol and marauding U-boats reporting surface activity. Operations became

more hazardous in the spring of 1917 as Turkish intelligence noted the preparations for an offensive in south Palestine and responded to reports of spies and sighting of British and French ships offshore. Lieutenant Salter was working with the French and when not using the *Veresis*, landed from French trawlers. One of Salter's more important agents was one who was landed at Mersina on a monthly basis so that he could collect information from a train-watching recording railway activity before trains reached the junction at Aleppo.

The *Managem* calling at Athlit became frequent. In mid-April, Weldon collected Sarah Aaronsohn, sister to Aaron, and took her to Famagusta. She then took the ferry to Egypt to meet her brother in Cairo where he was translating documents and still lobbying British officers and officials for a Jewish homeland. One of his handlers was Major Meinertzhagen, who humoured him with tales of derring-do. In April, the captain of the ship, Commander Morewood, handed command to Lieutenant Alan Cain RNR. In mid-May, after a particularly bad storm, Weldon landed three agents, including Sarah, at Athlit and the next night was rowed to the beach in the small harbour at Tyre because he needed to meet a contact who lived about 100 yards from the jetty. It was very dark and as he and one of his boatmen crept around the side of a house, they were challenged by an armed man. They both quickly returned to the beach and, finding their boat was no longer there and expecting shots, they waded into the sea and found their boatmen waiting 50 yards out. However, as they rowed to the *Managem*, a heavy squall roughed up the sea and as the boat shipped seawater, Weldon instructed the rowers to pull for a reef about 500 yards from the shore. Suddenly the wind dropped and they were able to reach the ship. On 31 May the *Managem* helped rescue survivors from a ship torpedoed about 20 miles from Port Said.

Throughout the summer of 1917, Captain Weldon regularly visited Athlit to meet informants, and, during the night of 15 June, to deliver arms and ammunition. Three nights later, Weldon returned to Tyre and although it was rough, he and two of his boatmen swam ashore and, going to the house of one his boatmen's relatives, learnt that the elderly Syrian 'beggar' was alive and well. On their way back to Famagusta, Weldon called in at Athlit to land a courier only to find the sea was too rough to launch a boat. One of his boatmen offered to swim ashore with the courier, but as they were swimming back to the ship, the courier shouted that he was drowning. Weldon pushed his head below the surface to keep him quiet. After the courier reported that NILI had asked if he could return in a couple of nights to collect their information, Weldon and two men were waiting ashore at the rendezvous when shots were fired, which sent them scampering back to the ship. At the suggestion of Major Smith, Weldon returned to Tyre and suggested to his contact that a submarine telephone cable be laid to a float offshore; the idea was shelved when it emerged that fishermen regularly waded past his house.

At the end of July Smith, Salter and Weldon went to Provincial Island, a rocky islet about a mile off Asia Minor, to collect Captain Salter and a colleague named Smithers manning an observation post watching for U-boat activity. When the French trawler tasked to extract them failed to turn up, Salter sailed to Cyprus in a small dinghy to seek help. Weldon then collected Smithers and sailed to a planned rendezvous to extract a Turkish official who wanted to desert. He sent three Greeks ashore to guide him but when he failed to turn up, the Greeks returned to their boat but missed the *Managem* in the darkness. They were eventually picked up by Weldon miles out to sea. In mid-August, his extraction of the elderly Syrian was nearly compromised when a schooner under full sail passed close to the boat waiting in the harbour. Soon afterwards, *Managem* was in Famagusta when Weldon's head boatman told him that a Turkish-Cypriot schooner had sailed for Syria and he was concerned for the security of his family in Tyre. Weldon agreed to evacuate them. During the course of more clandestine operations, *Managem* captured a suspicious Cypriot schooner heading for Turkey.

Between May and August, intelligence emerged that a German-Turkish army commanded by General Erich von Falkenhayen had been formed in northern Syria with the strategic intention of attacking General Maude in Mesopotamia. Known to the Turks as Army Group *Yilderim* ('thunderbolt') and to the Germans as Army Group F, it consisted of the new Seventh Army, Eighth Army and the German Asia Corps. The Eighth Army was originally the Sinai Defence Force. Information then emerged that its priority was to support the Fourth Army in Syria where the EEF was considered to be the greater threat. The German Asia Corps had a secondary objective to protect the Jewish community from genocide. In April 1917, the entire populations of Jaffa and Tel Aviv were deported. While the Muslims were allowed to return, the Jews, spread across Palestine, were not permitted to do, resulting in about 1,500 dying from disease and the effects of a hard winter.

In preparation for Allenby's arrival, Lieutenant-General Chetwode wrote an appreciation of the Gaza defences and, highlighting that the shortage of on the British right flank would govern operations, concluded: 'We must give the enemy every reason to believe until the last moment that he will contemplate renewing our efforts against his right. Subsidiary operations against the portions of his Gaza front, will, I think, be unnecessary.'

Deception and surprise is an ancient art of war that was infrequently practised on the Western Front in favour of questionable tactical management, but the manoeuvre warfare of the Palestine campaign presented opportunities. Factors contributing to successful deception included integrated operational planning with surprise the key strategy; an ability to control enemy reconnaissance; ensuring the enemy was allowed to see only what he was allowed to see, for instance by ensuring air superiority; creativity mixed with realism; good tactical intelligence to determine whether the bait had been taken; and effective field security.

Allenby agreed with Chetwode, particularly as credible intelligence indicated that Colonel Kress von Kressenstein believed that the British would attack Gaza a third time, and therefore he planned a strategy to employ a double bluff of attacking Gaza while opening the Gates of Levant by breaking through at Beersheba. Z-Day was set for 31 October. The plan was twofold: firstly, XXI Corps would demonstrate in front of Gaza, and, secondly, XX Corps and the Desert Mounted Corps would attack Beersheba and secure the wells.

When Aaron briefed Allenby in August that the Turks feared a third attack on Gaza and were equally anxious about a flank attack through Beersheba, he suddenly found himself in demand by the Arab Bureau on political conditions, by EEF Intelligence on meteorological conditions and by the RFC on flying routes.

When an attempt to equip NILI with a wireless failed, because it was impractical, and the group was given pigeons, Sarah Aaronsohn doubted their reliability. When bad weather prevented any landings and believing that a British offensive was imminent, she dispatched two courier pigeons on 30 August. Unfortunately, four days later, one bird landed in the coop of the provincial governor in Caesarea as he was feeding his pigeons. Discovering the coded message in its container although unable to decipher the code, Turkish counter-intelligence began investigations. One NILI agent was captured at Ruhama on the northern edge of the Negev Desert, apparently trying to take urgent information to the British. On 21 September Weldon learned from an agent at Athlit that the villagers were nervous and seeking evacuation. Two days later, the *Managem* returned with the *Veresis* to learn that the villagers wished to remain. On the same day, two Christian Syrians landed near Haifa were arrested carrying propaganda and British sovereigns minted after 1914 and, under interrogation, divulged information on French clandestine operations. As the reports reached Cairo, the two ships evacuated about sixty people from Zichron and then EMSIB refused to sanction further exfiltrations because the moon was full.

NILI operational security was weak and with Jews fearing genocide, not everyone in Zichron supported the mysterious activity around the research centre. In any event, during the Turkish investigation on Zichron and Athlit on 2 October, police and soldiers surrounded the village and over the next three days crushed NILI with arrests and ill-treatment of individuals for information. Sarah Aaronsohn endured four days of ruthless interrogation, but in an attempt to shoot herself with a pistol concealed in her house, was paralysed with a shattered spine. She died four days later. In spite of EMSIB anxieties that the Turks were alert, on 7 October Alexander Aaronsohn, who had returned from the USA and had taken over NILI from his older brother, and Liova Schneersohn landed at Athlit from the *Managem*. For three consecutive nights in mid–October they landed expecting to evacuate more people, but no one was waiting on the beach.

As Allenby's plans took shape, he commenced several deceptions to convince the Turks that Beersheba was his objective. The strategic element was to convince the Fourth Army that a landing in Alexandretta Bay to pin down the Turkish corps centred on Aleppo was a possibility, an option that had been considered as early as 1914 as a measure to disrupt communications between Anatolia and northern Syria. When he suggested that measures be taken to suggest a landing in Palestine from Cyprus, the small garrison increased wireless traffic to simulate increased military activity, built dummy camps, placed larger orders with local suppliers and prepared ports to handle more ships. However, Cyprus was porous and there was nothing to prevent the Turks from sending reconnaissance aircraft. Mounted reconnaissance patrols around Beersheba acclimatised the defenders to their presence and wireless transmissions sent in a compromised cipher indicated that Beersheba would be a feint to the 'main' attack on Gaza. Using another compromised cipher, Allenby asked the War Office for reinforcements. In the event, the 10th (Irish) Division was sent from Salonika. He also formed 75th Division from British and Indian units in Egypt.

On 5 October, Brigadier-General Salmond formed the Palestine Brigade RFC with:

- 5th (Corps) Wing: co-operation and close air ground support.
- No.14 (RE-8s) and No.17 Squadrons RFC (Nieuport-17s).
- No.1 Squadron, Australian Flying Corps (Martinsyde G100/102s). Also known as No.67 Squadron RFC.
- 40th (Army) Wing: interception, interdiction and air photo reconnaissance. Equipped with a Handley-Page bomber.
- Nos 111 (Bristol-F2Bs) and 114 Squadron (BE-2c).
- No.21 Balloon Company: Nos 40 and 50 Sections.
- Intelligence Sections attached to XX, XXI and Desert Mounted Corps

Both wings each had air intelligence sections of air photographic interpreters feeding information to GHQI(a) (Intelligence) and I(c) (Mapping). Some reconnaissance aircraft were fitted with wireless which allowed air-to-ground reporting.

Colonel Jacob, now promoted, had joined GHQ as an advisor on south-west Arabian affairs from Aden. Instructed by Allenby in mid-1918 to lead a diplomatic mission to the iman in Sana'a, tribesmen captured Jacob soon after landing at Hodeida, but failed to hand over the diplomatic negotiations to Major A.S. Meek, which had been agreed to secure the mission's release, and negotiated an agreement with the tribesmen without Foreign Office authority. The mission was released after several months of comfortable captivity.

In his *Secret Corps*, Captain Tuohy described probably the most famous and controversial deception of the First World War – the 'Haversack Ruse'. After Allenby had agreed with Lieutenant-Colonel Belgrave's seven-page memorandum to have a haversack containing plans left for the Turks to find, on 10 October, Colonel Abu Faud, commander of the Turkish XX Corps, reported to Army Group *Yilderim* that:

> One of our NCO patrols sent out to Abu Sahaita Tepi came back with some very
> important maps and documents left by a high ranking General Staff Officer of
> the British Army. The information contained in the documents is of such great
> value to us that we have been able to ascertain the date of the enemy's offensive
> and it will enable us to forestall him in that all our reinforcements will now be
> near Gaza in time for us to attack the arrogant English.

The haversack, a standard British army small pack, contained a British Staff Army
Book 155 filled with notes, including minutes from a commander-in-chief's
conference and maps of the coastal area near Gaza; a memo to Captain Lloyd
reporting that the ground around Beersheba was unsuited for mounted troops; a
chatty letter from a naval officer at sea; a letter from a wife telling her husband that
their son had been born; and a £20 note.

Tuoy claims that in a wallet was a note from Allenby to Meinertzhagen saying
that he was delaying their shoot as he was going to Cairo until 4 November.
During the day, a General Routine Order was circulated that a staff officer had
lost a haversack in the Girheir sector and, if found, it was to be returned to GHQ
without opening it. To add credibility, an enciphered memo instructed that troops
were to make determined efforts that night to find the haversack. Meinertzhagen
was also ordered to report to GHQ for an investigation into its loss. Next day,
two British soldiers captured in a clash said, under interrogation, that they were
part of a patrol sent to look for the haversack. A Turkish patrol found a copy of
the Desert Mounted Corps orders about the search wrapped around an officer's
lunch 'carelessly' being thrown away by a patrol. Although Colonel Kress von
Kressenstein believed that the winter rains would restrict a major British operation,
when the haversack eventually arrived on his desk he was sceptical of the validity
of the contents. Nevertheless he ordered that the defence of Gaza be strengthened
at the expense of Beersheba because, he believed, an attack on Beersheba would
require an advance across open desert and therefore another attack on Gaza was
more likely, possibly co-ordinated with an amphibious landing north of the town.

For years, Meinertzhagen claimed that he made up the content of the haversack
and that the letter about the birth had been written by a nurse based at Al Arish. Lloyd
is probably Captain George Lloyd, then heading Advanced Intelligence. He claimed
that he had left Khan Yunis with an Australian Light Horse patrol and then ridden
towards El Girheir on his own. Seeing Turkish cavalry, he dismounted and opened
fire from a range of about 600 yards and when they returned fire, he feigned being
wounded and in his 'struggle' to remount, dropped the haversack, having smeared
it with blood from a cut from his horse, and then watched from cover as a Turkish
soldier picked up his rifle, water bottle, binoculars and the haversack. The deception
became a classic example that others followed, including Operation Mincemeat
('The Man That Never Was') and Operation Fortitude to cover the Normandy

Landings. The subject of three biographies, Meinertzhagen's reputation soared until September 1956, when former Major Arthur Neate (Royal Artillery), who had been GSO2 (Intelligence) to Major-General Harry Chauvel, then commanding the Desert Mounted Corps, joined a debate in the *Spectator* and claimed that he had dropped the haversack. He claimed that it had been passed to the German intelligence officer in Beersheba, Lieutenant Schilling, who believed the information to be credible and sent it to Colonel Faud. Meinertzhagen replied that the haversack dropped by Neate had not been found, and that an attempt on 1 October by an Australian officer had also failed when the Turks failed to pursue him.

In 2007, the American author Brian Garfield dissected the legend and using Neate's diary concluded that it was he who dropped the haversack. His entry in his diary for 12 September 1917 reads: 'Left early in a borrowed horse and joined a Yeomanry Regiment in 5th Mounted Brigade. Reached el Geheir, saw Turks and dropped bag.' Garfield gives an interesting slant on the date by claiming that in 1917, Turkey was converting its Islamic calendar into the Gregorian system. When Garfield compared dates, he suggests that 10 October 1917 in the Islamic version equated to 12 September 1917. He believed he was able to prove this when a Turkish colonel wrote in October that 'in the second half of November, indicator of imminent British attack around Gaza'. The British attack had taken place almost a month earlier.

During early October, wireless intelligence suggested that Army Group *Yilderim* had been reinforced by the 19th Infantry Division and confirmed that the Seventh Army and HQ Eighth Army, totalling 50,000 infantry and a mounted corps, were in Palestine. As part of the first stages of the deception, on 20 October the Royal Navy started assembling landing craft near Deir el Belach, took soundings of beaches and bombarded targets at Wadi Hesi, 10 miles north of Gaza. Two days later, Allenby seized Karm railway terminal and neutralised two formidable redoubts. Although General von Falkenhayn sent a strong reconnaissance from Beersheba a week later followed by the Eighth Army attacking from Hareira, Kress von Kressenstein believed that the British would launch an offensive against Gaza during the first fortnight of November. He had not been entirely fooled by the haversack ruse because, tactically, Gaza was more important than Beersheba and British preparations did not match the intelligence being collected by his air and ground reconnaissance. However, he could not afford to take chances and had no alternative but to strengthen Beersheba and place his reinforcements between Gaza and Beersheba and ready to cover an advance from Wadi Hasi.

British artillery then shelled targets in Gaza to cover the transfer of XX Corps, the Desert Mounted Corps and 200 guns hopping from gun position to gun position to the right flank. The abandoned camps were occupied by a few soldiers. Railways and water pipes were extended at night and camouflaged at dawn. Two weeks earlier, Lieutenant-General Chetwoode had instructed his divisional commanders to measures be ensure Turkish reconnaissance aircraft were deceived:

Such as have your present bivouac areas looking as much occupied as possible by leaving tents standing and digging holes wherever you have blanket shelters, not pitching Brigade Field Ambulances or showing their flags, and allowing no new ground to be used whatever. I would ask that troops of the 60th, 74th and 53rd Divisions when east of the [Ghazze] Wadi should be kept concealed as much as possible, in wadis, gardens, near buildings etc, and that the strictest aeroplane discipline is enforced, all ranks lying flat when the whistle is blown, and remaining so until the 'carry on' is sounded. It is particularly important that no motor lights, either Ford or ambulance, should be shown east of the Wadi after Z Day, and then as little as possible.

Early on 31 October, as two infantry divisions attacked Beersheba, the ANZAC Mounted Division, on the right, ran into stiff opposition until a charge by the 4th Australian Light Horse shattered the defences. Next day, as XXI Corps, on the left, advanced toward Gaza, the Egyptian Labour Corps embarked on ships and then quietly disembarked during that night, leaving the ships to sail and hover off Wadi Hasi next morning. The targeting of enemy telegraph lines by shelling and patrols forced Turkish and German command posts to use wireless; however, British analysis of intercepts proved ponderous and, on several occasions, the intelligence arrived too late to be of use. For instance, when General von Falkenhayn ordered the Seventh Army to secure Beersheba against cavalry and weakened the central Tal al Sharai front by moving two reserve divisions, slow interpretation meant that Allenby missed an opportunity to exploit the gap.

As the defence crumbled on 6 November, wireless intelligence learnt that von Falkenhayn had ordered the Eighth Army to hold the Gaza flank while the Seventh Army would attack from Beersheba, but this contradicted the battlefield intelligence until 5th Wing then reported that Army Group *Yilderim* was retreating. Although the capture of Gaza the next day opened the gates into Palestine, within the week, the enemy had formed a defensive line along the road from Bethlehem to Jerusalem to Jaffa. Nevertheless, General Robertson instructed Allenby to relieve pressure on General Maude in Mesopotamia by pursuing the Turkish rearguards. Civilians, most glad to be rid of the Turkish yoke, proved to be useful observers, valued contributors to topographical intelligence and providers of information on climate, environment and infrastructure. Wireless signals indicated that Army Group *Yilderim* would not defend Jerusalem in favour of withdrawing to Nablus, 30 miles to the north. Although poor weather often grounded the Palestine Brigade RFC, the pilots were helped by a ground-to-air wireless intelligence station located with No.1 Squadron, Australian Flying Corps intercepting details of German artillery observation sorties. Enemy electronic warfare sometimes jammed British transmissions and imitated British pilots and forward air controllers.

12

Syria

By the end of November 1918, XX Corps was in the Judean Hills to the right of XXI Corps on the plains with the ANZAC Mounted Division anchoring the flanks. Clashes west of Jerusalem were interpreted as contact with the Turkish rearguard. Air reconnaissance reported enemy columns moving north, adding credibility to the reports. The first British soldiers to enter Jerusalem were two cooks from 2/20th London Regiment, who had become separated from their unit during the night of 9–10 December. The mayor then offered the city keys to two 2/19th London Regiments sergeants, an offer that was passed up the line until it reached Major-General Shea, whose 60th Division had attacked the city. Allenby famously entered the city on foot two days later and gave Prime Minister David Lloyd George his badly needed Christmas present after three years of stalemate on the Western Front. Next day, Allenby reported that the winter rains would restrict operations for at least two months. So far, the regional strategic objectives of the capture of Jerusalem and frustrating Ottoman-German operations against Baghdad had been frustrated. And British national morale had been boosted.

A week later, the Turks hanged two NILI members in Damascus and sentenced others to imprisonment. There is no doubt that NILI had provided a huge amount of intelligence which was highly regarded at GHQ, but Aaronsohn had done himself few favours by failing to acknowledge the British characteristic of reticence and that their prime objective was to defeat the Turks, not to provide a Jewish homeland. He did not like the principle of strict need-to-know and, unlike Lawrence, he was not a British officer.

Meanwhile, the War Cabinet gave General Allenby two objectives: to complete the conquest of Palestine, and to advance to Aleppo and cut the Turkish lines of communications to Mesopotamia.

Cyprus still remained a problem. On 31 December 1917 Lieutenant-Colonel Belgrave met High Commissioner Clauson to introduce Major Henry Lethbridge as the GSO1 (Cyprus) and said that both EMSIB and GHQI(b) (Secret Service) would be reporting to him. Clauson objected because he felt the Cyprus police could take responsibility for intelligence operations; in military matters, he would refer to OC Troops, Cyprus, as per King's Regulations. In an increasingly irritable meeting, when Belgrave raised the issue of a Turkish flag being flown at the main mosque in Nicosia, Clauson said that he had taken into consideration the flying of Greek flags. When Clauson then said he was always ready to assist in military operations, Belgrave suggested that the impression at GHQ was that 'his attitude towards the Intelligence Services in the Island was not sympathetic'. Belgrave, irked by Clauson's perceived weakness and his isolation from the war, recommended to Brigadier-General Bols that a strong military government should replace a weak civil administration for the duration of the war. The emergency regulations in force in Egypt should be applied to Cyprus and those associated with communicating with the enemy and interfering with the war effort should be prosecuted under the Proclamation under Martial Law in special courts. Belgrave had Lethbridge promoted to lieutenant-colonel to give him necessary authority. EMSIB endorsed most of the proposals. In January 1918, Captain Scott was relieved by Captain Melvyn, a former commissioner of police in Cyprus. In mid-summer Melvyn arrested seven suspects accused of helping ten German agents to land on the Karpas Peninsula.

Victory on the Western Front appeared to be remote, but the Palestine campaign provided a glimmer of hope that if Turkey could be knocked out, the Dardanelles could be breached and Germany would have to support the ailing Austro-Hungarian Empire, an analysis that provoked the 'Westerners' into arguing that the strategic focus should be the Western Front. The 'Easterners' agreed but argued that a policy of passive defence elsewhere made little sense. Early in February General Smuts, now a member of the War Cabinet, instructed Allenby that he was to defeat the Turks and would be reinforced by an Indian cavalry division from France and three infantry divisions from Mesopotamia to add to his existing seven infantry divisions and three mounted divisions. MI2 at the War Office believed Turkish forces in Syria numbered about 275,000 men of whom about 90,000 in eleven divisions were in Palestine. As the EEF prepared to advance, Allenby needed his intelligence assets to be offensively minded and enlarged, and the eight GSOs (Intelligence) he had in November 1917 had risen to nineteen by the New Year. The Intelligence Corps (Palestine) rose from the original thirty officers to sixty-two dispersed between the two Sections of Advanced Intelligence. Their areas of interests were wide ranging:

- The Turkish Army and Army Group *Yilderim*.
- Turkish political intelligence throughout the Turkish Empire and North Africa.
- Political intelligence in Palestine and Arabia.
- The Horn of Africa, Sudan and the interior of Egypt.
- Economic intelligence.
- Communication security of wireless, telegrams, postal and press censorship.
- Propaganda and publicity.

- Counter-espionage, port control and permit controls.
- Internment of enemy aliens.

The Economic Intelligence Section was formed in December 1917 with an officer and five clerks compiling blacklists of those with commercial links with the Germans and Turks, and collating technical intelligence through a trade intelligence bureau to assess whether the military and commercial blockades had degraded the manufacture of equipment. The section had expanded to thirty-five by May 1918.

As EEF had advanced, schools were reopened, the postal service recommenced, commerce and agriculture was reinvigorated and goods were sent by military railways. Liberated Palestine had been divided into four occupied enemy territory administrations with Brigadier-General Clayton appointed the senior administrator. On 15 January General Allenby reported to Brigadier-General Macdonogh that the Muslims in Jerusalem were generally ambivalent about the Arab Revolt but were worried by Jewish encroachment and varying Bedouin attitudes to the east of Jerusalem. The protection of sacred Muslim places was generally accepted as satisfactory. The Jews were overjoyed by the British political support for a homeland in Palestine contained in the 1917 Balfour Declaration. Meanwhile Georges Picot, the French representative in Palestine, was pressing Allenby for a share in the administration of the part of Palestine that France had enjoyed before the war (mainly modern Lebanon), but his presence was resented by Italy. EMSIB remained largely unchanged managing agents in Syria and Transjordan. The Palestine branch of the Arab Bureau operated east of the River Jordan.

While southern Palestine had been extensively surveyed, the area north of Jerusalem was less well known and it fell to 40th Wing to concentrate on collecting photographic intelligence, a relatively easy task as Allied aircraft had air superiority in January, destroying ten German aircraft at no loss. When two Australian pilots discovered on 3 January that boats were taking corn and hay produced on the plains to the south and east of the Dead Sea to the Turkish garrison in Amman, the supply was interdicted. Recent improvements included camera vibration in flight being further reduced, the introduction of wide-angle lenses and the Australians developing a system of three to five aircraft flying at the same height on consecutive days to provide overlapping air photographs. Two sound-ranging sections sent from France and attached to 7th Field Survey Company pinpointed guns tucked into wadis and caves. Information on trench maps included camouflaged enemy positions and motorable tracks, although some assessment later proved to be overestimated. Eventually, 16,000 negatives contributed to mapping covering about 2,000 square miles north of Jerusalem being produced by the Survey Company. RE-8 reconnaissance aircraft and 21st Balloon Company arrived in January to support XXI Corps and the Desert Mounted Corps. Allenby had concluded that balloons on his hilly right flank were of little value because of the amount of dead ground. Balloon operations were usually tethered to fly between 1,000ft and 3,500ft. The observer in one balloon that broke from its mooring in November 1917 and floated toward the Turkish lines parachuted to safety. Units generally used a technique developed on the Western Front of the observer passing his sightings and targets via a telephone to his controller on the ground and thus freeing him for further observations. Balloons also had psychological warfare value in that they harassed the enemy into believing they were under continual observation, particularly as they could stay in the air for long periods during the Mediterranean sun, which therefore limited activity. Agents were also directed to survey specific roads.

After the disaster at Athlit, Captain Weldon had been hospitalised with exhaustion for several days. When Major Ian Smith was posted to GHQ and Weldon was then appointed military intelligence officer at Port Said, he found that his new role sometimes prevented him from putting to sea, which he found frustrating. Nevertheless, he landed three Moroccan saboteurs near Sidon tasked to disrupt the Turkish rear area by leaving time bombs and devices disguised as eggs and cigarettes. Aaronsohn had always resisted NILI becoming involved in sabotage in case it brought retaliation against the Jews. The *Managem* was involved in another rescue, this time survivors from the HMS *Monitor 15* torpedoed by a U-boat.

Having been defeated at Beersheba and after failing to defend Jerusalem, General von Falkenhayn was replaced by Field-Marshal Liman von Sanders, the victor at Gallipoli, on 19 February 1918 as commander of Army Group *Yilderim*. In spite of adopting a strategy of 'active, flexible and unyielding defence' and with Anatolian troops sent to form the Army of Islam in the Caucasus, he was left with poor quality, dispirited conscripts. Reconfiguring his command and control, he extended telephone communications between Istanbul, Aleppo and Damascus and laid an additional line between HQ Fourth Army at Damascus and its subordinate HQs at Afula, Nablus, al-Salt and Tiberius and placed wireless units in every army and corps HQ. The Germans already had extensive ground and air signals units.

When the DMI reorganised wireless intelligence in early 1918, No.2 Wireless Operating Group replaced SWS (Cyprus) and a GHQ substation. Majors Lefroy and Clausen remained as the intercept and crypto-analysts co-ordinators respectively reporting to GHQI(e). To cope with the growing influence of intercept and direction-finding, the Royal Engineer Signals Service fitted equipment in lorries. Linguists arrived from Salonika. When the Turks introduced counter-measures and deception using phoney messages, such was the anxiety about losing the high value of wireless intelligence that 'a usually reliable source' was changed to either 'Agent X' or 'Agent Y' and then documentary intelligence or prisoner intelligence. Brigadier-General Macdonogh insisted that the recipients of wireless intelligence must protect it and, in instances of compromises, appropriate action was to be taken.

By the late spring, Army Group *Yilderim* had been forced to a line about 10 miles north of Jaffa with the Eighth Army facing XXI Corps on the coastal plain, the Seventh Army in the Judean Hills and west of the River Jordan, and the Fourth Army east of the river facing XX Corps and the Desert Mounted Corps. The irregular Northern Arab Army was raiding Turkish lines of communication and tying down garrisons throughout Palestine, Jordan, and Syria.

Von Sanders expected Allenby to attack the Fourth Army. The rapid advance by the EEF had largely outstripped existing tactical intelligence with most information coming from prisoners, refugees and local populations. In March, 24th Balloon Company arrived to support XX Corps. In April, the occupied enemy territory administration was reorganised and Clayton became Allenby's chief political officer. I(b) (Secret Service) also reorganised with the three corps intelligence sections being supported by two counter-intelligence officers authorised to detain suspects, conduct counter-intelligence and censorship, promote internal propaganda and collect political intelligence in occupied districts. Divisional counter-intelligence officers reported to the corps counter- and political intelligence officers and the divisional General Staff.

The launching of the German spring offensive on the Western Front on the same day as the advance to Amman persuaded the War Cabinet that Palestine was of secondary importance and consequently XX Corps lost 52nd (Lowland) and 74th (Yeomanry) Divisions and the equivalent of another division rushed to the Western Front. It received, in compensation, several half-trained Indian army battalions from Mesopotamia and Royal Engineer railway construction troops tasked to extend the railways into Russia. The advance convinced von Sanders that the strategic rail junction at Deraa must be defended. As this became evident, Allenby switched the focus of his strategy to his left towards Megiddo and Nazareth with the intention of destroying Army Group *Yilderim* before it left Palestine. In Hejaz, the Arabs attacked Ma'an between 15 and 17 April but failed to capture the main position.

When General Allenby reviewed the GHQ Intelligence Section in April and suggested that political intelligence should be renamed the Special Intelligence Section and be headed by a brigadier-general, Brigadier-General Macdonogh instructed Colonel Basil Buckley, then head of MI2, to review the entire intelligence function in the Middle East and Salonika. To give him credibility, Buckley was promoted to brigadier-general. Writing to senior intelligence officers in a letter entitled 'Near East Intelligence' dated 23 April 1918, Buckley observed that:

- Central control of the intelligence branches was lacking.
- Individual effort was dependent on individuals.
- Since control was lacking, there had been unnecessary expansion 'with the consequent waste of personnel and money, and lack of full co-ordination

in Egypt and Palestine between those areas and London'. This result was incomplete results and inefficiency.

• The intelligence culture had evolved around 'certain personalities' some of whom had usurped the functions of others or left their proper work.

Buckley visited between June and July and believed the size of the theatre of operations meant that the heads of military and political intelligence found it difficult to control activities. That four organisations dealing principally in human intelligence, namely GHQI(b) (Secret Service), EMSIB, the Arab Bureau and the chief political officer, collectively, he found to be counter-productive. The Army Council agreed with Buckley's proposals that EEF Intelligence should be divided into First Echelon supporting EEF and Second Echelon with the MEF in Egypt and the existing task-orientated system would be replaced by target-orientation against localised threats. Each echelon would have two branches: A Branch (operational intelligence and espionage) and B Branch (field security and political and economic intelligence sections). EMSIB A was to be fused into HQ EEF I(a) (Intelligence) while EMSIB B was merged into I(b) (Secret Service) into MEF Egypt.

Several incompetent officers were moved, but when Buckley recommended that Deedes be appointed head of intelligence, General Allenby rejected the recommendation and insisted that Brigadier-General Clayton should support his army from Jerusalem and that he be the chief political officer in Palestine. Buckley's view that Lieutenant-Colonel Meinertzhagen should command First Echelon was also rejected, as he had been posted to command the Camouflage and Security School in France. Buckley was appointed to be EEF brigadier, General Staff.

Meanwhile, Lieutenant-Colonel Deedes asked Alexander Aaronsohn, now an Intelligence Corps second-lieutenant in the Corps of Guides and Interpreters, to organise the collection of intelligence from behind Turkish lines and also to conduct covert internal security operations within the occupied enemy territory administration. Helped by Liova Schneersohn, he infiltrated about thirty-five Arab and four Jewish agents into the Seventh Army area of operations and targeted villages accommodating enemy headquarters. Insertion usually meant a long approach through a network of safe houses and avoiding guarded bridges and fords of the River Jordan, then slipping into enemy territory. Aaronsohn had heard about the Turkish crushing of NILI from a prisoner of war. He was awarded the DSO for an act of gallantry on 2 September.

In spite of winter storms and high surf, Captains Weldon and Salter continued their clandestine operations, which Weldon described as 'more agents, more landings, more talks with friends ashore'. The train-watching circuit west of Aleppo inserted by Salter produced valuable reports. Included in its reports were German and Turkish newspapers. When a U-boat was spotted on the surface off

Cyprus, *Managem* dropped a depth charge, but Weldon did not realise they are normally dropped at speed and consequently his ship reeled as it exploded almost underneath the vessel. A courier landed in the port of Latakia returned with reports and also an offer to take away the tobacco crop, which was rotting in warehouses. Weldon had to remind himself that he was not involved in commerce. In April, Captain Salter lost the *Veresis* and was given the HMS *Devaney*, the former 600-ton Plymouth-to-France ship *Devonia*, but it was slow and generally unsuited for clandestine operations. In May, Weldon landed an agent in a smuggler's cove near Ras el Nakura, a few miles north of Acre, that had been used by Syrian young men escaping conscription. Four days later, the agent returned with a local official who had been talent-spotted as a provider of information. However, Turkish security forces were suspicious of the cove and when, three months later, an ambush was spotted during the insertion there was a brief exchange of fire. The incident led to some agents becoming less valuable. Weldon resolved the dilemma by visiting the crew of a Turkish schooner imprisoned in Famagusta gaol and recruiting one of them. He landed the sailor at Nakura, north of Haifa, and although deeply suspicious that he could be betrayed, he was relieved when the agent returned with the contact.

Early in August, Captain Salter rescued an Indian soldier captured at Kut, who was with a working party repairing telegraph lines. He said that while Indian prisoners were treated badly, it was worse for the British. After EMSIB was warned by London that officers planning an escape intended to make for a cove in the Bay of Adalia, Weldon and Smith ran past the rendezvous but saw nothing. In September, eight escaped officers led by Lieutenant-Commander A.D. Cochrane RN had arrived in Cyprus. Cochrane had been captured in March 1916 when his submarine E-7 became entangled in anti-submarine nets as he tried to enter the Sea of Mamara. Confined to the prison camp at Yozgod, he broke out with twenty-six officers. All but eight were recaptured. Cochrane led the eight on a 400-mile march that took thirty-eight days to the Mediterranean coast where they stole a motorboat at Khorghos and made landfall at Kyrenia.

By August, Allenby was planning to deceive the Turkish Seventh and Eighth Armies into remaining in the hilly Jordan valley while he transferred the weight of the attack to the coastal plain overseen by the hills of Tel Meggido and then released the Desert Mounted Corps into the enemy rear to force him either to stand and fight or withdraw towards Damascus. Meggido was the site of two previous battles. Z-Day would be on 19 September.

By early September, 7th Field Survey Company had mapped the Turkish front to a depth of 30 miles from 42,000 prints and 1,500 prints had been taken in April. British air superiority was dominant. The arrival of two squadrons equipped with DH-9 and SE-5 fighters and a reconnaissance squadron gave a total 100 aircraft against fifteen German planes. As Z-Day approached, attacking units were provided with 1:40,000 scale maps covering the front line from Hadera to Samaria. To maximise the use of air photographs, unit commanders and General Staff officers attended two-day courses on air photographic reading. Mounted regiments were given smaller-scale Palestine Exploration Fund maps surveyed before the war.

By mid-September, XX Corps was visible in the Jordan valley, but XXI Corps and the Desert Mounted Corps had been smuggled to the coast, moving at night and using citrus orchards and woods during the day and for their assembly areas. To deceive enemy wireless intelligence the Desert Mounted Corps headquarters remained in the Jordan valley. To give impressions of full occupancy and yet allow for more arrivals, troop numbers were calculated to ensure that transfers were evenly spread. Troops marched in daylight from Jerusalem into new XX Corps camps occupied by men unfit for active service and then returned to the city in trucks after dark and repeated the deception next day. Dummy horse lines were constructed with the animals manufactured from fabric covering a wooden frame. Vehicles and mules dragging harrows raised dust to suggest troop movement. A Jerusalem hotel was ostentatiously commandeered for HQ EEF.

After agents, patrols and interrogations identified suitable wadi and river crossing points about marshes near Hadera, south of Haifa, the cavalry were given prescribed routes. Mendel Schneersohn was a member of NILI and brother of Liova who had been briefly arrested by the Turks in October 1917 and had returned to Hadera, where he continued to pass information to Captain Weldon. When the British reached the area, he was flown over the front line and then went into the trenches to verify his observations. He then joined his brother in Advanced Intelligence, then under command of Captain R. MacRury. While enemy aircraft were prevented from compromising the deception, the Intelligence Corps mounted a field security operation by assigning a Turkish-speaking officer, three Turkish and Arabic interpreters and an Arab assistant to every division with instructions to conduct counter-intelligence operations along the divisional lines of communications and also interrogate prisoners and defectors.

And as a final touch, British newspapers and private telegrams referred to a race meeting scheduled for 19 September, Z-Day. A German map dated 17 September shows that von Liman had been deceived. During the evening of 18 September, a discontented Indian army sergeant deserted and warned the Turks of the offensive. Although Refet Bey, commanding XXII Corps on the right flank of the Eighth Army, wanted to blunt the attack by withdrawing, von Sanders thought the sergeant to be part of an intelligence deception and ordered him to stand firm. It proved a fatal error of judgement.

At 4.30 a.m. on 19 September, artillery and naval gunfire support shelled the Turkish positions and then XXI Corps advanced through the shattered defences; by late afternoon they had overrun the headquarters of the Eighth Army and XXII Corps near Tul Karm. The only Handley-Page bomber in Palestine attacked the main Army Group *Yilderim* telegraph exchange at Afule and No.144 Squadron DH-9s twice attacked von Sanders' HQ in Nazareth and disrupted communications. Nos 142 and 144 Squadrons also raided the headquarters of the Eighth and Seventh Armies at Tul Karm and Nablus respectively while No.14 Squadron tackled three lower headquarters. On several occasions, Captain Weldon was landed to report on Turkish dispositions. Lieutenant-General Chetwode, commanding XX Corps, deceived the Seventh Army with raids and patrols into believing he would attack from the east and then at midday, Allenby released XX Corps to attack the Jordan valley from the south. As Army Group *Yilderim* began to fall back to the escape routes through the hills at El Affule, Beisan and Deraa, it was harassed by the Desert Mounted Corps, which had seized several defiles through Carmel Range on to the Plain of Sharon. The Eighth Army commander was cut off and spent the next week behind British lines before reaching safety. The Desert Mounted Corps netted scores of prisoners as it advanced in a generally northerly direction.

The 5th Cavalry Division had been instructed to capture Nazareth, von Sanders and his headquarters. Using a narrow, rough track, its brigades negotiated the Abu Shusheh Pass during the night of 19–20 September without incident and, crossing the Esdrealon Plain, a key Turkish road and rail lines of communications through the Judean Hills, blew up parts of the Haifa–Afula Railway. The slower divisional artillery was left to negotiate the pass. An early morning reconnaissance by No.1 Squadron reported three British armoured cars on their way to Afula, a cavalry brigade at Lejjun and two brigades advancing on a broad front. At about 7.15 a.m., 14th Cavalry Brigade seized Afula railway station and captured 300 prisoners.

Commanded by Brigadier-General Kelly, 13th Cavalry Brigade reached Nazareth at 5 a.m. minus a 9th Hodson's Horse squadron that lost touch during the night and brigade HQ requiring two 18th Lancers troops to clear Yafa. The remainder of the regiment captured 200 sleeping Turkish soldiers in El Mujeidil. The 15,000 people living in Nazareth were overlooked by the steep sides of a depression. On the left of the main road into the town was the Hotel Germania, which was the Army Group *Yilderim* mess, and 500 yards further on was the Monastery of Casa Nuova, which housed Army Group HQ. The only unit available was the 1/1st Gloucester Hussars and, in spite of the exhausting 50-mile night ride, they charged into the town at about 5.30 a.m., swords drawn, and captured prisoners at the Hotel Germania and bundled documents found in nearby houses into sandbags. German resistance then stiffened and the hussars found themselves fighting in the narrow streets further restricted by parked German lorries and were forced to withdraw under machine-gun fire from buildings on high ground, balconies and windows. At 8 a.m., two Gloucester Hussars squadrons, three 18th Lancers troops and a 9th Hodson's Horse squadron reinforced the attack and almost annihilated a fierce counter-attack organised by von Sanders using GHQ staff. After Divisional HQ advised brigade headquarters that 14th Cavalry Brigade could not be sent to Nazareth because of 'the state of the horses', Kelly withdrew south to El Afule, taking with them 1,250 prisoners. However, he was blamed for failing to capture Nazareth, failing to cut the road from Nazareth to Tiberias and failing to capture von Sanders; he was relieved from his command. Von Sanders escaped from Nazareth by car and eventually reached Damascus where he attempted to regain command and control, but in his absence, it had collapsed.

In the shadow of the strategically important narrow pass at Meggido guarding the trade route into Syria, Armageddon struck Army Group *Yilderim*. The Fourth Army was struggling in the narrow Wadi el Fara on 21 September to escape to Deraa, when, in an event mirrored in 1944 at the Falaise Gap, the RAF decimated the trapped Turks. Twenty Corps captured Nablus during the day. Arab irregulars attacked railways and aircraft raided isolated Turkish detachments. On the coast, the New Zealand Mounted Brigade captured HQ 53rd Division and 600 prisoners near Wadi el Fara the next day, including the divisional commander. Meanwhile Captain Weldon had been instructed to land in Haifa, Tyre, Sidon and Beirut to see if they were still occupied by the Turks and to send his report by wireless; most were devoid of enemy. In Beirut on 6 October he was welcomed by citizens reporting that the Turks had gone and he headed south until he saw the 5th Irish Lancers advancing north and landed to make his report. Weldon continued his clandestine landings until the end of the war and then returned to his family in 1919, the first time he had seen them for four years.

On the left, Chaytor Jordan Valley Force of the ANZAC Mounted Division, 20th Indian Infantry Brigade, two West Indies Regiment battalions and two Jewish battalions enlisted into the Royal Fusiliers entered Amman on 25 September. Next day, 5th Infantry Division and elements of the Arab Northern Army captured Aleppo and then advanced to Muslimie Station where the remnants of Army Group *Yilderim* were rallying. Meanwhile, the ANZAC Mounted Division captured Deraa and, climbing the Golan Heights, fought its way to Damascus, entering from the north-east and north-west on 30 September, followed later in the day by Lieutenant-Colonel Lawrence and elements of the Arab Northern Army.

Meanwhile, III (Indian) Corps were advancing towards Kurdistan from Baghdad. Lieutenant-Colonel Leachman had been to the 17th (Indian) Division and was attached to the Light Armoured Motor Brigade. Its role was to cut the Turkish retreat. The offensive was launched on 23 October and within days a large Turkish force had been surrounded north of Shergat. Leachman was tasked to find the airfield from which aircraft were attacking the British, and after finding, then attacked it. Leachman then attached a German Halberstadt aircraft to his armoured car for his driver to tow to British lines. On 30 October, the force surrendered and after the Treaty of Mudros had been signed, Leachman became involved in the surrender negotiations and then returned to his pre-war activities, but was murdered in 1920 during civil war in northern Mesopotamia.

13

East Africa

Ten days after their victory at Tanga, Lieutenant-Colonel Lettow-Vorbeck sent a small force of *Schutztruppe* across the border and captured the town of Taverta, against very light opposition. In strategic terms, he occupied a substantial portion of British East Africa. However, his troops fired so much ammunition that he changed tactics over the next six months to raiding the vulnerable Uganda Railway. The imperial strategy decreed by Lord Kitchener was to defend British East Africa and only cross the border when the risks were low.

Frequently seen as a sideshow, Edward Paice uses the analogy to cricket in his *Tip & Run* to summarise the East African campaign thus:

> The expense of the campaign to the British Empire was immense, the Allied and Germans 'butchers' bills' even greater. But the most tragic consequence of the two sides' deadly game of 'tip and run' was the devastation of an area five times the size of Germany, and civilian suffering on a scale unimaginable in Europe.

It was a catastrophe for the Africans. A *Schutztruppe* medical officer later wrote: 'Our track is marked by death, plundering and evacuated villages'.

The British formed the East African Expeditionary Force (EAEF) in early 1915, principally from South Africa. Since the South African constitution restricted the Union Defence Force to operating inside the colony, the South African Overseas Expeditionary Force was formed to support imperial operations. The EAEF was supported by the East African Intelligence Department with Lieutenant-Colonel Mackay and Major King remaining in Mombasa. A persistent intelligence failure at all levels was to underestimate the intentions, size and capability of the *Schutztruppe*. Major Meinertzhagen claimed that he infiltrated about 100 Africans into German East Africa. He suggests that he compromised a headman by writing a letter of thanks for information and enclosing a monetary reward and then ensured the letter was intercepted by his German handlers. One method he claimed to have used was 'DPM', an acronym that he never defined but describes thus:

My method was easy, reliable and inexpensive. It was known as DPM and so far as I know has never been used by anyone else nor do I intend to disclose a system which might easily be used against us. I also found that the contents of German officers' latrines were a constant source of filthy though accurate information as odd pieces of paper containing messages, notes on enciphering and decoding, and private letters were often used where lavatory paper did not exist. I continued to use DPM in the Sinai campaign and for many years after I left the Army I used it in connection with my 'other work' not only in this country but abroad.

Some suggest DPM to be the Dirty Paper Method and speculated that such was the shortage of toilet paper in the *Schutztruppe* that the German officers and NCOs recycled office wastepaper thrown into wastepaper baskets. His African agents then scooped the paper from latrine pits to be dried in the sun and scraped for information. Equally, DPM could be paper collected from wastepaper baskets.

In an early attempt to impose British supremacy on Lake Victoria, Bukoda on its western shores was attacked. Meinertzhagen claimed that he suggested the high-powered transmitter should be captured for wireless intelligence purposes. The town was overrun on 23 June 1915, but the Germans had dismantled the wireless station. An Indian force landing at Tanga on 7 July was the first of several landings designed to outflank the Germans and shorten lines of communication from Mombasa. Two months later, Dar-es-Salaam was captured.

Meanwhile, the machinery of the cruiser *Königsberg* was suffering badly from low-quality coal captured from a British ship. Accompanied by the supply ship *Somali*, it had slipped into vast swamps of the Rufiji Delta, about 80 miles south of Dar-es-Salaam, where its machinery was dismantled and dragged overland on rafts to the town for repair. Meanwhile, in late September, one of three Royal Navy cruisers searching for the ship captured the diary of a German naval reserve officer on Koma Island signalling station, which indicated that it might be in the Salale Channel. When HMS *Chatham* sent a boarding party to a German ship masquerading as a hospital ship in Lindi, they found a chart of the Rufiji Delta and discovered that lighters had taken coal into the delta. Meanwhile, German counter-intelligence was spreading disinformation, including that the cruiser had been at Dar-es-Salaam on 20 October. Ten days later, a naval landing party that landed at the mouth of the main channel learned from a headman and two villagers that a warship was indeed in Salale Channel. After the leader of the party was shown a masthead protruding from the jungle, HMS *Chatham* tried to shell both ships but was forced to retire as the tide ebbed. In November, the *Königsberg* tried twice to reach open sea but was prevented by the summer shallow water. The Royal Navy then blockaded the river.

Mr Gerrard Wright, a senior engineer at a diamond mine near Durban, then offered Rear Admiral Herbert King-Hall, who commanded South Africa Station, the use of two Curtiss F hydroplanes that he had bought in England to display at

galas and exhibitions. Wright suggested that his pilot Dennis Cutler fly the aircraft.
Cutler was a former sergeant in the London Balloon Company RE (TF) and was
one of the first British NCOs to qualify as a pilot. Commissioned into the RNAS
in 1912, he resigned a year later and was employed by Wright. Commissioned as a
temporary flight sub-lieutenant, his first attempt to find the *Königsberg* resulted in
being forced to ditch. Shortly before his second flight, the radiator was damaged
and replaced with one from a lorry sent from Mombasa. On his third flight Cutler
attacked the ship with bombs, but was shot down and spent the next three years
as a prisoner.

On board the *Königsberg*, as morale sank from low supplies and malaria, its
captain, Max Looff, transferred 220 sailors to the *Schutztruppe*. He had also created
Delta Force by landing guns, machine guns, torpedoes and patrols to defend his
ship. On 13 January Indian infantry captured the island of Mafia, at the mouth of
the Rufiji, for use as a base for intelligence operations managed by Lieutenant-
Colonel Mackay against German East Africa.

A recent arrival in Pretoria from German East Africa was a middle-aged big game
hunter of impeccable Boer extraction named Pieter Pretorius. An ancestor had led
a trek north during the nineteenth century to escape the British and his father had
twice fought the British. Pretorius had spent twenty-five years wandering across
Central and East Africa with the vague notion of walking to Egypt. During his only
journey from Africa, he had married in Palestine and took his wife to his new farm
on the River Rufiji but she died within months of arriving. Moving to be among
the Pygmies in the Belgian Congo, he killed several Africans who raided his camp
but was then arrested for murder when he returned to German East Africa. His
gun licence was cancelled and he spent the two years on bail pending inquiries,
until in 1906 he was convicted and immediately released, time served.

While on a hunting trip in Portuguese East Africa with a British friend, Captain
Hemmens, he learnt that German authorities had withdrawn his shooting licence
and that his property had been sold to a German officer. Pretorius had previously
told the authorities that if the farm was sold, he would shoot elephants for their
ivory without a licence until he had been fully recompensed. He and two colleagues,
one a former British army captain, then crossed the River Rovuma in German
East Africa and he had just recovered his cost when they learned that Great Britain
and Germany were at war. Deciding to return to British Central Africa, about
1,500 miles to the south, they were in camp on an island in the river when a 200-
strong German force attacked one night. While his two companions were captured,
Pretorius was badly wounded in both legs; nevertheless, he plunged into the river
and, with the help of Africans, staggered into a British Mission on the shores of
Lake Nyasa where he spent the next four months. He then reached Pretoria but his
application to join the army was rejected because he was thought to be a German
spy; the sister of a British army captain was detailed to watch his movements.

Meanwhile, the Admiralty sent Lieutenant-General Jan Smuts a telegram asking if he knew of an elephant hunter named Pieter Pretorius because 'we would like him for a special mission'. Within about a week. Pretorius was commissioned into the East African Protectorate Forces and posted to its intelligence department. After several meetings with intelligence officers, on a train that took him to Durban where he met Admiral King-Hall on board his flagship, the ageing battleship HMS *Goliath*. King-Hall explained that he knew *Könisgberg* was somewhere in the Rufiji Delta. When Pretorius suggested that the warship should first be located, King-Hall gave him a naval wireless operator. Pretorius said he would find it within eight days.

After Lieutenant-Colonel Mackay had helped Pretorius select six Africans whom he regarded as the 'biggest rogues on the east coast' and after two nights, Pretorius selected the low-lying Koma Island, about 100 miles north-west of Mafia Island, as his forward operating base. The absence of inhabitants led him to believe they had been relocated by the Germans to prevent loose talk. The following night the patrol paddled to the mainland in a dugout with the intention of collecting information from villagers at Kisiju, but the village was also empty. In spite of persistent heavy rain, the patrol waded about 8 miles and reached a new road that Pretorius recognised to have been a path to Dar-es-Salaam. The next morning the patrol watched German troops and a convoy of porters heading south toward River Rufiji and then they captured two Africans who agreed to guide them to the warship. The following night they took Pretorius to a small hill near the village of Batja and as dawn broke Pretorius saw, 300 yards from his perch at the top of a tree, several sailors, a green-painted and heavily camouflaged warship and several defensive positions and patrols. On the eighth night, the patrol reported to King-Hall that he had found the *Königsberg* about a mile south of the Simba-Uranga Channel.

King-Hall then told Pretorius he needed intelligence on Delta Force and the location of the torpedo tubes. Several nights later, Pretorius and his patrol returned to the tree and with one of the two prisoners, Pretorius plotted the Delta Force positions. He then contacted a village chief known to be friendly and supplying labour to the Germans to ask if he would help. In return for £5 a month and food supplies, he arranged for Pretorius to debrief his son, who was employed onboard as a stoker. Relying on twenty-five years of the African sun to give him a swarthy look, dressed as an Arab and accompanied by the chief acting as his 'boy' (servant), Pretorius met the son in a German camp alongside the ship. The son reported that the 'long bullets that swim in the water' (torpedoes) had been moved to the mouth of the River Rufiji to cover any enemy approaches.

Pretorius returned with the information to King-Hall, who then asked him to find a navigable channel for a warship. When King-Hall instructed that all shipping was to avoid the estuary mouth of the Rufiji and the instruction was printed in the German newspapers, a German officer on the *Königsberg* was accused of treachery. Masquerading as a fisherman, Pretorius began a very risky period of mapping the channels by paddling his dugout in daylight in and out of the channels and discovered the northerly 7-mile Kikunja Channel had an uninterrupted depth of 7ft of water until he reached a reef. He also placed a stick in the mouth of the channel and for the next month took hourly readings of the rise and fall of the tide, information he gratefully placed in front of King-Hall. Having been told by King-Hall that he was considering using monitors with 4ft draughts, Pretorius then paced the distance from the reef to the warship and found that the ship was within range of 6in guns.

Soon after the monitors HMS *Mersey* and *Severn* arrived, King-Hall told Pretorius that he planned to lure the *Königsberg* from its lair using two dhows, but the dhows were separated by a storm and the one used by Pretorius wrecked a mile off Koma Island in view of a German outpost. Their rescue by a German steam launch was interrupted by a whaler from a patrolling warship. The next night, Pretorius saw that the second dhow was tied alongside the *Königsberg*. Morale on board rose when a supply ship posing as a Dane challenged the British blockade until it was forced to beach by a destroyer; nevertheless, the Germans salvaged much of its cargo. Having heard a German patrol discussing the defences, Pretorius told his patrol that they would go inland for eight days to investigate whether the Germans had strengthened their defences and gave each man £1 in German coinage to be used for living among the local population and, if necessary, buying a boat in order to reach a patrolling warship. In a night heavy with rain, the patrol avoided the mangrove swamp in favour of a beach but had infiltrated no more than 500 yards when they were ambushed. Pretorius and three men raced back to the beach, under fire, and scrambled into the dugout. There was no sign of the other two men, until they were seen four days later, several miles out to sea in a small boat, exhausted after two days without food or water. The following day, Pretorius watched as several Royal Navy warships entered Rufiji estuary.

The relative success of Cutler had encouraged King-Hall to take a greater interest in air reconnaissance and at the end of March three Sopwith-807 Folder seaplanes and a ground detachment from No.4 Squadron RNAS, usually based on the Isle of Grain, arrived on Niororo Island, south of Zanzibar, under command of Lieutenant John Tulloch Cull. Although the aircraft were in poor condition and were temperamental in the conditions, on 25 April Cull and his observer, Able Seaman Boggis, took a panoramic photograph of the *Königsberg*. On 5 July, with Cull spotting, the monitors penetrated the delta and shelled the *Königsberg* but were damaged by return fire. Six days later, they reduced the cruiser to a wreck. The survivors and ten of the 105mm (4.1in) guns were converted into field artillery and joined the *Schutztruppe* as a second naval company.

By January 1916 the British, Belgian and Portuguese colonies had developed a strategy to surround Lettow-Vorbeck, but the Germans were fighting on their own ground and under his orders to 'harass, kill, fight, but don't get caught'. For the next three years, the Germans proved an elusive foe adept at occupying key ground for limited periods of time and then slipping away along prepared withdrawal routes, by living off the land and supported by village cottage industries, one particularly valuable resource being quinine. Shortly after defeat at the Battle of Salaita Hill, Lieutenant-General Jan Smuts assumed command of the EAEF in mid-February and commented: 'Swamps and jungles [...] what a dismal prospect there is in front of me'.

Captain Robert Dolbey RAMC wrote in his *Sketches of the East Africa Campaign*:

Of all the departments of War in German East Africa, probably the most romantic and interesting is the Intelligence Department. Far ahead of the fighting troops are the Intelligence officers with their native scouts. These officers, for the most part, are men who have lived in the country, who know the native language and are familiar with the lie of the land from experience gained in past hunting trips.

Often creeping behind the enemy, creeping along the lines of communication, these officers carry their lives in their hands, and run the risk of betrayal by any native who happens across them. Sleeping in the bush at night, unable to light fires to cook their food, lest the light should attract the querying patrol learning of their presence in the country had been out after them for days. Hiding in the bush, short of rations, the little luxuries of civilisation long since finished, forced to smoke the reeking pungent native tobacco; living off wild game (that must be trapped, not shot) and native meal; at the mercy of the natives, whom both sides employ to get information of the other, these men are in constant danger. Nor are the amenities of civilised warfare applied when capture is their lot [...] To this type of man, the African continent has offered a particular attraction and we should have fared badly in the East African campaign, if we could not have relied upon the services of many of them [...] Not the least of the assets of these men is the knowledge they have of the native and the hold they have obtained over them. The man will go furthest who relies upon the respect rather than the fear he inspires.

Major Meinertzhagen wrote in his diaries that he thought the East African intelligence department to be ineffective; he blames commanders for dereliction of duty by ignoring field service regulations which required them to 'reconnoitre his own front'. While respecting his opinion, his assertion fails to acknowledge that Smuts was using his experience of the Boer Intelligence Corps to install a screen of European intelligence officers leading detachments of African intelligence scouts screening the advance. Most of the intelligence officers lived in East Africa, spoke Swahili and while commissioned into either the King's African Rifles or East African Mounted Rifles, generally had a relaxed colonial approach to military etiquette.

The Mounted Rifles was formed from disparate groups of irregular horse and proved to be as effective as the best of the Boer War colonial units. Somali horsemen in Cork's Scouts were thoroughly at home in the arid bush but did not take kindly to military discipline. Seventy officers and men from 2nd Loyals and the 25th Royal Fusiliers (the Frontiersmen) were assembled into Driscoll's Scouts, a noted member being Cherry Kearton, a noted wildlife film-maker who recorded his service with the battalion. Belfield's Scouts, Grobler's Scouts and Botha's Scouts arrived from German South-West Africa. The 25th Royal Fusiliers (the Frontiersmen) recruited former military and naval personnel and those with experience in the colonies, reinforced by hardened African colonists such as the big game hunte, Frederic Selous, aged 64 years. One of its founders, Hugh Pollard, had plotted with two *Daily Express* journalists in mid-September 1914 to spread the word that a million Cossacks had landed in Scotland and would be reinforcing the BEF. A porter at Edinburgh station reported that the Russians 'had snow on their boots'. Pollard later joined the Intelligence Corps and was involved the development of propaganda.

Before Smuts crossed the border into German East Africa, he was introduced to Pretorius by Major Shakespear, his GSO2 (Intelligence) and appointed him as his chief scout. At a planning meeting about tackling Salaita Hill and forcing the Taverta Gap, Pretorius said that since the hill lacked water, the defenders were reliant on supplies being delivered via Taverta. He suggested that the attention of the defenders could be diverted while columns attacked Taverta from the north. But first, Smuts needed to know if there were any Germans on Mount Kilimanjaro and he sent a patrol of Pretorius and five men to investigate. Crossing the River Lumi south of the German positions anchored to the Zivane swamps, they crossed a road and headed up the slopes in increasingly cold drizzle before the warlike Wachaka tribe were aware. As the dawn crept across the mountain, Pretorius saw a German outpost in the Lake Chala crater and, further up the mountain, a wireless unit. With his left flank at very limited risk, during the afternoon of 7 August Smuts used the lake as his axis for launching a mounted brigade and an infantry brigade around Lake Chala in a pincer movement against the German positions. Pretorius was given a platoon to ensure safe passage through Wachaka territory. In danger of being outflanked, when Lettow-Vorbeck withdrew to high ground to the south, Smuts thought he was preparing a counter-attack and instructed Pretorius to infiltrate the German rear areas to see if they were bringing up reserves. In fact, the reserves were the rearguard. Pretorius remained behind German lines for eight days and, after watching them rip up the Northern Railway for 7 miles to Kahe, returned to Smut's HQ at Moshi, much to the surprise of those who had heard him reported as killed.

Smuts then instructed Pretorius to survey the bush astride the River Pangani, to the west of the Uganda Railway, as far as Buiko, and select drifts and bridging sites. His patrol of several former German *askaris* and ten porters was in frequent contact with the enemy, bumping into an outpost on the banks of a river and observing from what he thought was an abandoned trench, only to be saluted by two German *askaris* who thought he was a German officer. Pretorius collected intelligence from African villagers glad to see the last of the Germans and unwilling to betray them. Rarely camping in the same place on consecutive nights, he had several brushes with enemy patrols hunting for him. On one occasion, seven men whom he lost in an ambush were hanged.

In May 1916, Sergeant-Major Arnold Weinholt transferred from the East African Mounted Rifles to the African Intelligence Department and teamed up with an Australian and a British East African scouting for the column using the unknown terrain around Pangani River and reporting their intelligence to the advance guard. As the column approached the central railway in July, they ambushed a convoy using a track to supply German outposts and forced the porters to burn almost everything, including desperately needed uniforms. They also burned a railway depot and returned to their column 'half-starved and unkempt, bringing with them three prisoners and information of great importance'. The *Schutztruppe* retaliated and, surprising the scouts in their camp, wounded Weinholt. He was later captured by an Afrikaaner militia and was sent to the officers' prison camp at Liwale. The Australian was killed and the East African reached British lines. Lieutenant Dudley Groves had a leopard carry a scout into the bush. He was rescued, but the patrol were unable to use their weapons because the enemy were close.

At an engagement at Kissaki, about 200 miles south-west of Dar-es-Salaam during fighting around the River Ruvu, in September, South African cavalry charging to the rescue of the 2nd South African Brigade galloped into German reserves, as Lettow-Vorbeck had planned. One of his *askaris* masqueraded as a groom to infiltrate their lines. EAEF columns marched along the central railway and linked up with the Belgians and the British Lake Victoria Force. After Belgian-Congolese forces had captured Burundi and Rwanda, Smuts reminded them they were occupiers, not colonists.

By September, the advance through the rugged terrain south of Dar-es-Salaam was stalling, largely because the management of the logistic tail of hungry, understrength and overworked African porters had collapsed. During the campaign, 40,000 porters in British service died mainly from exhaustion and disease. Dependent on the railway from the port at Dar-es-Salaam, problems worsened when the German 3rd Field Company destroyed the bridge at Ruvu and wrecked twenty-one sluices of the railway embankment. Fearing that the Germans might be tasked with raiding the central railway, the Imperial Service Jind Infantry attacked the German base at Kissangire. Scouting ahead of the force were forty intelligence scouts commanded by Lieutenant George Howarth. Reporting that the German post was in a building on top of a steep conical hill around which two lines of trenches had been dug, Howarth recommended an approach from the west and south-west. On 9 October, the Sikhs overran the two trench line, but were held in front of the building by heavy fire that neutralised the machine guns and killed two British officers with the force. When the commanding officer decided to withdraw, Howarth took command and withdrew the infantry under heavy fire. He was awarded the MC. When General Smuts ordered troops from 1st Division into the area, in mid-October, the 57th Wilde's Rifles (Frontier Force) commanded by Lieutenant-Colonel T.J. Willans and a detachment from 2nd North Loyals marched over 80 miles across densely bushed, unmapped territory. Willens, who was compelled to leave fifty soldiers behind because their boots were beyond repair, was guided by a King's African Rifles Mounted Infantry platoon commanded by Captain George Hurst, a professional game hunter. The column crossed the swift River Ruvu twice. The mounted infantry captured a German small patrol that had become hopelessly lost in the bush. For his work with the column, Hurst was awarded the MC.

Meanwhile Lettow-Vorbeck ordered Captain Stemmerman to hold Kissangire with 11 Field Company until crops to the south were harvested. There were several clashes as the Germans raided the railway. In early November, twenty intelligence scouts and fifty Zanzibar African Rifles landed on Kwale Island and crossed to Kisiju, from where they extended their intelligence operations toward Kongo to Msanga until they were attacked by three field companies under Captain Liebermann three weeks later and withdrew to Kwale Island. Shortly before Kilwa was captured, the Germans marched their prisoners inland to Mangangira on the River Luwego. Using a small compass, Sergeant-Major Weinholt and three officers escaped and reached Kilwa. Weinholt was shipped to Nairobi to recuperate.

During the early stages of the Battle of the Rufiji River in early January 1917, Pretorius was guiding a 1st Cape Corps column and two guns commanded by Colonel Morris through 30 miles of bush with the intention of surprising General Lettow-Vorbeck. They were within 2 miles of crossing the river at Makalinso when Pretorius's instinct led him to advise Morris to cross about 2 miles upstream west of Kipenio. Later that day, Pretorius scouted downstream and found that the planned crossing was defended by a strong enemy position. During the day, signallers collected information by tapping into an enemy telephone cable discovered by one of Pretorius's scouts. When a herd of hippopotami charged through their position, the force assumed an enemy force was attacking. The only casualties were several meat-on-the-hoof cattle that stampeded into the bush. A dawn bayonet attack cleared Makalinso.

By the New Year Smuts was still struggling to regain momentum. The advance through dense bush and tropical forests soaked by the rainy season took its toll, particularly among the South Africans, more acclimatised to the bracing chill of the veldt than marching, wading rivers, building roads and erecting bridges on limited rations in heavy rain with the ever-present threat of 'tip and run' raids and attacks by animals. Shorts and short-sleeved shirts offered no protection to cuts, which quickly turned sceptic. Dysentery and malaria were rife with ten soldiers hospitalised for every one killed in action. Tsetse flies were the kiss of death for thousands of horses, mules and oxen. Smuts had no alternative but to halt and medically evacuate thousands of soldiers to South Africa. When he asked the War Office if gas could be used, he was told it could, provided that it was on a frontage of 1,280 metres. There the matter rested.

Smuts was replaced by Major-General Arthur Hoskins, formerly King's Africa Rifles; he was forced to rebuild the EAEF with a greater number of African troops and introduced wirelesses and lorries, but, accused of lacking energy, he was replaced by Lieutenant-General Jacob van Deventer in May. He had been Smut's deputy during the Boer War and his English was poor. Hoskins later commanded a division in Mesopotamia. Deventer was no more successful in trapping the *Schutztruppe*. Meanwhile, Lettow-Vorbeck had assembled his field companies into battalion-sized *Abteilungs* of Main Force and West Force. In the fierce battle at Mahiwa on the River Lukuledi in October, about 60 miles west of Lindi, he lost 519 men killed against 4,900 EAEF casualties, half from the Nigerian Brigade.

When Deventer landed at the southern port of Lindi in mid-September 1917 much of the fighting centred around the Makonde plateau between the Lukuledi and Rovuma rivers to the south. Lettow-Vorbeck sent Captain Looff and 600 men and a *Königsberg* gun to contain the landing. Marching 200 miles through tangled bush in three weeks, he destroyed a weak Portuguese incursion and surrounded Lindi, which was being transformed into a major base. British aircraft scouted the bush for his gun but failed to find it. Two British intelligence officers, Captains Hallam and Best, operating near the Portuguese East African (now Mozambique) border, heard about the landing and decided to offer their services, but were ambushed by a German patrol hunting for them. Hallam, shot in the leg, plunged into a river, distinctly fearful that crocodiles would surely smell his blood. None investigated. When the Germans lost his spoor, he persuaded several Africans to carry him to Portuguese East Africa. Best reached Lindi and later served in Palestine as an intelligence officer.

Meinertzhagen claims that when he heard that a *Königsberg* force was being hunted in the forested misty, high ground overlooking the Masai steppes, he sent 160 scouts under command of a Dutchman named Linton to track them. Linton ambushed the seamen near Ufiome and captured an ensign. After being loaned to the Intelligence Corps Museum, it was returned to the National Maritime Museum in 1979. Captain Looff later claimed that he had buried the original near his ship.

Intelligence scouts and irregulars under Captain Lionel Cohen MC cleared the enemy from a western stretch of the Rovuma River and absorbed several captured *Schutztruppe askaris* into 1/4th Kings African Rifles. Major Brian Hawkins, from the same battalion, occupied Liwale on 29 November 1917 and captured a 14th Field Company officer. An officer using an old and inaccurate British survey map and who had become lost in the dense bush was also captured. Hawkins linked up with a Congolese battalion and an attached cyclist platoon that had been landed at Kilwa. Captain Egerton Seymour, previously Belfield's Scouts, was supporting the 1/4th Kings African Rifles west of Negomano and was also awarded the MC:

> He has repeatedly performed marked acts of courage and initiative, and he has on two occasions attacked and routed enemy patrols, though greatly outnumbered. Within the last two months he has himself accounted for sixteen of the enemy during various patrol encounters, and has burned large quantities of enemy supplies, his work being magnificent throughout.

In November a South African topographical section commanded by Sergeant Quigley arrived. German attempts to deliver essential supplies to Lettow-Vorbeck using the naval Zeppelin L-59 from Bulgaria turned back.

Several months after Lindi had been captured, Pretorius was sent to the port because its intelligence department was having little success in obtaining information. Meeting with Captain Donner, he learned that the hostility of Africans was a problem and that several intelligence officers and scouts had not returned from missions. Pretorius was discussing the situation with the garrison commander when a dishevelled intelligence officer named Engelbert arrived reporting that the 25th (Frontiersmen) Royal Fusiliers had been defeated attacking a German outpost 15 miles north-west of the port. The battalion was part of Brigadier-General O'Grady's Lindi column.

Pretorius immediately selected sixteen captured *askaris* and eight to be porters from the prison camp and learnt from a reluctant chief that there was a German camp on the Makonde Plateau that could only be approached by using a narrow track along a narrow ridge. The following night Pretorius pinpointed the outpost and then, moving west, found the Germans were in scattered positions ready to resist the British advance. They were also ensuring that food was reserved for the *Schutztruppe* and were paying for it with worthless money. Pretorius made contact with O'Grady and suggested that as long as the Germans had access to food, they were in a strong position but were vulnerable to being cut off from the coast. Pretorius then devised a plan to convince the Germans that the chiefs were on side by reporting them reporting that he was raiding their villages for food. After smuggling sufficient rifles to arm 2,000 people, in a co-ordinated assault the Africans attacked the German garrisons.

Pretorius avoided capture by keeping on the move, but had a horse shot underneath him and survived three days without food while being harassed by German patrols. After another patrol, he collapsed seriously ill during a visit to army headquarters. Even so, his African couriers arrived with reports, including a letter seized from a German courier written to General Lettow-Vorbeck by Captain Theodor Tafel, commanding Western Force, that he intended to march to a path crossroads about 2 miles north of where the Rivers Bangala and Rovuma met. Pretorius knew the area and wrote to Deventer suggesting the area be cleared of Africans and that the German column be denied food by a scorched earth policy. Deventer agreed and when he sent his car to collect Pretorius to plan the detail, a doctor cheerfully told his patient that he would be dead within the week. Several days later, Pretorius and his patrol reached the River Bangala to find it dry and that a large pond near the crossroads was undisturbed, except for animal spoor. He immediately sent couriers to villagers instructing them to leave by 5 p.m. or risk arrest, and that any food they could not carry was to be destroyed. A scout reported that the Germans had arrived at the pond and then captured two *askaris*, who said that West Force had not found any food for several days and was at the crossroads in expectation that it would be resupplied with food captured by Lettow-Vorbeck after raiding a Portuguese supply dump.

Unaware that his letter had been intercepted and watched by Pretorius from high ground, Tafel waited at the crossroads for two days and then headed south to a gorge through which the Bangala usually flowed. When someone fired a shot from the south, Pretorius scrambled to a ridge and saw Tafel's column on one side and Lettow-Vorbeck's main force approaching the river junction to the south. Suddenly, Tafel's column halted at the entrance to the gorge. Below him, Tafel consulted with his officers and led his column south across the River Rovuma during the morning of 28 November and missed linking up with main force. Having not found food for several days and not realising that Lettow-Vorbeck was near, Tafel sent a message to his commander that he was 'ceasing hostilities at 6 p.m.', as he wished to 'surrender on best possible terms'. The courier was intercepted by one of Pretorius's scouts and the letter was sent to Brigade-General J.A. Hannyngton, then commanding Han Force, who intercepted the Germans. The surrender of 1,371 troops was a severe blow to Lettow-Vorbeck.

Promoted to major-general, Lettow-Vorbeck crossed into Portuguese East Africa but lack of supplies forced him to trim the size of the *Schutztruppe* by ordering 1,000 men to surrender. Scouting ahead of British forces was Weinholt, promoted to lieutenant, and a detachment of forty intelligence scouts; they faced hostility from Africans and settlers sympathetic to the Germans and were forced to withdraw to the coast when they lost everything in an attack on their camp. Weinholt was later awarded the DSO and MC and bar, one for escaping. Lettow-Vorbeck crossed into Northern Rhodesia in August 1918 and worked into an advantageous position to attack the copper mines in Northern Rhodesia and the Belgian Congo. When the Armistice was signed in Europe he surrendered at Abercorn on 25 November, twelve days later, with 155 Germans and about 1,160 Africans, all that remained from the 10,000 men who had fought 250,000 Allied troops for four years.

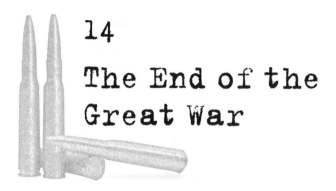

14

The End of the Great War

When the guns literally fell silent on the Western Front at 11 a.m. on 11 November 1918, the world had changed dramatically since 1914. The monarchies of Austria–Hungary, Germany and Russia had disappeared and the Turkish Empire was in ruins. Chaos, bitterness and political instability was infectious as the high hopes of the 1919 Paris Peace Conference ended in disillusionment, not least in the Middle East where Lieutenant-Colonel Lawrence's sensible solution was discarded in favour of Great Britain and France carving up the region as agreed in the Sykes–Picot Agreement, a consequence that still resonates today. The League of Nations was formed to promote peace, but the failure of member nations to meet demands led to frustration.

Meanwhile, Allied forces had intervened in the chaos of a disintegrating Russia. After the 1917 Treaty of Brest-Litovak had released German divisions to be transferred to the Western Front, the collapse of the Russian army exposed parts of Russia to German occupation and Bolshevik exploitation. This led to the Allies dispatching several expeditionary forces to protect their geopolitical interests. To meet the threat to the Mesopotamian and Syrian military fronts and to India, the North Persia Force was raised in January 1918 to support a coalition of anti-Bolshevik and anti-Turkish groups and to protect the railway from the Russian cities between Baku and Tiflis and to secure the Baku oilfields. The force consisted of a British brigade and Australian, Canadian, New Zealand and South African volunteers commanded by Major-General Lionel Dunsterville. He had considerable expertise of Russian affairs and was fluent in several dialects. His force became known as Dunsterforce and its intelligence officer was Major Martin Donohue (Intelligence Corps).

Regional instability meant that in late January the force advance guard reached Enzil after a two week 600-mile drive through wintery, inhospitable territory. When Dunster found that the town and Baku were both occupied by belligerent Bolsheviks, he concentrated his force at Hamadan. When it became evident that Donohue was unable to make the best of the intelligence, Brigadier-General Macdonogh sent Brigadier-General R. St George Gorton (late Royal Artillery) to be the force brigadier-general, General Staff (Intelligence). Brigadier-General

Beach gave him access to his III (Indian) Corps Intelligence Section in Baghdad and introduced him to military attachés. He also supplied a GSO1, a GSO2, two GSO3s, one for I(b) (Secret Service) and one for I(c) (Mapping), and nine Intelligence Corps Special Service officer linguists. One was Captain Francis McCullagh, a journalist in Russia before the war, who spoke ten Russian and Eastern European dialects and who had fought with the Caucasian Brigade in the Manchurian War before being commissioned into the Royal Irish Fusiliers in 1914. Transferring to the Intelligence Corps, he served in the Dardanelles, Salonika, Serbia and Macedonia.

After the main body arrived by train and vehicles, Dunsterforce entered Enzeli and Baku on 27 June, but its tactical positions were never totally secure and on 1 September 14,000 Turks attacked Baku and Hamadan and first drove it from Enzeli and then slaughtered the indigenous Armenians. A fortnight later, the force withdrew and was disbanded. Dominion officers were quick to blame Dunsterville for the perceived failure; nevertheless, Field-Marshal Sir Henry Wilson, the CIGS, considered that while intervention had been a gamble, the stakes had been sufficiently high to make the mission justifiable.

Elsewhere during the summer of 1918, a mission commanded by Major-General Wilfred Malleson assisted the Trans-Caspian government by curtailing German and Turkish subversion and reduced the threats to Afghanistan and India by organising a spy network in the city of Meshed. Malleson had previously fought in East Africa. The small Macartney mission entered Bolshevik Russian Turkestan from Chinese Turkestan and based itself in the city of Tashkent on the Trans-Caucasus Railway. The Tashkent Bolsheviks were under pressure from Cossacks claiming independence and from White Russians. A mission in Siberia included Japanese soldiers. While most of the British Military Mission were declared unfit for active service, their role was to guard the Trans-Siberian Railway. An Intelligence Corps officer attached to the mission was McCullagh, who was briefly captured when the city of Omsk was overrun by the Red Army in November 1919. The French entered South Russia and Ukraine. British forces also landed in North Russia at Murmansk and Archangel. Although the anti-Bolshevik 'White' army valued the support, the intervention was muddled and a drain on war-strapped European economies, and by the summer of 1919, it was evident that war-weary public opinion did not support the interventions.

A fortnight after the signing of the Treaty of Mudros on 30 September, an Intelligence Corps detachment accompanied the army of occupation to Constantinople to assist in the demobilisation the Turkish and German armed forces. Given the resurgence of Turkish nationalism, fears of Bolshevik intrigue and the outbreak of hostilities between Greece and Turkey over disputed territory, the detachment of about 100 British intelligence officers sent from Palestine and Macedonia was the largest in any of the occupied countries. Their presence led to

General Sir Tim Harington, commanding the Army of the Black Sea, mentioning to Wilson: 'I don't know what all these intelligence officers do. The place stinks of them. Every café is full of them. I must say since I've arrived I've got very little intelligence.' Colonel Gribbon, previously the head of MI2, was sent to resolve the problem, but hardening tensions erupted into civil war and victory for the nationalists.

Germany was divided into three zones governed by the British and Canadians from Cologne, the Americans in Koblenz and the French in Mainz and Wiesbaden. In March 1919, the BEF reformed as the British Army of the Rhine (BAOR). The military government of Cologne was supported by intelligence officers and a 250-strong security section capable of handling cipher, photo interpretation, wireless security and press censorship. Its principal threat was the German secret service promoting resistance and sedition, particularly spreading communism among British troops. When the Treaty of Versailles came into force the Rhineland became the British-occupied zone. Armed forces reductions led to the GSO1 taking command of an Intelligence Corps in Germany that, by 1921, had shrunk to ten officers and sixty-two other ranks. The military government was replaced by the Inter-Allied Rhineland High Commission empowered to 'secure the safety and requirements of the Allied Forces of Occupation'. When HQ BAOR moved to Wiesbaden in December 1925, the civil administration was transferred to two Intelligence Corps sections of General Staff (Civil Affairs) and Intelligence. Civil Affairs consisted of detachments of NCOs advising British military authorities on relationships with the German authorities, their terms of reference including political associations, the arts, marriages and labour disputes. One organisation warned about its practice of wearing uniforms was the *Nationalsozialistische Deutsche Arbeiterpartei* (NDSAP), the forerunner of the Nazi Party; however, it was considered not to be a subversive threat and therefore was not proscribed.

During this period, the word 'intelligence' was replaced by 'security' because it was deemed more acceptable in a political and social environment of pacificism. The BAOR Intelligence Corps was renamed 'Civil Affairs and Security Branch' until the following year when both branches were amalgamated into General Staff (Security) with a remit still to ensure the 'dignity and security of the Army of Occupation' and forbidden to admit its association with any intelligence organisation. The intelligence police became the field security police. Always wearing civilian clothes, their immunity from arrest enabled them to carry out more in-depth investigations. As Russia began to emerge as an ideological threat, the Intelligence Directorate was reorganised. MI5 handed the Passport Control Department to MI6 and was confined to monitoring evidence of Bolshevism within the armed forces.

Meanwhile, with labour unrest, disillusionment among discharged service personnel and talk of revolution on the social agenda in Great Britain, GHQ

Home Forces instructed intelligence officers to gather information without raising suspicions, particularly during the seven-day railway strike in September 1919. When Sir Basil Thomson, head of the Special Branch, suggested to Field-Marshal Haig, then commander-in-chief home forces, that army intelligence and Special Branch should operate together, Haig replied: 'I would not authorise any men being used as spies. Officers must act straightforwardly and as Englishmen. "Espionage" amongst our own men was hateful to us Army men [...] Thomson's machinery for getting information of sedition must work independently of the Army and its leaders.'

Notwithstanding the War Office stance, the DMI established a domestic intelligence network for 'emergency home defence' but dared not risk paying for information. In Ireland, the British army fought a bitter war against the Irish Republican Army led by Michael Collins, in which both sides targeted intelligence officers. The most notable incidents were the co-ordinated murders of fourteen members of the Cairo Gang on 21 November 1920 and the assassination in June 1920 of Field-Marshal Wilson in London. Retaliation for the Cairo Gang was swift when thirteen spectators were shot by security forces at Croke Park sports stadium in an event that became known as Bloody Sunday.

War Office contingency planning for war in Europe accepted that the BEF would be accompanied by a 175-strong Intelligence Corps, a figure calculated on the size of the organisation that had existed in France between 1917 and 1918. It would be commanded by the commandant and would consist of 300 FSP and air photographic support to the RAF.

During the winter of 1928 it became clear that the troop withdrawals would start sooner than the planned date of 1935, and during 1929 the drawdown began when civil matters were transferred to the French and German authorities. In December, the organisation described by Major Piggot, the former 2nd Army GSO2 (Intelligence) as having 'reached its apotheosis' departed from the army order of battle when the BAOR GSO2, Major Kenneth Strong, an intelligence officer and an Intelligence Corps FSP NCO, left Germany by car. Nevertheless, the 1931, 1936 and 1937 War Establishments required Home and Overseas Commands to form an Intelligence Corps. When MI5 formed E (Port and Border Security) Branch to address the threat of hostile infiltration, Major Strong, now posted to the DMI, and Major-General Vernon Kell, still head of MI5, persuaded Captain Frank Davies MC (Glosters), a former Intelligence Corps officer, to accept two months' consultancy to raise home port security sections at large ports as a counter-intelligence function to support port security officers and security control officers, as had been done in 1914. In 1938, Davies developed Defence Security courses under the cloak of the Corps of Military Police at their depot at Mytchett for regular army other ranks nearing the end of their service and liable to be recalled to the colours in the event of mobilisation. Subjects included interrogation, the maintenance of morale through security awareness and counter-propaganda and developing orders of battle, in particular of Germany. Course notes were destroyed at the end.

Intelligence was regarded as a crucial operational requirement during the Second World War, as it had been in the first. Although its covert capability was taken over by other organisations, the Intelligence Corps was widely represented in its traditional roles. Nevertheless, the War Office, true to form, predicted in 1947:

> By about 1952, intelligence commitments of the Active Army are likely to be too small to justify the retention of an Intelligence Corps for officers, for the principal reason that it would not be possible to guarantee a normal Army career for more than a very few officers. It is probable that a very small Intelligence Corps, for other ranks only, would be retained permanently.

The assessment quickly unravelled as the independence, counter-revolutionary and internal security campaigns and the Cold War broke out, forcing the Standing Committee on Army Post-War Problems to accept in 1948 that 'there was a need for a permanent Intelligence Corps in the Regular Army'. When the large pool of manpower disappeared with the ending of National Service in the early 1960s, the Intelligence Corps added operational intelligence to its security and counter-intelligence skills, leading to the development of multi-disciplined intelligence sections at all levels, including the Ministry of Defence. The Royal Signals and Royal Military Police have both made attempts to absorb the application of intelligence and security, without success.

15

Conclusion

Many of those who first went to war in 1914 believed that they would be home by Christmas. Instead, the fighting in Europe developed into a stalemate, while elsewhere in East Africa and the Middle East it was largely a war of manoeuvre. However, during the first two years of the war, the role of the General Staff was largely sidelined by a general, Lord Kitchener, whose career had been fashioned fighting small colonial wars. When Field-Marshal Haig took command of the BEF in 1916, the intelligence system on the Western Front had developed into one which was providing masses of quality information. Commanders from platoon level upwards were familiar with the need for intelligence through intelligence officers at battalion level to GSOs (Intelligence) at formation level and through associations with the Intelligence Corps. By the end of the war, virtually every military organisation – from battalion upwards to army, theatre of operations HQs to the War Office – was supported by an effective intelligence department. The Intelligence Corps had expanded from fifty-five in August 1914 to 3,000 in 1918. At least the green and grey of Intelligence was not as abused as the red insignia of the General Staff!

The development of the Intelligence Corps as a pool for intelligence specialists providing a range of expertise in an era of intelligence technology proved crucial. The observations of pilots and then cameras and air photographic interpretation proved crucial in providing intelligence from the very early days and were developed throughout the war. This includes systems familiar to troops today – maps marked with grid references and the clock system to give direction. While the Royal Navy led in wireless intelligence, the development of I-Tocs in the front line providing tactical communications intelligence was a crucial innovation that re-emerged in the British army during the 1970s.

Human intelligence and the extraction of information from willing and unwilling sources is the oldest and best method. It is also the most flexible because the subject talks. Interrogation is an extension of the battlefield and the interrogators proved able to extract masses of information from prisoners, sometimes in face-to-face conversations shortly after capture, sometimes by using ploys, such as stool pigeons in prison camps and talking with captured casualties in hospitals. Those interrogators had a single aim – that of winning the war and thereby contributing to shorter casualty lists. At least, they were not at the mercy of an unsympathetic judicial system and naïve journalists.

Of particular success were the army covert intelligence operations conducted in Europe and the Middle East which are not well known. The difficulties of the long front line in Europe were solved by recruiting circuits and sources in occupied Europe and asking them to count railway trains carrying troops and equipment. It was simple, relatively safe and reliable enough that a special map, the railway map, was maintained at BEF GHQ to track reinforcements and calculate the German order of battle.

While there is a tendency to focus on Lawrence of Arabia, the years that Lieutenant-Colonel Leachman spent in the desert in Mesopotamia before and during the war and the four years that Captain Weldon spent landing on beaches to contact sources and collect information in Asia Minor and Syria is barely known. The rejection of the Jewish organisation NILI by an inexperienced intelligence officer was fortunately resolved to the advantage of General Allenby and his advance through Palestine and Syria.

Three weeks after the evacuation from Dunkirk in mid-1940, several First World War intelligence officers transferred their skills to help reform the Intelligence Corps on 19 July 1940 ,taking as its motto *Manui Dat Cognitio Vires* ('knowledge gives strength to the arm'). The new corps adopted the unofficial badge devised by the Censorship Division for its cap badge. During the 1970s, the corps adopted the Cypress green beret.

An Intelligence Corps director suggested in 1990 that he was the only director in the army able to send a soldier, of any rank, anywhere in the world at short notice, sometimes alone, often in civilian clothes, and for that soldier to use his initiative and experience to achieve the objective, a culture that began in 1914 when Major Torrie told his officers to 'make yourself useful'.

Extract from *The Wipers Times*, 25 December 1916

INTELLIGENCE
Summary Measures

'O' the Observer who stood at his post,
and at 3 on the 10th saw a small German host
Going east with a cart, so he had a good look,
And proceeded to make – a note in his book.

'D' the Division who read the next day
The Report 'O' had rendered, and sent it away
To Corps, where it rested, until bye and bye
The Army decided that those Huns should die.

So a mandate was sent to Corps as a start,
To slaughter those Huns going East with a cart,
Which mandate was with decision and ease
Pushed onto Division, 'for action, please'.

Division post-haste, or as near as could be,
Sent word to the gunners of what 'O' could see.
The gunners prepared with shot and shell,
To blow those said Germans from here to Hell.

With lanyard in hand, and with cool flashing eye,
They scanned all the landscape, they scanned the sky.
And here we will leave them, gazing apart
For the Huns who – a week ago – passed with a cart.

Anonymous

Bibliography

General

Andrews, Christopher, *Secret Service: The Making of the British Intelligence Community* (London: Heinemann, 1985)

Beach, Jim, *Haig's Intelligence; GHQ and the German Army 1916–1918* (Cambridge: Cambridge University Press, 2013)

Beesley, Patrick, *Room 40: British Naval Intelligence 1914–1918* (London: Hamish Hamilton, 1982)

Brown, Malcolm, *The Imperial War Museum Book of the First World War* (London: Sidgwick & Jackson, 1991)

Chaussard, Peter, *Mapping: The First World War* (Glasgow: Collins, 2013)

Clayton, Anthony, *Forearmed: A History of the Intelligence Corps* (London: Brasseys, 1993)

Croxson, Paul, 'The Birth of Signals Intelligence', *The Rose and Laurel*, 175 (2013)

Eaton, Captain H.B., 'APIS: An Account of the Development of Aerial Photographic Interpretation in the British Army' (The Intelligence Corps Museum, 1978)

Ferris, John, 'The British Army and Signals Intelligence in the Field during the First World War', *Intelligence and National Security*, 3:3

Gibson, Hugh, *Journal for the Legation in Brussels 1915* (New York: Grooset & Dunlop, 1917)

Gilbert, Martin, *First World War* (W&N, 2008)

Grant, R.G., *World War 1: The Definitive Visual Guide* (London: DK, 2014)

Haswell, Jock, *British Military Intelligence* (London: Weidenfeld and Nicolson, 1973)

Herbert, Aubrey, *Mons, ANZAC & Kut: A British Intelligence Officer in Three Theatres of the First World War, 1914–1918* (Leonaur, 2010)

Jeffrey, Keith, *MI6: History of the Secret Intelligence Service 1909–1949* (London: Bloomsbury, 2010)

Lee, Bartholomew, 'Radio Intelligence Developments during the First World War', *The Journal of Intelligence History*, 5 (Winter 2005)

Macdonald, Lyn, *1915: The Death of Innocence* (BCA, 1993)

Miller, Charles, *Battle for the Bundhu: The First World War in East Africa* (London: Book Club Edition, 1974)

Nash, David, *German Infantry 1914–1918* (Mitcham, Surrey: Almark Books, 1971)

Parritt, Brigadier Brian, *The Intelligencers: British Military Intelligence from the Middle Ages to 1929* (Barnsley: Pen & Sword Military, 2011)

Pritchard, Major H.L., *History of the Corps of Royal Engineers. Volume VIII: Mesopotamia, East Africa and Inter-War Years* (Institute of Royal Engineers, 1952)

Taylor, A.J.P., *The First World War: An Illustrated History* (Norwich: George Rainbird, 1963)

Tuohy, Ferdinand, *The Secret Corps: A Tale of Intelligence on All Fronts* (London: John Murray, 1920)

West, Nigel, *Historical Dictionary of World War 1 Intelligence* (Lanham, Maryland: Rowman & Littlefield, 2014)

Winegard, Lieutenant Timothy, 'Dunsterforce: A Case Study of Coalition Warfare in the Middle East 1918–1919', *Canadian Army Journal*, 8.3 (2003)

The Western Front

Liddle, Peter, *The 1916 Battle of the Somme* (Ware: Wordsworth Editions, 2001)

Morgan, Janet, *The Secrets of Rue St Roch: Intelligence Operations Behind Enemy Lines in the First World War* (London: Allen Lane, 2004)

Van Emden, Richard, *The Trench: Experiencing Life on the Front Line, 1916* (London: Bantam Press, 2007)

Dardanelles and Gallipoli

Boswell, L.A.K., 'The Naval Attack on the Dardanelles', *Royal United Service Institute Journal*, 110 (1965)

Carlyon, L.A., *Gallipoli* (Transworld Publishers, 2002)

Mackenzie, Compton, *Gallipoli Memories* (London: Panther Books, 1929)

Monick, S., 'Gallipoli: The Landings of 25 April 1915', *Military History Journal*, 6:4

Steel, Nigel and Hart, Peter, *Defeat at Gallipoli* (London: Macmillan, 1994)

Mesopotamia

Barker, A.J., *The First Iraq War, 1914–1918: Britain's Mesopotamian Campaign* (Enigma Books, 2009)

Erikson, Edward J., *Ordered to Die: A History of the Ottoman Army in the First World War* (Westport, CT: Greenwood Press, 2001)

Popplewell, Richard, *British Intelligence in Mesopotamia: Intelligence and Military Operations* (London: Frank Cass, 1990)

Arabia, Palestine and Syria

Bruce, Anthony, *The Last Crusade: The Palestine Campaign in the First World War* (London: John Murray, 2002)

Bullock, David L., *Allenby's War: The Palestine-Arabian Campaign 1916–1918* (London: Blandford Press, 1988)

Carver, Field-Marshal Lord, *The Turkish Front 1914–1918: The Campaigns at Gallipoli; in Mesopotamia and in Palestine* (London: Sidgwick and Jackson in association with National Army Museum, 2003)

Dimitrakis, Panagiotis, *Military Intelligence in Cyprus: From the Great War to Middle East Crises* (Tauris & Co. Ltd, 2010)

Eddoves, Lt Cdr (US Navy) Andrew W., *The Haversack Ruse and British Deception Operations during World War 1* (Newport: US Naval War College, 17 June 1994)

Finnegan, Col (USAF9R) Terrence, 'Military Intelligence at the Front; Origins of Modern Intelligence, Reconnaisance and Surveillance', *Studies in Intelligence*, 53:4, December 2009

Florence, Ronald, *Lawrence and Aaronsohn: T.E. Lawrence, Aaron Aaronsohn and the Seeds of the Arab-Israeli Conflict* (London: Penguin Books, 2007)

Freeman, John, *A Planned Massacre? British Intelligence Analysis and the German Army at the Battle of Broodseinde, 4 October 1917* (Birmingham: University of Birmingham, 2011)

Hamm, Geoffrey, 'British Intelligence and Turkish Arabia: Strategy, Diplomacy and Empire' (Toronto: University of Toronto, 2012)

Lawrence, T.E., *Revolt in the Desert* (Ware: Wordsworth Editions, 1997)

Lawrence, T.E., *Seven Pillars of Wisdom* (London: Penguin Modern Classics, 1963)

Mohs, Polly A., *Military Intelligence and the Arab Revolt: The First Modern Intelligence War* (Abingdon: Routledge, 2008)

Povlock, Paul, *Deep Battle in World War I: The British Offensive in Palestine* (Pickle Publishing, 2014)

Sheffy, Yigal, *British Military Intellligence in the Palestine Campaign 1914–1918* (London: Frank Cass, 1998)

Sheffy, Yigal, 'Institutionalized Deception and Perception Reinforcement: Allenby's Campaign in Palestine', in *Intelligence and Military Operations* (London: Frank Cass, 1990)

Varnava, Andrekos, 'British Military Intelligence in Cyprus during the Great War', *War In History*, 19:353

Weldon, Captain L.B., *Hard Lying: Eastern Mediterranean 1914–1919* (London: Herbert Jenkins, 1925)

Africa

Dolbey, Robert Valentine, *Sketches of the East Africa Campaign* (John Murray, 1918)

Harvey, Maj. (US Army) Kenneth J., *Battle of Tanga, East Africa, 1914* (Fort Leavenworth: Faculty of the US Army Command and General Staff College, 1991)

Miller, Charles, *Battle for the Bundu: The First World War in East Africa* (London: Purnell, 1974)

Mosley, Leonard, *Duel for Kilimanjaro* (London: Weidenfeld and Nicolson, 1966)

Paice, Edward, *Tip & Run; The Untold Tragedy of the Great War in Africa* (London: Weidenfeld and Nicolson, 2007)

Pakenham Thomas, *The Boer War* (London: Weidenfeld and Nicolson, 1979)

Britain at War

Hadaway, Stuart, 'The Royal Flying Corps goes to War' (September 2014)

'Western Front Battlefield: Twenty Iconic Sites' (October 2014)

The Rose and Laurel (Journal of the Intelligence Corps)

Beach, Jim, 'Extract from "Intelligence Civilians in Uniform: The British Expeditionary Force's Intelligence Corps Officers 1914-1918"', 17:4 (2008)

Condon, John, 'Centenary of the First World War & a Celebration of the Birth of the Intelligence Corps in 1914', 57 (2013)

Croxson, Paul, 'The Birth of Signals Intelligence', 75 (2013)

Fecitt, Harry, 'Captain Arnold Wienholt DSO MC and Bar, Busah Scout and Intelligence Officer', 72 (2010)

Harvey, A.D., 'Intelligence Officers at the Front', 175 (2013)

Hawker, Maj. D.S., 'An Outline of the Early History of the Intelligence Corps', 27 (1965)

Judge, Fred, 'The East African Intelligence Department', 17:4 (2008)

Parritt, Major B.A.H., 'Intelligence corps to INTELLIGENCE CORPS', 8:29 (1967)

Online Sources

Gawrych, Dr George, 'The Rock of Gallipoli'

Kelleher, J.P., 'The Royal Fusiliers (London Regiment) and the Intelligence Corps 1914–1920'

Raid on the Suez Canal

www.kaiserscross.com/intelligence

Index